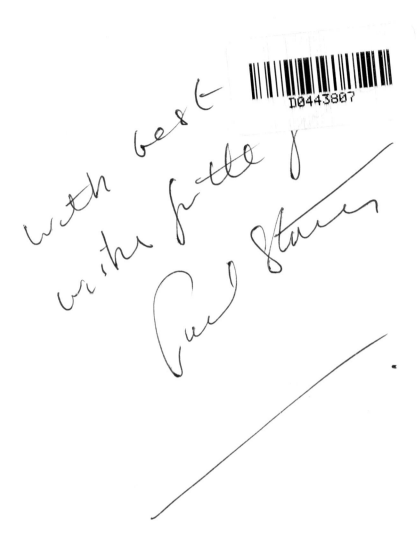

with best
wishes fully

Paul Stares

D0443807

PREVENTIVE ENGAGEMENT

A COUNCIL ON FOREIGN RELATIONS BOOK

The Council on Foreign Relations (CFR) is an independent, nonpartisan membership organization, think tank, and publisher dedicated to being a resource for its members, government officials, business executives, journalists, educators and students, civic and religious leaders, and other interested citizens in order to help them better understand the world and the foreign policy choices facing the United States and other countries. Founded in 1921, CFR carries out its mission by maintaining a diverse membership, with special programs to promote interest and develop expertise in the next generation of foreign policy leaders; convening meetings at its headquarters in New York and in Washington, DC, and other cities where senior government officials, members of Congress, global leaders, and prominent thinkers come together with CFR members to discuss and debate major international issues; supporting a Studies Program that fosters independent research, enabling CFR scholars to produce articles, reports, and books and hold roundtables that analyze foreign policy issues and make concrete policy recommendations; publishing *Foreign Affairs*, the preeminent journal on international affairs and U.S. foreign policy; sponsoring Independent Task Forces that produce reports with both findings and policy prescriptions on the most important foreign policy topics; and providing up-to-date information and analysis about world events and American foreign policy on its website, www.cfr.org.

* * *

The Council on Foreign Relations takes no institutional positions on policy issues and has no affiliation with the U.S. government. All views expressed in its publications and on its website are the sole responsibility of the author or authors.

PAUL B. STARES

PREVENTIVE
ENGAGEMENT

How America Can Avoid War, Stay Strong,
and Keep the Peace

Columbia University Press / New York

Columbia University Press
Publishers Since 1893
New York   Chichester, West Sussex
cup.columbia.edu
Copyright © 2018 Columbia University Press
All rights reserved

Library of Congress Cataloging-in-Publication Data
Names: Stares, Paul B., author.
Title: Preventive engagement : how America can avoid war, stay strong, and
    keep the peace / Paul B. Stares.
Description: New York : Columbia University Press, [2017] |
    Includes bibliographical references and index.
Identifiers: LCCN 2017016724 (print) | LCCN 2017037375 (ebook) |
    ISBN 9780231544184 (ebook)| ISBN 9780231182461 (hardcover : alk. paper)
Subjects: LCSH: Conflict management. | Peace-building. | War—
    Prevention. | Conflict management—United States. | United States—
    Foreign relations. | United States—Military policy. | National security—
    United States. | Security, International. | Conflict management—
    International cooperation
Classification: LCC JZ6368 (ebook) | LCC JZ6368 .S735 2017 (print) |
    DDC 355/.033573—dc23
LC record available at https://lccn.loc.gov/2017016724

Columbia University Press books are printed on permanent
and durable acid-free paper.

Printed in the United States of America
Cover design: Chang Jae Lee

For Nick, Justin, Isabel

and

Peter Stares

(1953–2015)

As a very important source of strength and security, cherish public credit. One method of preserving it is to use it as sparingly as possible, avoiding occasions of expense by cultivating peace, but remembering also that timely disbursements to prepare for danger frequently prevent much greater disbursements to repel it.

—George Washington, Farewell Address, September 19, 1796

CONTENTS

PART 2
A U.S. STRATEGY OF PREVENTIVE ENGAGEMENT

PREFACE

*In politics, the belief that certain facts are unalterable or certain
trends irresistible commonly reflects a lack of desire or lack of interest
to change or resist them.*

—E. H. CARR

*Great powers like the United States need a sound grand strategy if
they are to protect themselves and preserve the international order
that they have labored hard to construct. Get the pieces of the puzzle
right, and even grave threats can be turned back. Get the pieces of
the puzzle wrong—or worse, fail to recognize that there is a
puzzle—and those same threats can bring great nations to their
knees.*

—CHARLES KUPCHAN

HISTORIANS OFTEN MARK the beginning and end of a century not by
the turn of the calendar but by pivotal events that bookend the
distinctive character of the period in between. Thus for some, the
nineteenth century began not in 1800 but in 1789 with the French Revolution and only ended with the outbreak of the First World War in 1914.
Despite its turbulent beginnings, the "long" nineteenth century was characterized by the ascendance of Great Britain as the predominant global
power and, for the most part, no major outbreaks of international conflict.
In comparison, the twentieth century is often portrayed as relatively short
and certainly more violent in that it encompassed two catastrophic world
wars and the dangerous Cold War confrontation between the United
States and the Soviet Union that only ended with the latter's formal dissolution in 1991.[1] Over this period the United States also succeeded Britain

as the preeminent global power and principal standard bearer for what is widely referred to as the liberal international order—today's rules-based system broadly committed to the promotion of democratic values, open capitalist economies, and the peaceful resolution of disputes.

How the twenty-first century will come to be defined now seems much less certain than it did at the end of the twentieth. The general consensus then was that the world would grow progressively more peaceful and prosperous, driven in large part by the irresistible forces of globalization and broad acceptance of the liberal international order as its default operating system. America's paramount standing in the world also seemed assured; the demise of the Soviet Union left it without a serious rival and with no new peer competitors in sight. The willingness, moreover, of successive U.S. administrations to exert America's unmatched power and moral authority as a benign hegemon to lead "coalitions of the willing" in response to various challenges to international peace and security—whether repelling Iraqi aggression in Kuwait, managing famine in the Horn of Africa, halting (for several years, at least) North Korea's nuclear weapons program, and bringing peace to the Balkans and other conflict-stricken parts of the world—likewise bode well for a better, more orderly future.

That positive outlook, it is fair to say, no longer holds sway. Commentators now routinely talk of a "world in disarray," a "great unraveling," and an "unmistakable sense of disintegration" to describe their growing fear that the liberal international order, and America's commitment and capacity to maintain it, are irrevocably waning.[2] The twenty-first century is expected to become much more unstable and dangerous as a consequence. This dramatic shift in outlook can be attributed to three mutually reinforcing developments since the turn of the century.

The first concerns the consequences of the September 11, 2001, terrorist attacks and in particular the reaction of the administration of President George W. Bush—or, some would contend, overreaction. The costly U.S. "global war on terror" launched in the aftermath of 9/11 destabilized several regions of the world, disaffected the American public about the need for active engagement overseas, and arguably distracted U.S. leaders at a critical juncture from addressing the larger challenge posed by a rising China and a resurgent Russia. Not surprisingly, some now consider 9/11 as the real beginning of the twenty-first century.[3] Although it remains debatable whether the administration of Barack Obama made matters worse with its comparative caution and restraint in managing several later international crises, it certainly fed the perception of growing American indifference and detachment.

The second broad development relates to the uneven effects of globalization. The widespread belief that an increasingly borderless world where goods, people, and information circulate freely would produce broad benefits for everyone has given way to deep discontent and fear in much of the West. Indeed, globalization has come to symbolize not greater prosperity and security but the opposite. Such feelings are especially acute in communities where globalization is seen to have either advantaged a few, to produce extreme disparities of wealth, or where the prospects for employment and a better life have been destroyed by the remorseless forces of technological change and foreign competition.[4] As a result, public sentiment in the United States and Europe has become increasingly inward looking and protectionist.[5] The shocking British referendum in 2016 to leave the European Union (commonly known as Brexit), and the even more surprising election of Donald Trump to the White House in the same year on a platform based on the slogans "Make America Great Again" and "America First" are symptomatic of these shifting sentiments.

The third development has been the rise or resurgence of various actors on the world stage that are viewed as antithetical to the core tenets of the liberal international order. The seemingly inexorable ascent of China, which surpassed Japan as the world's second largest economy in 2010, clearly presents the biggest challenge in that the nation remains undemocratic and wedded to state capitalist principles. Moreover, China's growing military power and assertive behavior in various territorial disputes has done nothing to reassure those who fear its ultimate intentions. Similarly, the aggressive actions of an increasingly authoritarian Russia in Georgia, Ukraine, and Syria, not to mention its alleged interference in the 2016 U.S. elections—all of which have taken place without serious reaction— have given validity to the argument that the West is weak and getting weaker. And last but not least, the growing potency and virulence of various nonstate actors—whether terrorist groups, transnational criminal syndicates, or cyberhackers—represents another, if different, challenge to the prevailing international order. Their ability to exploit open societies and ungoverned spaces and to cause immense disruption and harm out of all proportion to the resources at their disposal is expected to only grow in the years ahead.

These developments are all undoubtedly real and serious, but in the grand scheme of things do they really warrant the apocalyptic fears that they have engendered? Will later historians look back at the recent conjunction of events as the pivotal moment that forever changed the course and character of the twenty-first century, or as just a transient period of turbulence? This is not the first time, after all, that parts of the world have been racked by violent conflict, only for them to eventually burn out and subside. Nor is it unprecedented for the West to feel besieged by multiple crises—whether political, economic, or military in nature—that at the time appeared to pose grave, even existential threats but likewise passed without lasting consequences. Indeed, for the most part, the norms and institutions of the liberal international order built up over more than seventy-five years have proven to be remarkably resilient; in short, they may bend, but they do not often break. Similarly, the world has suffered periodic economic downturns over the same period, but human development has still managed to steadily advance on virtually every major yardstick of progress.

In the same positive vein, reports of America's demise have also been greatly exaggerated on more than one occasion in the past. Putative challengers to its predominant position have come and gone, along with episodic bouts of anxiety and self-doubt about its leading role in the world. The United States has invariably bounced back, reenergized, and recommitted to the task. Why, then, should this moment be any different? For all the talk of its diminishing influence, America still has immense economic and military resources at its disposal while it enjoys many geostrategic advantages that are not likely to change any time soon. Although it clearly faces the prospect of *relative* decline—something that is inevitable as other actors emerge on the world stage—there is no reason to believe the United States will relinquish its preeminent global position for many decades to come.[6]

These are compelling (not to mention reassuring) arguments, but they do not wholly dispel the fear that this time things may be different and that the world—and America's leading place in it—could indeed be moving in a highly undesirable direction. The liberal international order is not pre-ordained to survive any more than earlier international arrangements designed to promote peace and stability were. Indeed, one does not have to look back very far in history to find examples of how the course of world affairs quickly and decisively changed for the worst, in large part because of the failure of the leading powers at the time to properly appreciate and manage the emerging threats to the prevailing international order. Some contemporary observers, for example, believe that the centrifugal forces at work today bear more than a passing resemblance to those that emerged in the first half of the twentieth century and eventually tore the world apart. While the parallels between then and now should not be pushed too far—the world today is different in several important respects—the dangers are nonetheless just as real. In short, it is not hard to imagine how recent developments could continue to gather momentum in a highly destabilizing and dangerous fashion.

As the most powerful country in the world, the United States has the greatest capacity to avert the potential unraveling of the liberal international order, and it is without question in its security and economic interests to do so. The United States, moreover, has not only the most to gain by perpetuating the liberal international order but also arguably the most to lose if it mismanages this task. As the principal guarantor of global peace and security, America is—like no other country—at great risk of being drawn into potentially costly military engagements to counter emerging threats to international order. The United States simply cannot afford to underestimate those threats or respond to them in an ad hoc, improvised, or impulsive manner. America's future as a world power depends on it. In this respect, while the parallels are inexact, Britain's experience in the twentieth century offers a salutary tale for the United States in the twenty-first.

The conventional wisdom is that Britain's decline as a world power was largely inevitable once several continental powers began to industrialize and overtake it economically at the end of the nineteenth century. Furthermore, Britain's leaders, having seen the writing on the wall, adroitly managed its subsequent global retrenchment: they wisely acquiesced to U.S. ascendency in the western hemisphere, skillfully suborned American military power to prevail in the two world wars and subsequent Cold War, and successfully divested their colonial possessions in a timely manner that was also in many respects handled more humanely and responsibly than most of their European counterparts.[7]

There is, however, an alternative, more damning explanation of Britain's retreat from primacy. Although it had indeed been surpassed economically at the beginning of the twentieth century, Britain was still, on the eve of the First World War, the leading global power by virtue of its enormous financial resources, productive capacity, imperial possessions, and naval strength.[8] No one—least of all, its leaders—expected that Britain would decline in the way it did and as rapidly as it did; the sun, after all, was never going to set on the British Empire. Multiple factors played their part, but the exertion of fighting two ruinously costly wars against Germany and trying to maintain Britain's pretensions to be a major player during much of the Cold War was the most decisive.[9] Rather than having a clear vision for the future and coherent strategy to conserve Britain's strength in the face of emerging challenges to its global position, its leaders essentially ended up lurching from one crisis to the next for most of the twentieth century, depleting its power in the process.[10] As one historian has concluded, "The record shows that Britain's decline was far from graceful, much less 'managed.' The British were reactive, not far-sighted, and inconsistent rather than careful. Imperial descent, while preordained in certain respects, unfolded in fits and starts over the course of decades. If the British experience does indeed 'hold some valuable lessons,' . . . it is as an example of what *not* to do."[11]

Although the United States is undoubtedly in a much stronger position today with advantages that Britain either never had or enjoyed only fleetingly, its global responsibilities are at the same time more extensive and critical to world order. The risk of America becoming drawn into costly new military entanglements and other onerous commitments in defense of that order is much greater as a consequence. The inclination of the American public to shoulder these responsibilities is also not limitless. It is not hard to imagine how the United States could grow increasingly disenchanted and disengaged from playing the crucial global role it assumed in the twentieth century, leaving the liberal international order it so assiduously built to an uncertain fate. There is, after all, no obvious emerging great power for America to hand the baton of enlightened global leadership to should it falter as Britain once did.

It falls then to the Trump administration to navigate what is likely to be an extremely challenging and potentially fateful period in the nation's history. The initial signs, however, have not been encouraging that President Trump understands what is at stake or has a coherent vision for America's place and role in the world beyond what was proclaimed during the election campaign. Putting "America first" is not in itself objectionable unless it translates into a narrow-minded, self-interested, and short-term approach to U.S. foreign and security policy. This includes, among other things, peremptorily dismissing the value of long-standing military alliances, free trade agreements, and multilateral institutions out of the misguided conviction that the United States has been exploited by its partners or given more than it gets in return for being a member of such arrangements. Likewise, strengthening the U.S. military (as the Trump administration has declared its intention to do) is not in itself wrongheaded, but believing that it will be sufficient to keep the United States secure and—more to the point, here—out of harm's way so that it can focus on "making America great again" at home is to fundamentally misread the external challenges the nation is now facing and the likely demands that these will place upon it.

In short, the Trump administration must devise a comprehensive long-term strategy that harnesses *all* elements of U.S. power to preserve the liberal international order in a way that advances its national interests and core values without becoming drawn into costly new military engagements that drain its power and risk compromising its long-term standing in the world. This strategy, furthermore, has to be sustainable and adaptable beyond the Trump administration in much the same way as the policy of containment toward the Soviet Union during the administration of Harry S. Truman set the basic course for U.S. policy during the Cold War.

This book offers just such a strategy. Doubtless, not all will find its argument convincing or its recommendation compelling; that is their prerogative. But if it stimulates debate and, moreover, inspires others to come up with a better and more practical solution to the challenges that the United States will likely face in the years ahead, it will have served a useful purpose. What cannot be condoned, however, is fatalism and passivity. Hoping for the best is neither a policy nor a prudent approach. Likewise, faith in the notion that the United States can weather any adversity, come what may, or that a special providence will always shine beneficently upon it is also not a dependable plan of action. For all its immense strengths and advantages, the United States faces growing risks and narrowing margins for error. In short, it cannot afford to be either naïvely passive or impulsively reactive to emerging international challenges. It needs to think and act ahead in a timely and precautionary manner. In this respect, Theodore Roosevelt's admonition at the beginning of the twentieth century remains just as relevant in the twenty-first: "In foreign affairs we must make up our minds that, whether we wish it or not, we are a great people and must play a great part in the world. It is not open to us to choose whether we will play that great part or not. We have to play it. All we can decide is whether we shall play it well or ill."[12]

PREVENTIVE ENGAGEMENT

1

AMERICA'S PREDICAMENT

*It is the vital national security interest of the United States to reduce
these conflicts because whether we like it or not, we remain a dominant military superpower, and when conflicts break out, one way or
another we get pulled into them. And that ends up costing us significantly in terms of both blood and treasure.*

—BARACK OBAMA

*One of the most serious weaknesses that has hampered the long-range
effectiveness of American foreign policy . . . is the over emphasis upon
our role as "volunteer fire department" for the world. . . . The role, to
be sure, is a necessary one; but it is not the only role to be played, and
the others cannot be ignored. A volunteer fire department halts, but
rarely prevents, fires. It repels but rarely rebuilds; it meets the problems of the present but not of the future.*

—JOHN F. KENNEDY

AMERICA FINDS ITSELF in an acute predicament with no obvious or
easy solution. The international order it has championed and
helped build over many decades for the benefit of itself and many
others around the world is under growing stress from multiple challenges.
As by far the strongest military power and principal guarantor of international peace and security, the United States is expected to respond to
these challenges, whether it be resisting Russian and Chinese territorial
assertiveness in Eastern Europe and the South China Sea; rolling back
nuclear proliferation from Iran and North Korea; stabilizing war-torn
Iraq, Syria, and other places; or countering terrorist threats in virtually
every corner of the globe. The maintenance of order, however, ultimately

rests on America's willingness and ability to use its immense power—including, ultimately, the use of force when all else fails—to uphold the fundamental rules and norms of international behavior from which it derives. Therein lies the American predicament.

More specifically, if the United States responds reflexively or impulsively to every challenge to international order or heeds each request for assistance, it risks becoming overextended and progressively enervated by its exertions to the point at which it has neither the resolve nor the resources to perform its critical global role. Yet if the United States signals one way or another that it is less than fully committed to fulfilling its many responsibilities and obligations, or is widely perceived to be growing detached or indifferent to the fate of the world, it could trigger a self-fulfilling loss of confidence in its global leadership. Without the United States as a credible underwriter of global peace and security, and with no other power visible on the horizon that is capable or committed to shouldering this burden, the very international order that it has expended so much effort to build could start to unravel with potentially very dangerous consequences.

The purpose of this book is to show how America can address this predicament in a way that avoids strategic insolvency on the one hand and the possibility of growing global disorder on the other. It argues that the United States should adopt a comprehensive *preventive* strategy to manage the risks of a more turbulent world so as to lessen the likelihood that it will be increasingly confronted and potentially overwhelmed with excruciating and hugely consequential choices about the use of military force. *Preventive engagement*, as this strategy is known, essentially has three mutually reinforcing components: first, the promotion of policies known to lower the general risk of conflict and instability over the long term; second, a deliberate and prioritized effort to anticipate and avert those crises most likely to precipitate major U.S. military engagement in the medium term; and, third, the ability to react rapidly to mitigate—and, better still, resolve—those conflicts that erupt in the short term before they escalate and increase the pressure for U.S. intervention.[1]

The chapters that follow will discuss in detail what preventive engagement requires the United States to do in practice. To appreciate why such a strategy is desirable at this time, it is important first to understand the nature of the growing challenge to international order and how America's predicament could very well grow more acute in the future. It is also important to recognize why the most commonly proposed alternate strategies do not offer satisfactory solutions and may actually exacerbate the challenge the United States now faces. In crude terms, they essentially rest on America committing itself to expend either more or less military power to uphold international order. As such, these two alternatives can be characterized as "supply-side" strategies, whereas preventive engagement is focused essentially on reducing the overall *demand* for U.S. military power. This approach is sure to raise some initial skepticism, possibly based on misconceptions about the intent and scope of preventive engagement and, ultimately, its feasibility. Thus it is important at the outset to address such concerns before turning to the substance of the book.

EMERGING CHALLENGES TO INTERNATIONAL ORDER

Until relatively recently, the world appeared destined to grow steadily more peaceful. Certainly the trends tracking the incidence of deadly conflict all looked promising. For over seventy years, the major powers have managed to avoid going to war with one another, a period that some now refer to as the Long Peace.[2] Over the same period, interstate conflict—certainly for the purpose of territorial conquest—also became exceedingly rare and seemingly obsolescent as a rational instrument of statecraft.[3] And while incidents of intrastate or civil war continued to blight several regions of the world, the number of such conflicts appeared to peak in the immediate aftermath of the Cold War before steadily declining thereafter. These trends are illustrated in figure 1.1.

The prospect of an ever more peaceful world, however, no longer appears so assured for several reasons. The first, and arguably most worrisome, source of concern is the growing geopolitical friction among the major powers. Relations between the United States and Russia have grown increasingly

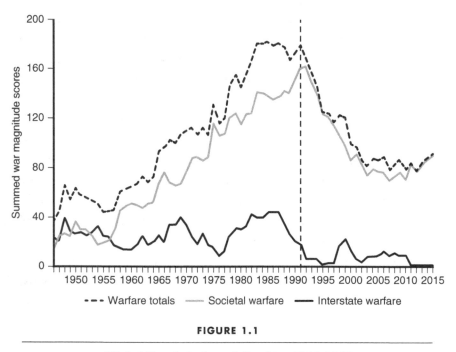

FIGURE 1.1

Global Trends in Armed Conflict, 1946–2015

Source: Center for Systemic Peace © 2016.

distrustful and at times tense as a result of the 2014 Ukraine crisis and the Russian military intervention in Syria that began in 2015. Led by the United States, NATO is now bolstering its defenses against Russia to counter potentially aggressive moves in eastern Europe. Several points of contention along Russia's periphery could nevertheless escalate into a serious U.S.-Russian confrontation with unpredictable consequences. America is also increasingly engaged in what can only be described as militarized hedging behavior in response to China's rise as a major power and, in particular, its increasingly assertive behavior in the East China and South China Seas. Given that these territorial disputes directly or indirectly involve U.S. allies in the region and could, if they escalate, affect freedom of navigation along vital international trade routes in the Pacific, relations between the United States and China could quite easily grow more adversarial if not overtly hostile. Similarly, tensions between India and

China have in recent years also flared up periodically over contested territory and other concerns. They, too, are engaged in an increasingly competitive strategic relationship.

The likelihood that growing friction between the major powers will lead to outright hostilities still seems remote, but this trend is unwelcome even if it does not lead to open warfare. Russia, China, and the United States are all upgrading their military forces (including nuclear arsenals) while adapting their operational doctrines and developing new security partnerships with other states—with the possibility of war very much in mind. Such preparations are not only distracting and costly at a time when many domestic priorities demand attention in the United States, but they also risk opening up dangerous new areas of rivalry that undermine strategic stability—that is, the sense of security among the major powers that comes from having effective nuclear deterrent capabilities. These areas include the exploitation of various emerging technologies (robotics, synthetic biology, three-dimensional printing, genetic engineering, and hypersonic propulsion, to cite some obvious examples) as well as new operational domains—notably, cyberspace and outer space. All this will create new insecurities and opportunities for misperception and miscalculation, especially during crises which will almost certainly arise. It is easy to forget, as the Cold War recedes in memory, how close the world came to catastrophe on several occasions for these very reasons.

The second broad source of concern is the deteriorating security outlook in several regions of the world that also poses a growing risk to the United States. Some long-standing international conflicts have not ameliorated and, if anything, are becoming more dangerous. The armed confrontation on the Korean Peninsula is especially worrisome now that North Korea has developed an arsenal of nuclear weapons and the ballistic missiles to deliver them, threatening not only U.S. allies in the region but also, increasingly, American territory. The conflict between India and Pakistan has not abated and has arguably become more unstable as both sides have not only developed the means to quickly mobilize and attack one another, but also possess nuclear weapons. Meanwhile, in the Persian Gulf, fears of a regional nuclear arms race have lessened with Iran's acceptance of constraints on its nuclear power programs, but when these begin to expire after ten to

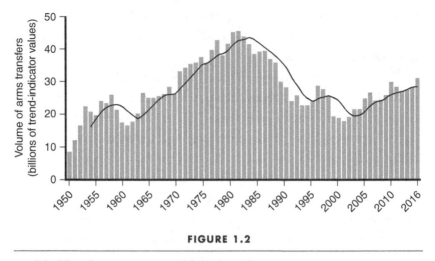

FIGURE 1.2

The Trend in International Transfers of Major Weapons, 1950–2016

Source: Stockholm International Peace Research Institute, "International Arms Transfers," https://www.sipri.org/research/armament-and-disarmament/arms-transfers-and-military -spending/international-arms-transfers.

fifteen years, the latent mistrust of Iranian intentions among U.S. allies in the region will almost certainly resurface. These and other growing regional insecurities are manifested in the recent increase in arms sales around the world, as figure 1.2 indicates.[4]

Although new weapons acquisitions can help deter potential aggression and thus contribute to regional peace and stability, the net effect could also be to heighten the underlying insecurities that prompted them in the first place. The likelihood that some states will seek nuclear weapons as the ul-timate deterrent will almost certainly grow as a consequence. While some experts believe that the proliferation of nuclear weapons would help deter war among an expanding group of major powers—as it is judged to have done between the United States and the Soviet Union during the Cold War—many others consider this a highly dubious proposition.[5] It is by no means clear that the imputed restraining effect of nuclear weapons on U.S. and Soviet behavior during the Cold War would be replicated in the future between other protagonists with different histories, cultures, and geopo-litical contexts. There is also the danger of such weapons falling into the hands of terrorists and other groups who may have few, if any, inhibitions about using them. As more countries acquire nuclear weapons, that risk inevitably increases.

Many parts of the Middle East and North Africa have also clearly become more unstable and violent, which accounts for the recent upturn in the number of internal conflicts indicated in figure 1.1. The situation in Afghanistan and parts of central Asia is also not improving. Though usually classified as societal or civil wars, these conflicts are effectively internationalized in that regional and sometimes major powers play an active military role in one way or another, including providing support and sustenance to local combatants who act as their proxy forces in pursuit of other goals. Figure 1.3 illustrates the recent increase in internationalized civil wars.

FIGURE 1.3

**Internationalized Civil Wars as a Portion of Total Intrastate
Conflicts, 1945–2015**

Source: Uppsala Conflict Data Program and Peace Research Institute Oslo Dyadic
Dataset and Uppsala Conflict Data Program Non-State Conflict Dataset, in
"Shifting to Prevention," UN–World Bank Study on Prevention of Violent Conflicts.

The growing rivalry between the predominantly Sunni states of Saudi Arabia and the Persian Gulf, on the one hand, and Shiite Iran and its partners, on the other, could easily intensify and play out in various regional flash points for decades to come. Indeed, some now refer to this rivalry as a generational conflict, or the modern-day equivalent of the Thirty Years' War.[6] The costly intervention in Iraq has made the United States leery of becoming drawn into major new military commitments in the Middle East, but due to the security commitments it has already made and the pressure to contain dangerous spillover effects into neighboring states and Europe, it is not difficult to imagine how it could become more deeply involved in the future.

The third and related concern is the growing threat posed by armed nonstate actors. Terrorism is hardly a new phenomenon, but the number of recorded attacks has grown in recent years, as illustrated in figure 1.4. Much of this growth can be attributed to the growth in militant Islamist groups, as indicated in figure 1.5.

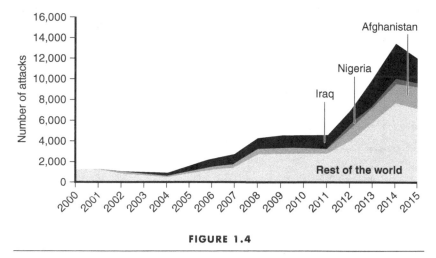

FIGURE 1.4

Terrorist Attacks, 2000–2015

Source: Institute for Economics and Peace, *Global Terrorism Index 2016* (New York: Institute for Economics and Peace, 2016), http://economicsandpeace.org/wp-content/uploads/2016/11/Global-Terrorism-Index-2016.2.pdf.

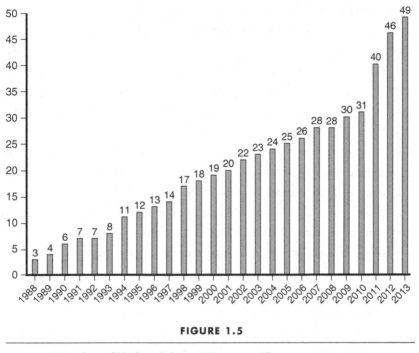

FIGURE 1.5

Number of Violent Islamist Extremist Groups, 1988–2013

Source: Seth G. Jones, *A Persistent Threat: The Evolution of al Qa'ida and Other Salafi Jihadists* (Santa Monica, Calif.: RAND, 2014).

These trends have important implications for the United States. There are now many more terrorist groups that are hostile toward America and its allies than there were before 9/11. The threat from al-Qaeda—the perpetrators of 9/11—has seemingly diminished as a result of numerous defensive counterterrorism initiatives that have made it harder for terrorist groups in general to penetrate and operate within U.S. borders, as well as a relentless offensive campaign overseas notably in Somalia, Yemen, Afghanistan, and Pakistan to kill and capture its leaders—including Osama bin Laden in 2011. Al-Qaeda has, however, spawned numerous offshoots and affiliates that operate in many other areas of the world and pose a threat to U.S. regional interests.[7] The most dangerous of these—the self-proclaimed Islamic State of Iraq and Syria (ISIS, also known as ISIL or Daesh), which suddenly emerged in Iraq and Syria in 2014, has also demonstrated the capacity to not only strike several European allies but also to inspire individuals to carry out attacks within the United States.

Given the typical life cycle of previous terrorist groups, the threat posed by ISIS will in all likelihood recede in the coming years, especially after the military campaign to destroy its presence in Iraq and Syria is completed. But the underlying threat posed by militant Islamist groups will not soon disappear, even if such groups do not control territory. Their ideology will continue to resonate across borders aided and amplified by new personal information technologies that are becoming globally ubiquitous. New groups and coalitions will surely emerge in the wake of ISIS, perhaps refining their techniques for radicalizing and recruiting disaffected individuals inside Western states, as well as in other areas of the world that have become more or less ungoverned spaces or were never really under state control. Moreover, the emergence of new terrorist groups with very different grievances and political agendas cannot be discounted.

How the potency of dangerous nonstate actors could evolve in both quantitative and qualitative terms is the question that most concerns security experts. Al-Qaeda—and, reportedly, ISIS—have tried to acquire nuclear materials and other deadly substances to carry out truly catastrophic mass-casualty attacks. The use of less lethal but still highly disruptive methods of attack, including cyberwarfare, on the critical infrastructure of states—such as essential services like financial systems, power supplies, and health systems—could also conceivably grow in the future. To many experts, it is just a matter of time before such attacks happen.

All these concerns could be exacerbated over time, moreover, by the interacting effects of population stress, resource scarcity, climate change, and environmental degradation caused by human progress and development. Many scenarios can be imagined in which international rivalry, internal instability, and the threat posed by dangerous nonstate actors worsens as a result of these factors. Assessing their likelihood is hard given the many intervening variables—some local, others global—that could conceivably affect the severity of the challenge.[8] This uncertainty is, however, no excuse to discount or disregard the latent risks. Disputes over potable water and access to potential hydrocarbon reserves, fish stocks, and rare metals are already a source of worsening tensions in many parts of the world. And we know that the competition for sought-after resources has been a driver of violent conflict in the past.

To be sure, many of these concerns may never gain momentum or evolve in such extreme, dystopian ways. But this cannot be reliably assumed. History is certainly not very reassuring on this score, as prolonged periods of peace in the past have often been followed by intense spasms of violent conflict.[9] Even the impressive longevity of the current Long Peace among the major powers is not considered by some who have studied it to be very significant, at least in statistical terms.[10] In short, we could be entering a very dangerous period.

THE LIMITATIONS OF SUPPLY-SIDE STRATEGIES

Most of the policy recommendations for how the United States should respond to a world growing more dangerous and disorderly can be viewed as efforts to close what is sometimes referred to as the Lippmann Gap, named after the famous American foreign policy commentator Walter Lippmann and his oft-quoted invocation that foreign policy "consists in bringing into balance, with a comfortable surplus of power in reserve, the nation's commitments and the nation's power."[11] Thus, some believe, the United States needs to recalibrate its national interests and contract its global commitments accordingly in order to reduce its exposure to growing disorder in the world. For others it is about building up military capabilities and being prepared to use them to perform the role the United States has assumed as the principal guarantor of global security, whether that means upholding the fundamental rules and norms of international behavior, safeguarding universal access to the global commons (the high seas, outer space and, increasingly, cyberspace), ensuring general compliance with numerous arms control agreements (particularly those relating to weapons of mass destruction), protecting endangered populations against the deliberate privations of their governments, and last (but by no means least) guaranteeing the national security of dozens of countries in virtually every region of the world. Both approaches can be classified as supply-side strategies in that they essentially hinge on whether the United States should provide more or less power—particularly military power—to the maintenance of international order. Each offers compelling arguments to make its case, but on further examination, supply-side solutions have serious limitations.

Pulling back from the world, steering clear of its many problems, and focusing on reviving the domestic sources of America's power—what President Obama memorably called "nation-building at home"—is certainly appealing.[12] The recent U.S. military interventions overseas have seemingly accomplished little and arguably made matters worse—at considerable cost in blood and treasure. Well over six thousand American servicemen and -women have been killed, and another fifty-one thousand have been wounded in action, many maimed for life—mostly in Afghanistan and Iraq, but also in in numerous smaller counterterrorism operations around world.[13] Though the final bill will not be clear for some time given uncertainties over how some expenses will come due in the coming years (notwithstanding that military operations in Afghanistan and Iraq are still ongoing), it could end up costing somewhere between $4 trillion and $6 trillion—an extraordinary outlay of national financial resources.[14]

Furthermore, while the United States has now mostly rebounded from the Great Recession that was triggered by the 2008 financial crisis (and which caused the sharpest American financial downturn since the 1930s), there is still much to be concerned about in the general state of the nation. Deficiencies in education, infrastructure, and critical areas of science and technology, among other concerns, have been well documented. Meanwhile, the long-term outlook for the economy remains worrisome. Current projections from the Congressional Budget Office (CBO) indicate that national debt will rise substantially due to growing health-care and insurance costs associated with an aging population. Under some CBO projections, it could reach nearly 150 percent of gross domestic product (GDP) by 2046.[15] The implications of extreme levels of national indebtedness on inhibiting economic growth (not to mention the potential strategic consequences of ceding leverage to creditor nations) are generally accepted by most economists.[16]

For all its undeniable appeal, pulling back from the world has proven to be harder than imagined when the United States has attempted to do so in the past. America's diplomatic disengagement after the First World War is the most well-known example of U.S. retrenchment, but there have been other, if less extreme, periods when the United States became more inwardly oriented—notably, following the end of the wars in Korea and Vietnam, and in the immediate aftermath of the Cold War.[17] Each of these brief periods, however, ended with a shocking or alarming event that caused public opinion to swing back in support of—and in some cases even clamor for—greater American activism. The Japanese attack on Pearl Harbor in 1941, North Korea's invasion of South Korea in 1950, the launch of Sputnik in 1957, the Soviet invasion of Afghanistan in 1979, the 9/11 terrorist attacks and, to a lesser extent, the Taliban resurgence of 2015 and the emergence of ISIS, are all examples of how the United States was rudely stirred into a new cycle of overseas military engagement as a result of a wholly unforeseen crisis. In short, history is not very encouraging to those who believe the United States can stay above the fray. To paraphrase Leon Trotsky, America may not be interested in war, but war is interested in America.[18]

To be clear, few if any foreign policy experts believe in or advocate for the United States retreating completely from the world—even if it could. Geographical distance has long since ceased to be a barrier to foreign attack, and the nature of the world's economy, with its global supply chains, means that America is exposed to the effects of international instability as much if not more so than any other leading industrialized country. Rather, many experts now argue that the United States should be more "restrained," "calibrated," and "modest" in how it conducts its foreign and security policies.[19] To some this entails America being more selective and discriminating about when and where it decides to commit its armed forces. Since 1945, every American war save one has been a "war of choice"—that is, optional—rather than a "war of necessity" in which vital national interests are at stake to the extent that the use of force is unavoidable.[20] Accordingly, the United States should cure its addiction to questionable foreign excursions and "just say no."[21]

Similarly, others have advocated that the United States should at the same time deliberately reduce its worldwide military footprint, with an associated effort to encourage other countries to bear more of the burden of defending themselves, not to mention doing their fair share as members of the international community to contribute to global security. In the process, the United States would adopt what is sometimes referred to as an "offshore balancing" role.[22] Though the policy and operational implications of this strategy are rarely spelled out in detail, it equates broadly to the United States maintaining its security commitments to key allies around the Eurasian land mass but reducing the size of its military deployments, particularly of ground forces, in Europe, Northeast Asia, and the Persian Gulf. U.S. power would essentially be ready and available "over the horizon" in the form of naval, amphibious, and air power to deter potential threats and intervene when deemed necessary.

These arguments for restraint and retrenchment have been criticized by conservatives and liberals alike, albeit for different reasons. Some focus on the difficulty of determining what constitutes a war of choice from one of necessity due to the subjective nature of U.S. interests. Most critics, however, typically focus on the potentially harmful implications of U.S. retrenchment on the security calculations of both America's long-standing allies and, more important, its potential adversaries.[23] Would allies become increasingly unsure of the credibility of U.S. security guarantees—or worse, fearing abandonment, be more willing to accommodate the wishes of other powers to the detriment of U.S. interests? Would they acquire more arms and adopt more independent and conceivably nationalistic security policies to compensate, ultimately undermining regional stability and making them less likely to partner with the United States in other endeavors? Similarly, would some powers, sensing that the United States was no longer fully committed to the security of specific areas or countries, become more assertive and even aggressive in the pursuit of their goals? And would the costs of U.S. reengagement to restore order and equilibrium when it is threatened be considered so prohibitive as to dissuade Washington from doing so, thereby effectively ceding U.S. influence in those places?[24]

These are all mostly "realpolitik" criticisms of strategic retrenchment, but there are also other concerns to ponder. Would a retraction of U.S. security commitments also translate into curtailing America's promotion of democracy and human rights around the world? Would local human rights advocates be demoralized and authoritarian regimes become more emboldened by such a retreat? And would the hard-earned advances in establishing global norms of behavior start to fray should the United States—hitherto their most vociferous champion—be perceived as faltering?

In contrast to those who would have America do less in the world are those who argue that the best strategy to meet the challenges of a more dangerous world is to do much more—in essence, for the United States to maintain the strongest possible military to dissuade major challengers of the status quo while being prepared to intervene to manage lesser threats before they turn into bigger ones. Such thinking has clearly shaped American defense investments since the United States became a global power after the Second World War and has, if anything, grown more influential in the post–Cold War era.[25] Although a U.S. defense posture that explicitly sets global military dominance as its aim has never been formally embraced, decades of intensive investment in the U.S. armed forces has essentially produced this result. America not only spends more on defense than any conceivable rival, but also somewhere between 40 and 45 percent of the world's total military expenditure.[26] The cumulative effect has given the United States extraordinary power projection capabilities and an unmatched readiness to conduct what is sometimes called "full spectrum" military operations, ranging from relatively small missions involving U.S. Special Forces to high-intensity conventional campaigns—and ultimately global thermonuclear war.

But maintaining military preponderance is an expensive undertaking with considerable opportunity costs.[27] By some calculations, a dollar spent on defense makes less of a contribution to the economy than other types of government spending.[28] In periods of fiscal austerity, these opportunity costs—whether investments in infrastructure, health care, education, science and technology, or other areas—take on added political significance. Yet in terms of their actual burden on the U.S. economy, defense expenditures in the post–Cold War period are not especially onerous.[29] The U.S. national defense budget as a percentage of GDP has ranged between 5.7 percent (in 1988) and 3 percent (in 2001). The guns-versus-butter trade-offs are defensible, moreover, if they help avoid the much greater economic and societal costs of fighting a major war. Certainly a good case can be made that America's security guarantees and associated global military presence have helped reassure allies, dampen regional rivalries, and deter aggressive behavior on the part of certain states in important areas of the world.

Yet those critical of maintaining U.S. military preponderance and its forward presence in the world also make some valid arguments. One is that it makes other powers fearful of U.S. intentions, causing such powers to take offsetting moves that ultimately undermine U.S. security. Certainly the global extension of U.S. military power since the end of the Cold War has antagonized Russia and China, who have expressed concern over what they view as unacceptable U.S. encroachment of their national borders and their traditional spheres of influence. Some commentators also contend that the "forward presence" of U.S. forces inevitably increases the risk of the United States becoming ensnared in local grievances and conflicts. Resentment at the physical presence of American forces in certain countries, moreover, can breed dangerous animosities among their citizenry that make them—and ultimately the U.S. homeland—targets for attack. The desire to expel American "infidels" or "crusaders" from the Muslim world (and, particularly, areas considered sacrosanct) is now generally accepted as having been a prime motivator for the 9/11 al-Qaeda attacks.[30]

Another unintended consequence of the United States' dominant military posture that critics emphasize is that it encourages others to do less not only for their own defense but also for the "common good"—essentially collective security missions in support of broader international security goals. The "free rider" problem endures: The United States spends 3.3 percent of its GDP on defense, while its NATO allies spend an average of 1.45 percent, Japan spends 1 percent of GDP, and South Korea spends 2.6 percent.[31] As a result, allies have become even more dependent on the U.S. security blanket, while the task of forming effective "coalitions of the willing" is becoming harder as the gap in capabilities and standards of readiness grows wider.[32] The demands placed on the United States to underwrite international order have only increased as a consequence.

THE ADVANTAGES OF A DEMAND-SIDE STRATEGY

Managing the growing challenges to international order before they gather momentum and present the United States with unpalatable choices that have potentially costly consequences is clearly desirable. At a time of fiscal austerity when the United States is facing many competing demands, both foreign and domestic, a more preventive strategic posture designed to conserve U.S. power has even greater appeal. In contrast, adopting a reactive posture increases the risk that the United States increasingly becomes hostage to world events. As Stephen Hadley, former U.S. national security adviser, has acknowledged, "When you have a series of crises and . . . all you end up doing is crisis management . . . then all you're going to get is more crises because you're not going to be shaping events and the future direction of our interests."[33]

Appreciating the strategic logic of preventive action is one thing; understanding where, when, and how to carry it out is quite another. U.S. policy makers need not look very far for inspiration and guidance, however. Preventive strategies have long been employed in other areas of public policy in response to more or less the same basic imperatives. Managing life-threatening infectious diseases probably represents the first example of a deliberately conceived preventive approach to a public policy problem. The now standard evidence-based techniques developed for preventing the onset and spread of infectious diseases have since been replicated in other areas of public health as well as for numerous public safety concerns ranging from combating violent crime and illicit drug use to firefighting and natural disaster management. For each of these challenges, painful experience has taught that reactive and remedial approaches are too easily overwhelmed and exhausted in times of crisis—and especially multiple, simultaneous crises. As a consequence, the imperative to fashion early preventive approaches has grown. Though there are variations in how preventive action has evolved across different areas of public policy, they essentially all use the same mutually reinforcing layered approach that can be readily adapted to create a comparable strategic framework to guide U.S. foreign and security policy. This consists of, in broad terms, three successive levels of prevention.

The first level of preventive action—conflict risk reduction—entails actively promoting conditions generally understood to be conducive to peace and stability both within and between states. The public health care equivalent is dietary and lifestyle guidelines to promote healthy living and lower the likelihood of debilitating disease. Conflict risk reduction includes promoting generally accepted norms and rules that regulate the behavior of states to lessen the inherently "anarchic" nature of the international system—most notably those relating to national sovereignty, proscriptions on the use of force, and access to and use of the global commons. International mechanisms that facilitate the peaceful resolution of disputes—particularly competing territorial claims, but also miscellaneous global regulatory regimes that control potentially destabilizing weapons—also fall into this category. Less obvious as conflict risk reduction measures are numerous international initiatives and programs that promote broad-based economic development, international trade, public health, literacy, democratic forms of governance and, increasingly, improving the economic and social condition of women around the world; all have had a demonstrable benefit in promoting peace and stability. Diminishing the possible negative impact of anticipated demographic trends, natural resource exploitation, or environmental degradation can also all be considered risk reduction initiatives.

Within states, conflict risk reduction entails deliberate efforts to promote the rule of law as well as civil and human rights, which can mean anything from encouraging independent judiciaries, broadening electoral rights, and limiting political and economic discrimination to strengthening policing and improving general access to the justice system. Other elements of what is now often called good governance designed to improve the "social contract" between state institutions and the citizenry also help reduce the risk of political instability and conflict. Such measures, moreover, can be broadly applicable (in what is sometimes called systemic risk reduction) or more narrowly focused on redressing a specific source of concern (known as structural risk reduction).

The second level of preventive action are deliberate measures to avert an extant dispute or source of tension (again, within or between states) from erupting into a violent conflict. The health equivalent is early medical treatment to prevent the onset of a disease where the warning signs are already evident. Depending on the nature of the conflict, a variety of preventive measures can be directed at addressing—and, better still, resolving—the source of the dispute. External mediation and arbitration directed at achieving, for example, an acceptable domestic power-sharing arrangement or satisfactory demarcation of a territorial dispute constitute one kind of crisis prevention. If the source of the conflict cannot be resolved, at least in the short term, then other preventive measures can be employed to shape the calculus of the parties in dispute so that a resort to violence is seen as neither attractive nor necessary. Various military, economic, and diplomatic measures can be targeted to constrain or otherwise positively influence the motives, means, and opportunities of the parties not to engage in violent behavior.

At the interstate level, these can range from confidence-building measures designed to reduce mistrust and avoid unintended military escalation to unilateral actions intended to deter aggressive behavior through military assistance, security guarantees, and the threat of various types of sanctions for noncompliance, all with the goal of raising the likely cost of such action. Similar techniques can be used for intrastate disputes to shape the behavior of governments as well as nonstate actors. For example, precautionary measures can be taken to address a predictable increase in tensions, such as those that might occur around an election or transfer of power, as well as known flash points like existing disputes over access to such resources as oil, arable land, or water.

The third level of preventive action is conflict mitigation measures intended to de-escalate a dispute after parties have resorted to the use of force. Emergency care would be the medical equivalent. The techniques of conflict mitigation are broadly similar to crisis prevention in that positive and negative inducements would be employed to convince the parties to the conflict to halt—and preferably reverse—the actions that escalated the dispute in the first place. This includes, on the one hand, *coercive de-escalation* measures, such as the use of various sanctions (e.g., diplomatic pressure, travel bans, trade embargoes, and withholding foreign aid, as well as legal and military threats) and, on the other hand, *consensual de-escalation* measures such as offering various rewards for compliant behavior (e.g., economic assistance, diplomatic recognition, military support, and domestic power sharing). These tactics are not mutually exclusive, and more often than not they are used together in a complementary, mutually reinforcing manner (as "sticks and carrots"). Where de-escalation is not immediately feasible, containing the conflict and minimizing the human costs may be the best that can be accomplished in the short term.

These three levels of preventive action would form the basis of a comprehensive U.S. strategy of preventive engagement to manage long-term, medium-term, and short-term risks to international order. Although this strategy would encompass many programs and activities that the United States already pursues, preventive engagement would amount to a much more coherent and systematic effort that also encompasses several new initiatives.

ANSWERING THE SKEPTICS

The premise and practicalities of preventive engagement are sure to elicit some initial skepticism—and perhaps even concern over its potential costs and risks—among readers. More specifically, the notion that the United States can shape the forces that cause instability and conflict in the world so as to lessen the likelihood that it may be called upon to use its military power could be considered the height of conceit. There are many deep and powerful—not to mention complex—drivers of disorder at work that, to put it mildly, are difficult enough for American policy makers to comprehend, much less to tame. Pursuing this goal, moreover, could lead the United States to take on even more risky and expensive commitments that lead to the very outcome preventive engagement is intended to avoid—namely, strategic overstretch. Alternatively, other readers may fear that preventive engagement could have the opposite effect in fostering what might be called strategic "understretch" by constraining and delimiting U.S. foreign and security policy in such a way as to be self-emasculating.

With regard to the first set of concerns, it is important not to misunderstand or exaggerate the core objective of preventive engagement. It is not about eradicating conflict from the face of the earth, a goal that would be truly grandiose and in some instances even undesirable. Regrettable though the loss of life is when disputes turn deadly, societal conflict has in many instances served a positive role in bringing about desirable change in the world. Rather, the goal is to lessen the risk of the United States being drawn into costly military interventions that could have been avoided and that will not advance American interests or demonstrably improve global security.

Here the record of U.S. conflict management efforts is encouraging regarding the feasibility and, moreover, larger rewards of a more deliberate and comprehensive preventive engagement effort. Indeed, as will become clear, much of preventive engagement entails adjusting and extending long-standing U.S. policies that have clearly contributed to the near absence of major interstate conflict since 1945—the aforementioned Long Peace. These include various initiatives to promote strategic stability among the major powers, dampen regional rivalries, foster global development, stimulate free trade, and extend democracy and human rights around the world. The United States, moreover, has on many occasions made bold and timely interventions to defuse dangerous international crises and avert conflict. Deftly managing the Cold War's endgame, dissuading on several occasions Indian and Pakistani leaders from going to war, and mediating in numerous deadly disputes in the Middle East, Africa, and Latin America are just some of the examples.

Some skeptics will likely still be doubtful that the United States can "scale up" its preventive efforts and do significantly better than it has in the past. Detecting signs of incipient instability—and with it, larger geostrategic risks—is difficult at the best of times given all the uncertainties of political forecasting, as the United States has found out to its surprise on many occasions. Likewise, mobilizing the political will to act given other demands and interests even when there are compelling warning signs has, if anything, proven an even bigger obstacle since the end of the Cold War. And even when the commitment exists, orchestrating all the moving parts of a preventive engagement strategy can seem a formidable challenge.

These are all reasonable questions to ask, yet there are ample reasons to believe the United States can implement such a strategy using tools it has been refining for many decades. Not all kinds of preventive action, moreover, depend on the early detection of potentially dangerous contingencies.

Just as in everyday life we take precautionary measures to lower the risk of plausible events that could do us harm—whether car accidents, household fires, illnesses, tooth decay, or criminal acts (all without clear indication that these will happen to us anytime soon)—so the application of best practice applies to long-term preventive engagement. At the same time, our capacity to assess the likelihood of specific events happening in the near future, at least, is improving all the time with the development of new forecasting and risk-assessment tools. So, too, is our ability to monitor current hot spots around the world in close to real time by virtue of new and publicly accessible surveillance technologies and personal communication devices. Generating the will to act will always be a challenge but, here again, various organizational strategies can be implemented to overcome inertia and resistance. More routinized and rigorous policy planning that produces feasible options at an early stage, as well as crisis management techniques based on lessons learned, can also go a long way toward generating timely and effective responses. Properly trained and resourced personnel can likewise make a big difference. And while there have been many obvious failures of preventive action, there have been enough successes to suggest that much more can be achieved with the appropriate level of effort, if not always and everywhere.

It is also important to acknowledge when discussing issues of practicality, preventive engagement should not be pursued in an undisciplined or undifferentiated manner. Not every plausible source of instability and conflict poses the same set of risks to the United States and is thus deserving of equal attention and resources. U.S. preventive engagement should be prioritized, therefore, to focus most on the challenges that would matter most; otherwise its execution would indeed court strategic overstretch and national exhaustion. How to determine what is important and also what could become important if left unaddressed is not a straightforward exercise, but strategic discrimination must increasingly be practiced by the United States. This book offers guidelines on how to make those judgment calls, since there are remarkably no accepted criteria for classifying how specific threats or contingencies relate to the *national interest*, despite the frequency with which this term is invoked. Viewed this way, preventive engagement actually has more in common with the tenets of realism than

22

liberal idealism. In a similar vein, the job of maintaining international order is not one the United States can or should take on alone. The magnitude and complexity of the emerging challenges described herein are too great and their potential impact too far-reaching. Preventive engagement should thus be a shared imperative and responsibility. This would entail the United States enhancing and harnessing the capacities of like-minded actors, whether they be other major powers, allied countries, international institutions, nongovernmental organizations, or private business interests. Forging effective partnerships with these actors will not only lend broad legitimacy to U.S initiatives but also help sustain domestic support for continued engagement.

As for the second set of concerns, it is equally important to emphasize that preventive engagement does not mean that America would, a priori, eschew the use of force to achieve its objectives. There are clearly instances in which the United States will feel compelled to take military action, including those for preventive purposes. The purpose of a preventive engagement strategy is to make it feel so compelled less often. This does not mean, however, that force would only be used when all other options have been tried and exhausted—in other words, as a last resort. Although it is clearly desirable to pursue peaceful preventive measures when they still offer the prospect of success, the early use of military force may be necessary in some instances to preempt a larger harm to U.S. interests. This is an accepted principle of policing in law enforcement. Finally, preventive engagement should not be construed as limiting the United States to taking action only when its strategic interests are imperiled. Risks that appear low or inconsequential can become more menacing if left unattended. While prioritization is essential for the reasons discussed, it should thus endeavor to address lesser concerns when and where it can, even if that only amounts to exhorting and pressuring others who have more of a stake to take action.

Finally, some may believe that preventive engagement is simply too complex and demanding a strategy for the United States to implement. Grand strategies that have many moving parts to manage and orchestrate—as does preventive engagement—are certainly easier to formulate in the abstract than carry out in practice. This is especially true for advanced democracies like the United States whose entrenched interests and multiple power centers pursue their own agendas and often keep one another in check.[34] Yet the United States has demonstrated that it can pursue multifaceted foreign initiatives in the past, and it certainly has the organizational resources to do so today. Nevertheless, preventive engagement would require the current machinery of foreign policy to undergo a significant change in operational posture—from one that is overwhelmingly shortsighted and reactive to world events to one that actively seeks to anticipate and manage them to America's benefit.

AN OVERVIEW OF THE BOOK

The case for a U.S. strategy of preventive engagement will be laid out more fully in the chapters that follow. This book is organized into two parts. The first discusses the conceptual foundations of preventive action as the basis for a new national strategy. Chapter 2 examines more closely the commonly recurring problems that bedevil the early detection and warning of threats that can preclude early preventive responses. A different approach to triggering preventive action is proposed—one that emphasizes the assessment of changing geopolitical risk through the rigorous application of what is termed *preventive foresight methods*. Foresight is a necessary, but not sufficient, ingredient to preventive action. Numerous other obstacles can still inhibit policy makers from taking timely action regardless of how compelling the need may seem. Chapter 3 discusses these impediments and how they, too, can be overcome. This includes having a full understanding of the available options so that choices do not become artificially restricted, embedding preventive policies in other public policy initiatives and creating dedicated structures to facilitate early action.

The second part of the book lays out what a U.S. strategy of preventive engagement would look like in practice. Chapter 4 assesses the long-term preventive priorities of the United States and what can be done to lessen the general risk of global disorder. Chapter 5 examines the medium-term contingencies that could plausibly arise and trigger U.S. military engagement. Specific measures for how this risk can be lessened through deliberate crisis prevention efforts are proposed. Chapter 6 focuses on how to manage the short-term risks posed by ongoing conflicts that already involve or threaten the United States.

How well the United States executes these different but interconnected elements of preventive engagement will depend greatly on how well it both encourages and harnesses the help of potential international partners who also have a stake in managing sources of conflict and disorder. These actors can not only help share the burden but also lend legitimacy to U.S.-sponsored initiatives. Chapter 7 assesses the opportunities and challenges to working with a range of potential "partners in preventive action" and proposes ways the United States can enhance their contribution.

Much of the assessment and associated prescription within these latter chapters will inevitably become dated; the world is, after all, a dynamic place, and U.S. preventive priorities must change accordingly. The basic approach, however, will remain valid, and thus readers can take the same generic strategies and tactics and adapt them for new contingencies that arise.

The book concludes with chapter 8, a discussion of the organizational changes required to make a preventive engagement strategy work. The United States does not need to carry out a wholesale or costly overhaul of its current foreign policy machinery. What is needed most of all is a reorientation of existing structures to make them more forward looking and less reactive, as well as a rebalancing of existing resources devoted to U.S. foreign and security policy away from the current heavy reliance on military measures toward other instruments of statecraft.

PART ONE

THE BUILDING BLOCKS OF PREVENTIVE ENGAGEMENT

R EDUCED TO ITS bare essentials, preventive engagement requires that the United States anticipate how it could be drawn into potentially costly military commitments in the foreseeable future and then take precautionary measures to lessen that risk. In practice, preventive engagement entails several discrete steps—four, to be precise. The first is discerning how certain trends could evolve or circumstances coalesce in plausible ways as to threaten U.S. interests and increase the likelihood of military force being used in response. Such assessment—what can be termed preventive foresight—then has to be rendered actionable in the sense that it is sufficiently specific and compelling to garner the attention of policy makers otherwise consumed by day-to-day issues. The second step, therefore, is effectively conveying the results of preventive foresight to those empowered to respond. How they use this information constitutes the next step. Much hinges on their appreciation of what strategies and instruments can be employed to mitigate specific risks, since inertia is likely to prevail otherwise. The fourth and final step is orchestrating and implementing the chosen policy. Here, being adaptable to changing circumstances and opportunities that arise is especially important. The first two steps—abbreviated here as "thinking ahead"—will be addressed in chapter 2, whereas the last two—"acting ahead"—are discussed in chapter 3.

2

THINKING AHEAD

From Warning to Anticipation

A man who does not think and plan ahead will find trouble right at his door.

—CONFUCIUS

For the far-sighted, nothing is unexpected; there are no tight spots for those who are prepared. Don't save your reason for when difficulties arise, use it well before that. Anticipate critical times with mature reflection. The pillow is a silent Sibyl and sleeping on things is better than lying awake under their weight.

—BALTASAR GRACIÁN

N ONE OF his last major speeches as U.S. secretary of defense in early 2011, Robert Gates addressed the cadets at the U.S. Military Academy at West Point, New York, and made a remarkable admission: "When it comes to predicting the nature and location of our next military engagements, since Vietnam our record has been perfect. *We have never once gotten it right*; from the Mayaguez to Grenada, Panama, Somalia, the Balkans, Haiti, Kuwait, Iraq, and more—we had no idea a year before any of these missions that we would be so engaged."[1] Gates could easily have gone back further than Vietnam to the Korean War as well as to Pearl Harbor and America's entry into World War II. And, had he spoken just a few weeks later, he would doubtless have cited the completely unforeseen U.S. military intervention in Libya as yet another example. Indeed, as he would later ruefully admit, this time to U.S. Marines at Camp Lejeune, North Carolina, "If you'd asked me four months ago if we'd be in Libya today, I would have asked you what you were smoking."[2]

Although Gates's remarks were clearly intended to admonish the U.S. military about the perils of wishful thinking when planning for the next war, he touched on a larger, more uncomfortable truth: the United States has repeatedly found itself involved in major conflicts and many lesser military contingencies that it never saw coming—at least not very far in advance. How, then, can U.S. leaders hope to avoid potentially costly military engagements in the future if they have regularly failed to foresee them in the past?

The usual response is through better early warning. Indeed, virtually every postmortem of an acknowledged strategic surprise or intelligence failure has recommended that the United States improve the various early warning systems it relies on to detect threatening developments and alert policy makers in a timely fashion.[3] This has resulted in numerous initiatives over the years that, among other things, have upgraded the collection and sharing of intelligence, enhanced the quality of analysis, and sped up the transmission of critical information to senior decision makers to give them the opportunity to respond. Despite these efforts, however, the United States continues to be blindsided by threatening developments. Some of these were genuinely unpredictable, but not all.

As will be discussed in greater detail, numerous problems can bedevil how well early warning systems work. The biggest limitation, however, is what can be described as their inherent confirmation bias. More specifically, those responsible for either conveying or responding to warning information are understandably reluctant to do so until they are certain or near certain that the threatening development or event will actually occur. Such a high threshold of proof effectively means that early warning systems are essentially *reactive* in how they function: threats more or less have to materialize before action is taken in response. This does not mean that all early warning systems are worthless and should be abandoned, but rather that their limitations for triggering early *preventive* action must be recognized and a different approach found.

This chapter will argue that the answer lies in being able to anticipate potentially dangerous developments or contingencies in terms of the risk they pose to U.S. interests so that precautionary measures can be taken to lessen their likelihood or reduce their potential harm should they occur. Thinking ahead in this fashion can be accomplished through *preventive foresight*, a process that draws on forecasting and risk assessment techniques commonly used by public policy practitioners in other areas as well as by many private businesses to evaluate how the future might unfold for good or bad. The second half of this chapter will describe how preventive foresight would work in practice and how its results can be conveyed to policy makers in a way that motivates them to act in a precautionary fashion.

THE LIMITS OF EARLY WARNING

Much has been written about the challenges that early warning systems face, particularly in the context of trying to avoid a surprise military attack.[4] These challenges are typically dissected and organized into discrete phases of the warning process, from the initial tasking of intelligence collection on potential threats to the eventual alerting of policy makers. The most common and relevant challenges are reproduced here to underscore the limits of early warning systems for preventive action:[5]

- Missed Signals: Early indications of danger can be overlooked because intelligence collection efforts are focused elsewhere or technical problems and environmental constraints compromise their early detection. Deliberate denial-and-deception measures by adversaries to evade or mislead intelligence collection can pose an additional challenge. Since gathered intelligence usually has to be processed from its raw state to render it accessible for subsequent interpretation and analysis, technical issues, human error, and the sheer volume of information to be sifted can also affect whether critical information is extracted and identified amid the "background noise"—again, in a timely manner.
- Dismissed Signals: How well the collected information is analyzed and interpreted can depend on another set of factors. Bureaucratic silos and the common practice of compartmentalizing sensitive intelligence for

31

security reasons can sometimes prevent analysts from being able to assemble all the available pieces of the puzzle and "connect the dots." These same analysts (like all humans) are subject to well-known cognitive biases when it comes to filtering and interpreting information, and this may cause them to dismiss or ignore important warning signs.[6] In particular, as Thomas Schelling noted in his oft-quoted foreword to Roberta Wohlstetter's famous account of U.S. failings prior to the Japanese attack on Pearl Harbor, "There is a tendency. . . . to confuse the unfamiliar with the improbable. The contingency we have not considered seriously looks strange; what looks strange is thought improbable; what is improbable need not be considered seriously."[7] Procedures to counter such biases, including having multiple groups and designated "red teams" review the intelligence,[8] can help but may come at the price of delaying the transmission of warning information to the appropriate decision makers. Major differences of opinion may have to be reconciled or resolved in some way before the warning process can proceed. Analysts, moreover, ultimately have to grapple with the classic overwarning versus underwarning dilemma—essentially whether to sound the alarm for something that may later prove to be unfounded (potentially damaging the credibility of subsequent warnings, not to mention triggering costly and unwarranted countermeasures) versus refraining from alerting policy makers about concerns that may later prove to be warranted (with potentially even graver consequences).

- Missed Warnings: Human error, technical snafus, and organizational silos that regulate the flow of information in any government bureaucracy can all delay or derail the transmission of warning information to the appropriate officials. Even when channels exist for senior officials to be alerted, simple agenda overload caused by the press of current events can hold up the timely consideration of warning information.

- Dismissed Warnings: Policy makers are subject to the same set of cognitive biases as analysts, and these inevitably shape how they assimilate warning information and whether they absorb and appreciate it.[9] Studies indicate that much hinges on how reliable and trustworthy the source of the warning intelligence information is and the perceived credibility of the messenger bearing it. Time pressures and other distractions are additional factors.[10] For harried policy makers typically consumed by the immediate tasks at hand, less than fully confident warnings—which given typical levels of uncertainty is commonplace—can provide an excuse to discount and even ignore information about as yet unrealized developments. This tendency will be strongest the further into the future the warning pertains.[11] The availability of other information acquired from the media or personal contacts with nongovernmental experts or foreign leaders that either reinforces or contradicts the warning message can also be critical.

In general, early warning systems tend to work better when the provenance and nature of the threat is well known and accepted as a priority concern. Intelligence collection efforts can be focused and refined in a way to reduce the likelihood that critical danger signals will be missed. Analysts are less likely to wring their hands over the meaning of ambiguous indicators. And the recipients of warning information are also more predisposed to react when the signs of potential hostile behavior start to manifest themselves since they are already primed about the significance of the threat. As Alexander George and Jane Holl note, "Policy makers have already determined that some set of observable hostile actions would be an unmistakable threat and have the strongest possible incentives to acquire timely warning and to respond to that threat in some way."[12]

Such clarity about the threat more or less prevailed in the Cold War, certainly with regard to the main focus of concern. Besides the possibility of a "bolt from the blue" missile attack by the Soviet Union, the principal warning priorities consisted of a few relatively discrete contingencies in Europe, East Asia, and later the Persian Gulf. Following the fall of the Berlin Wall and especially the demise of the Soviet Union, the early warning challenge eased dramatically in one sense but grew much harder in others. More specifically, aside from a few unresolved conflicts left over from the Cold War—notably on the Korean Peninsula and between China and Taiwan—the need to detect early signs of offensive military preparations more or less disappeared. In its place, however, an expansive list of new and much more ambiguous security concerns emerged that policy makers increasingly demanded had to be monitored. This included would-be nuclear proliferators, terrorist groups, transnational criminal gangs, and

33

miscellaneous political and humanitarian problems associated with what came to be categorized as weak or failing states. In effect, as one former U.S. intelligence official described the shift in focus, the United States went from having to carry out the equivalent of a small number of police stakeouts of known criminal haunts where the telltale signs of potential unlawful intent are well known and relatively easy to identify at an early stage, to having to carry out many neighborhood watch patrols where it is inherently difficult to discern what is going on and thus what could happen next.[13]

THE POST–COLD WAR WARNING CHALLENGE

The mixed record of the United States in detecting and responding to miscellaneous threats in the post–Cold War era underscores the strengths and weaknesses of early warning systems. Not long after the fall of the Berlin Wall, the U.S. intelligence community successfully warned the George H. W. Bush administration about rising military tensions between India and Pakistan. Senior officials were subsequently dispatched to the region in early 1990 to mediate between the two countries, and the crisis was defused.[14] That both countries had gone to war several times in the past clearly made the warning signs more credible and thus harder to discount. In contrast, when the intelligence community later warned more or less the same group of officials that Iraq was preparing to invade Kuwait in August 1990, they dismissed the likelihood of this happening virtually right up to the moment it occurred.[15] This scenario had not been considered in earlier U.S. policy planning toward the Persian Gulf, and thus the United States was caught completely unprepared for its eventuality.[16] As Richard Haass, then the senior director for the Near East and South Asia on the National Security Council later acknowledged, "There was no playbook or contingency plan for dealing with this scenario or anything like it."[17]

The U.S. response to the early signs that Yugoslavia might break apart violently reflects a similar story. The U.S. intelligence community correctly interpreted the centrifugal forces at work and warned policy makers that the Yugoslav Federation would inevitably dissolve amid considerable "intercommunal conflict."[18] Not until Yugoslavia began to unravel, however, did the United States begin to respond. Besides the distractions of what was happening in the Persian Gulf and the Soviet Union at the time, several senior officials who had firsthand experience working in Yugoslavia evidently discounted the likelihood of it breaking up, while others felt there was nothing much the United States could do about it in any case—certainly not without contradicting long-standing U.S. policy favoring national self-determination.

In contrast, U.S. intelligence failed to warn the William J. Clinton administration about the potential for mass atrocities in Rwanda in 1994 and was slow to grasp the scale of the genocide even after it had commenced. Central Africa was not a priority focus for intelligence gathering, and to the extent that those monitoring the situation appraised the risk of a civil war in Rwanda, the likelihood of a massive genocide had simply not been imagined.[19] The Indian and Pakistani nuclear tests of 1998 also came as a surprise to the Clinton White House. Having seen India make earlier preparations to test and then back off, mostly as a result of U.S. pressure, the pledge by the new Indian Bharatiya Janata Party government to move forward with developing an operational nuclear capability appears to have been interpreted as no more than nationalistic bluster by U.S. officials. It also did not help that the intelligence analyst responsible for monitoring the Indian test site was off duty immediately prior to the first blast.[20]

The 9/11 terrorist attacks represent a more complex story. Although it is clear that signals were missed and potentially crucial information was not shared among various intelligence agencies that might have made a difference in thwarting the attacks, senior U.S officials were nevertheless given strategic warning of al-Qaeda's intentions to carry out a major and potentially catastrophic strike on the United States on multiple occasions well before September 11, 2001. By summer 2001 the warnings of an imminent attack and even details of the potential method were conveyed to President George W. Bush and his senior advisers, though the location and precise timing remained uncertain. While some actions were taken during this period to counter al-Qaeda, it is fair to say that the prevailing assessment—certainly among senior Bush administration officials—discounted the likelihood and certainly magnitude of a potential attack.[21] There is no indication, moreover, that those who did worry about a mass casualty terrorist attack gave much if any thought to how the United States might have to respond if what they feared actually happened.[22]

A similar pattern of denial occurred in the lead-up to the Russian invasion of Georgia in early August 2008. As tensions grew between Georgia and Russia throughout spring 2008, the U.S. intelligence community warned U.S. officials of the danger of conflict, especially after it was observed that the Russian forces seen undertaking military exercises on the border with Georgia in July had not returned to their barracks thereafter. This prompted Secretary of State Condoleezza Rice to warn Georgian president Mikheil Saakashvili to desist from actions that might provoke Russia. The delivery of this message appears to have convinced the White House that Georgia would not do anything so foolish, while at the same time it also presumed that Russia would not risk broad international opprobrium by invading a sovereign country. Thus the initial Georgian artillery bombardment of the breakaway republic of South Ossetia and the subsequent but apparently preplanned invasion of Georgia by nearby Russian forces caught everyone by surprise. As Damon Wilson, then a director at the National Security Council later admitted, "Our analysts missed it on Georgia." He added, "We had plenty of warnings in 2008 that Russia would provoke a confrontation with Georgia and end up invading, but we still didn't believe they would actually do it."[23] As a result, the United States had to improvise its response from a hastily prepared set of options.[24] These included supplying Georgia with antiaircraft missiles and even bombing the tunnel used by Russian forces to support their invasion. Though these military options were quickly rejected, the subsequent U.S. airlift of Georgian troops that had been deployed to Iraq back to Georgia, along with the presence of U.S. advisers in the country, did increase the risk of a U.S.-Russian military incident that might have escalated the conflict in a dangerous manner. As Angela Stent, former U.S. national intelligence officer for Russia later argued, "American and Russian troops came closer to facing each other on opposite sides of an armed conflict than at any time during the Cold War. American troops were in Georgia, training soldiers who were going to Iraq and Afghanistan. This sobering fact was fully appreciated only after the war was over."[25]

More recently, the Arab uprisings that began in December 2010 following the self-immolation of Mohamed Bouazizi, a lowly fruit vendor in Tunisia, to protest the harassment and humiliation he had felt at the hands of the local authorities caught everyone by surprise. The public outrage over his death triggered widespread unrest that would eventually bring down the government in Tunis and spark rebellions throughout the Arab world that would result in the demise of two more heads of state, Egypt's Hosni Mubarak and Libya's Muammar al-Gaddafi, the latter through NATO intervention. Though the U.S. intelligence community can hardly be faulted for having failed to predict the precise trajectory of events in Tunisia, it clearly failed to appreciate the growing vulnerability of the region to political instability, apparently in large part because its principal sources of information were the regimes that would eventually fall.[26] Subsequent events in Syria and in Iraq with the rise of the Islamic State, as well as the Houthi rebellion in Yemen, also came as a surprise to U.S. policy makers, though it remains a subject of contention as to whether they were properly informed about these developments or did not take the warnings from the intelligence community seriously enough.[27]

The United States also seems to have been blindsided by Russia's annexation of Crimea and its support for rebel forces in eastern Ukraine in 2014. Although parts of the U.S. intelligence community have insisted that they warned the Obama administration about Russia's intentions, the former deputy director of the CIA, Michael Morrell, acknowledged that the single-minded focus on preventing another 9/11 contributed to the United States being surprised by what eventually transpired.[28] As he later wrote in his memoirs, "Perhaps the biggest downside to our necessary focus on terrorism was the cost to the Agency's ability to be a global intelligence service—to have the access around the world to be able to warn the president in advance that could undermine US national security. There is no doubt in my mind that the resource shift and focus on terrorism were in part responsible for our failure to more clearly foresee some key global developments such as Russia's renewed aggressive behavior with its neighbors."[29] Russia's subsequent military intervention in Syria in September 2015, as well as

China's rapid island reclamation activities in the South China Sea at more or less the same time, are also thought to have caught senior U.S. officials off guard.[30]

THE MERITS OF PREVENTIVE FORESIGHT

The recurring instances in which the United States failed to either detect or respond to threatening developments since the end of the Cold War strongly suggests that this pattern will continue unless a different approach is used to sensitize policy makers to incipient dangers and motivate them to take precautionary measures in response. The remedy lies in having the ability to not just warn about known *threats* but also to assess and appreciate evolving *risks*. This distinction between threats and risks may seem trivial, but it is important.

Threats are typically viewed in binary terms—they are either present or absent—and, moreover, have agency in that they derive from someone's intention to do harm. The magnitude of a threat is usually calculated as

$$Threat = Capabilities \times Intentions$$

Risks, on the other hand, are generally understood to be the product of a double calculation—an estimate of the likelihood that something harmful could happen in a defined time frame and its probable impact or consequences if it does. This is sometimes represented as

$$Risk = Probability \times Impact^{31}$$

Unlike threats, risks are generally seen as latent, albeit variable in magnitude. Human agency is also not assumed in that harmful events can occur as a consequence of accidents and unintended actions. This is why threat terminology is more frequently attached to human-driven phenomena, whereas risk is more often associated with naturally occurring and thus more random hazards.

This difference has important psychological effects: people are predisposed to respond to threats only when they become evident, whereas they typically view it as desirable to actively manage risks through precautionary measures before they materialize and cause harm. For example, many car drivers will behave more cautiously at nighttime and in adverse weather, without needing confirming evidence that the road surface is more hazardous or that others are driving recklessly. City neighborhoods known to be high crime areas will also typically induce precautionary behavior in those passing through them. Likewise, many people will not wait for signs of incipient disease or ill health before they do things that are perceived to lower their risk of illness. They may appreciate the chance of succumbing to specific ailments based on known rates of prevalence in specific demographic groups and also find healthy living to be rewarding in other ways. By contrast, unless there are good reasons to assume that a threat may emerge in the future or that it will evolve from its current form to become more dangerous at some later point, the default response is typically to wait and see, hoping for the best.

Risks can be assessed in a variety of ways depending on the nature of the putative danger or hazard being studied. In general, quantitative and qualitative judgments are made about the likelihood of the risk materializing and the magnitude of the potential harm if and when it does. The former typically entails looking for statistically robust correlations between identifiable risk factors and the incidence or onset of the phenomenon under study and then making estimates about the future. Such efforts can be supplemented with active surveillance for known risk factors or by monitoring them when they are already evident. Similarly, to the extent that the impact or harmful consequences of a phenomenon has been recorded from prior experience, reasoned estimates can be made about what might happen in comparable cases in the future. Where statistical assessments are hard to make because of deficiencies in the data, qualitative judgments can be used.

Risk assessment techniques are now regularly used in many areas of public policy, from epidemiology to criminology and environmental science. Although some of this work has been criticized for reductionism (oversimplifying complex processes), determinism (underestimating the role of human agency as a factor), and imputation (conflating correlation with causation), the underlying approach has become accepted in virtually every area of public health and safety. Moreover, it is widely credited with helping to fashion programs to reduce or minimize relevant risk.[32]

Preventive foresight adapts and uses similar techniques for the purpose of gauging the risk of specific events or contingencies arising that could be considered sufficiently threatening to U.S. interests as to trigger a military response. The goal is not to predict such events or contingencies but rather to reach an informed judgment regarding their likelihood and potential significance. Preventive foresight involves a three-step process. Step 1 entails understanding in general terms those contingencies likely to trigger U.S. military engagement based on historical experience. Step 2 involves assessing when, where, and how these generic triggering contingencies might plausibly arise in defined time periods by evaluating identifiable risk factors known to heighten (or lessen) the likelihood of such events occurring in the future. Step 3 requires evaluating the potential impact and significance of these specific contingencies for the United States since some pose a greater threat than others and could plausibly precipitate more extensive and costly levels of U.S. military engagement as a consequence. From these steps, an overall picture or "risk matrix" of U.S. military engagement can be produced, which plots various contingencies on a grid that indicates relative probability and impact. This matrix can in turn be used to prioritize specific preventive or mitigating measures. Each step will be discussed more fully below.

STEP 1: UNDERSTANDING TRIGGERING CONTINGENCIES FOR U.S. MILITARY ENGAGEMENT

What has motivated the United States to use force in the past represents the most reliable guide for gauging how it is likely to respond in comparable situations in the future. There is arguably no better and simpler encapsulation of the range of potential triggers than Thucydides' classic formulation of "fear, honor, and self-interest."[33] For the United States, as with any other country, fear derives most directly from perceptions of harm to life and property from either a prospective attack on its sovereign territory or one that has already materialized and that could be repeated and cause further harm. Fear can also derive from losing something deeply valued—an acquired standard of living or cherished way of life—and usually defined in terms of economic vitality and political freedom. Such concerns clearly overlap with interests in that America's general well-being depends heavily on its underlying economic health and standard of living. This in turn derives from (among other things) trading relationships, access to foreign markets and vital resources overseas, as well as the nation's relative political and economic influence in the world—all of which may be deemed worthy of protecting by force if necessary.

Honor, in comparison, would appear to be the weakest of the three triggers for the United States, though for Thucydides it was the most potent.[34] While conceived in his day as essentially about acquiring fame and glory, nowadays honor has come to mean self-esteem and international standing; these are sometimes expressed by the term *credibility*. More specifically, honor means living up to nationally proclaimed values and standards as well as fulfilling commitments and promises made to others. The United States sees itself as both the exemplar and standard bearer for what it believes to be universal human values. At the same time, it has taken on an unparalleled set of international security obligations that it now views as in its national interest to uphold. Perceptions of these obligations and the potential cost of not meeting them can exert a powerful and unpredictable influence on U.S. decision making in crisis situations.

The likelihood of U.S. military engagement will clearly be highest in situations when sentiments of fear, honor, and interest all come into play simultaneously. Obviously, when the territory of the United States is either overtly threatened or physically attacked, public pressure to retaliate forcefully will be greatest, as political and reputational concerns will also come into play. A similar contingency involving a close U.S. ally—especially one where many U.S. military personnel and civilians are living and thus in harm's way—would have a similar effect, if not with quite the same level of emotional intensity. In contrast, the violation of an important international agreement or norm that could have broad systemic or global consequences if ignored is a less predictable trigger for U.S. military engagement. Much depends on other contextual factors as the different U.S.

reactions to Iraq's invasion of Kuwait in 1990, Russia's seizure of parts of Georgia in 2008, and Russia's annexation of Crimea from Ukraine in 2014 indicate. All three entailed violations of state sovereignty, but the threat to U.S. strategic interests was perceived to be much higher in the first case than the latter two. Finally, contingencies involving countries that are not U.S. allies but where there are important political and economic interests at risk or where large numbers of civilians are threatened in some way can also trigger military intervention—as seen in Libya in 2011, in Iraq in 2014 to protect the minority Yazidi community on Mt. Sinjar from the depredations of ISIS, and in 2017 with the U.S. cruise missile strike on the Syrian airbase responsible for using chemical weapons against civilian targets. In such cases, the personal influence of specific advisers as well as the strength of certain domestic constituencies and pressure groups can affect how public opinion and ultimately U.S. decision makers react. The probable impact of these kinds of contingencies on U.S. behavior are thus the hardest to assess in advance, as the quote from Robert Gates during the 2014 Libya crisis attests. While historical examples provide useful precedents about when, where, how, and why the United States has intervened militarily in the past, it goes without saying that patterns will undoubtedly shift as norms develop, leaders change, and the nature of war evolves. Additionally, perceived lessons—both negative and positive— from prior cases of military intervention can color subsequent decisions on the use of force and must therefore be taken into account when making assessments.

STEP 2: ASSESSING THE LIKELIHOOD OF POTENTIAL TRIGGERING CONTINGENCIES

Although it is impossible to predict the precise events or scenarios that could lead to U.S. military intervention, it is possible to reduce the level of uncertainty in useful ways. Statistical analysis of observable variables is now increasingly used to assess the likely onset of certain types of conflict and political instability—in other words, the preconditions of most, if not all, of the likely triggering contingencies of interest. Judgments about the risk of specific states going to war, for example, can be assessed in broad-brush terms, at least, by the level of cross-border trade and investment. More dense economic relationships are generally positively correlated with a lower risk of international conflict.[35] Governance is another recognized risk factor. It is widely accepted that democracies rarely go to war with each other, though relatively new ones or those making the transition from authoritarianism have a higher risk of being involved in conflict than more established democracies.[36] At the same time "a new democracy is safest in a neighborhood mostly populated by other democracies."[37] How developed a state is in terms of its standard of living and level of institutional performance is yet another important risk factor. Less developed states are more susceptible to political instability and violent conflict than developed ones, though the precise reasons for this are a matter of dispute. In general, though, the poorer the country, the greater the risk. As political scientist James Fearon argues, "Per capita income is the single best predictor of a country's odds of civil war outbreak, empirically dominating other factors."[38]

Elaborate efforts have been made to build on these statistical associations and design formal predictive models. The most prominent is the work of the CIA-supported Political Instability Task Force (PITF). Over two decades of work has steadily refined this modeling effort to produce forecasting accuracies of around 80 percent on the basis of four leading indicators: regime type, infant mortality (seen as a proxy for level of development), armed conflict in neighboring countries, and state-led political discrimination. The PITF has applied its model with some additional modifications to specific subtypes of conflict, such as ethnic war and genocide, as well as specific regions and country types—sub-Saharan Africa, or countries with predominantly Muslim populations—with equally impressive results. Similar models have been developed to forecast state failure or risk of acute political instability.[39] Several indexes ranking fragile or failing countries are now published annually on the basis of these models. Collectively, these modeling efforts help to identify countries that are particularly susceptible to political instability and conflict without pretending to predict the precise onset or proximate causes of such events.[40]

Long-Term Assessments

These insights into the risk factors associated with certain kinds of instability and conflict can help inform more focused or tailored "horizon-scanning" exercises. For long-term assessments, one commonly used technique—sometimes referred to as cone of plausibility analysis—assesses how broad trends (political, economic, demographic, technological, environmental, etc.) could unfold and interact in ways that increase or lessen known risk factors to produce certain outcomes. An expected business-as-usual projection of the future is made based on the uninterrupted continuation of existing trends. This serves as a baseline from which to then explore how changing the core assumptions could alter the expected future in significant ways—whether that be in a potentially positive or negative direction (see figure 2.1). More profound departures from the baseline trajectory due to potential "shocks" or "wild card" developments—events of low probability but potentially high impact—can also be considered.

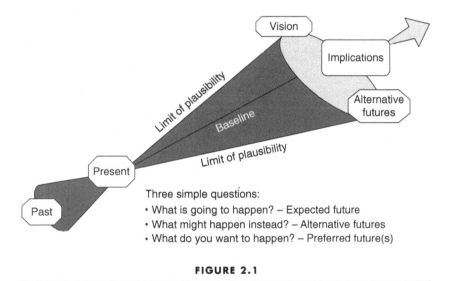

FIGURE 2.1

The Cone of Plausibility

Source: Josh Calder, concept by Charles W. Taylor, Army War College, "What Is Foresight?," Foresight Alliance, http://www.foresightalliance.com/resources/foresight-maturity-model /what-is-foresight/.

The scope of this kind of foresight analysis can be very broad for the purpose of understanding potential systemic global risks, or it can be more narrowly focused on a specific region or subregion or even a specific country where the key variables or drivers may be clearer and where a wider range of assumptions can be tested for their probable implications.

The forward-looking orientation of cone of plausibility exercises can be complemented by backcasting exercises. These entail positing future events or outcomes (whether positive or negative) and tracing a logical chain of events backward to the present day. The goal is not only to explore how different futures could plausibly transpire but also to identify potentially useful policy interventions to reverse engineer the preferred one.[41]

Medium-Term Assessments

For medium-term assessments where the goal is to reach more precise judgments about a particular country or region or the likelihood of a specific contingency, more refined foresight techniques can be employed. For example, the United States and several European governments have developed a variety of assessment methodologies for estimating the general susceptibility of individual countries to instability and conflict and to anticipate specific windows of vulnerability to guide potential precautionary measures. The approach used by these tools is broadly similar in that an initial assessment is made of the institutional capacity and performance of the country to carry out basic governance functions and also its underlying ability to withstand notional systemic shocks, whether from inside or outside the country. The principal actors—political leaders, factions, and groups—are also assessed on their potential motivations to resort to violence in prescribed circumstances, how and when they might do so given potential opportunities that could plausibly arise, and the means at their disposal to do so. The role of potential "enablers" and "inhibitors" is also often addressed this way. Particular attention is given to known upcoming events, such as an election or other political transition that may provide either a period of vulnerability or opportunity. The approach is captured in figure 2.2,

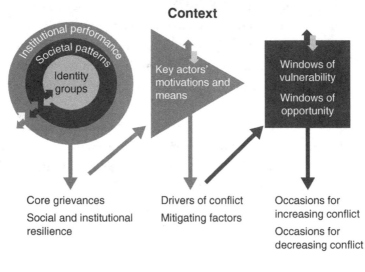

FIGURE 2.2

Evaluating the Dynamics of Conflict

Source: U.S. Department of State, *U.S. Interagency Conflict Assessment Framework* (Washington, D.C.: U.S. Department of State, 2008), http://www.state.gov/documents /organization/187786.pdf.

which is drawn from the U.S. Interagency Conflict Assessment Framework (ICAF) developed by various government agencies to better understand the risk of violent instability.

Although the ICAF and related assessment methods were designed with internal or civil conflict in mind, the basic approach can easily be adapted to assess the risk of interstate conflict. The same three core variables—the motives of the disputants, the means at their disposal, and perceived opportunities to resort to violent action—can be assessed in a similar fashion. Just as police investigators or forensic scientists will try to re-create the events leading up to a crime *after* the event, so a similar "pre-forensic" assessment of specific contingencies can be carried out to gauge their likelihood and consequence. Moreover, as will be illustrated in the next chapter, this same methodology can be used to devise preventive strategies that address each of the three variables.

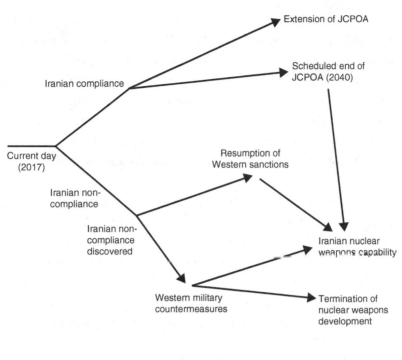

FIGURE 2.3

Joint Comprehensive Plan of Action (JCPOA) Scenarios

Source: Paul Stares, Washington, D.C., June 2017.

Branch analysis is another useful foresight technique, particularly in cases where the goal is to try to anticipate what might happen in the wake of an important and potentially pivotal event that is either planned or considered plausible. This projects different chain reactions from a single event, such as an upcoming election or referendum, a coup, or an armed clash between two protagonists. Figure 2.3 illustrates this approach with reference to the 2015 nuclear agreement with Iran.

Short-Term Assessments

Gauging whether one branch or outcome is more likely than another can also be augmented through statistical analysis of the kind described above, as well as by polling acknowledged experts (for example, using the so-called

Delphi technique and predictive markets, where participants make bids on specific futures). Exploiting the collective wisdom of nonexperts through regular questioning has also developed into a promising area of forecasting—at least for relatively short-term horizons.[42] Gaming exercises that simulate possible triggering events for specific contingencies to evaluate not only their likelihood but also their outcome is another well-developed approach. Different scenarios can be rigorously examined and tweaked in ways to ascertain what are likely to be the critical variables or drivers of certain outcomes.

From these different assessment methodologies, specific contingencies can be categorized according to their relative likelihood. For long-range assessments, probability judgements will necessarily be quite general, whereas for medium- and especially short-term horizons greater precision should be sought. This can take the form of specific bands of estimative probability with associated language to convey relative likelihood to policy makers. The schema in table 2.1 developed by CIA analysts illustrates this approach.[43]

Using this many increments of probability to evaluate the likelihood of a specific contingency may be considered excessive on the grounds that the level of uncertainty simply precludes such refined differentiation. It could also inadvertently suggest a false level of estimative confidence to policy makers that the analysis doesn't really support. These are important concerns but to avoid making even relatively crude probabilistic judgements because of the inherent analytical uncertainties would invalidate the whole logic of trying to be more anticipatory rather than reactive. For this reason, three general bands of likelihood derived from table 2.2 will be used here and in subsequent chapters: High (probable to almost certain), Moderate (even chance of occurring), and Low (improbable to highly unlikely).

STEP 3: EVALUATING THE IMPACT AND CONSEQUENCES OF PLAUSIBLE TRIGGERING CONTINGENCIES

Contingencies that carry the latent risk of triggering U.S. military engagement will vary not only in their likelihood within a defined time period but also in their immediate impact and, moreover, the type and scope of

TABLE 2.1 TERMS OF ESTIMATIVE PROBABILITY

100% CERTAINTY		
The General Area of Possibility		
93%	give or take about 6%	Almost certain
75%	give or take about 12%	Probable
50%	give or take about 10%	Chances about even
30%	give or take about 10%	Probably not
7%	give or take about 5%	Almost certainly not
0% Impossibility		

Source: Central Intelligence Agency, "Words of Estimative Probability," http://cia.gov/library/center-for-the-study-of-intelligence/csi-publications/books-and-monographs/sherman-kent-and-the-board-of-national-estimates-collected-essays/6words.html.

military operations that could plausibly ensue. Clearly some contingencies can be judged to be potentially more harmful and consequential to U.S. interests than others. Various assessment criteria can be used to evaluate the impact of a contingency besides its propensity to precipitate a U.S. military response. These include loss of life and other injuries (notably to American citizens), destruction of property (in particular U.S. property), temporary or prolonged effects on the quality of life (e.g. economic, environmental, and health prospects) in the United States, and other less tangible or subjective factors having to do with American values and political goals in the world. Harder to evaluate are the potential political and strategic costs of a contingency. The United States could conceivably lose international influence (in broad terms or with specific countries), international backing, or geographical access to certain countries or regions. The relative power and influence of other countries might grow as a consequence, which could have economic as well as security consequences for the United States.

When it comes to evaluating the significance of a potential contingency for U.S. military engagement, several criteria can again be used to assess the underlying risk. These include most obviously the nature of the potential adversary or adversaries, its/their capabilities (particularly the capacity to inflict harm on the U.S. homeland), the likely nature of the military engagement (from the use of weapons of mass destruction to low-intensity operations), the scope of operations (global, regional, or relatively local), and the potential duration of hostilities (from days to years).

Using these evaluation criteria, specific contingencies identified as plausible within certain time frames can in turn be broadly categorized for their relative impact and potential consequences for U.S. military engagement as follows:

- Category 1. High Consequence Contingencies: These would include contingencies that could cause or expose the United States to one or more of the following: high levels of fatalities (measured in the 10,000s), widespread physical destruction (measured in trillions of dollars to repair or replace), and high intensity military operations (measured in comparable terms). Potential armed conflict with one or more major powers that have the capability to attack the American homeland with weapons of mass destruction would constitute the most serious risk. The use of such weapons would have catastrophic—and in extremis existential—consequences for not just the United States but also the rest of the world. Attacks by nonstate actors that use or have the capacity to use weapons of mass destruction or other means to inflict comparable harm to the United States pose a lesser risk but still belong in this category.

- Category 2. Medium Consequence Contingencies: These would include contingencies that cause or expose a specific region to high levels of fatalities and physical destruction (including American citizens and property) and which are likely to involve the United States in a major regional military intervention. Events that could lead to war with a regional power represent the highest risk contingency in this category given that states in general have the capacity to mobilize significant national resources (conceivably including nonstate proxy forces) to wage war and may also be willing to resort to extreme measures if their leaders perceive that the outcome of the conflict has existential consequences for them. It cannot be assumed that the U.S. homeland and certainly U.S. citizens and/or military personnel living abroad would be safe from attack in such circumstances. The recent U.S. military operations to change the political regimes in

TABLE 2.2 RISK MATRIX FOR ASSESSING
CONTINGENCIES

	HIGH	MODERATE	LOW
Category 1			
Category 2			
Category 3			

Afghanistan and Iraq also illustrate how costly major regional military interventions can become after the defeat of a state adversary.

■ Category 3. Low Consequence Contingencies: These include contingencies that would cause minimal harm to the United States or likely affect its security and other interests in a marginal way if at all. Only very limited forms of military intervention would likely follow as a consequence. Examples are counterterrorism and counterproliferation strikes, limited humanitarian interventions, and peacekeeping missions. While such contingencies pose the least risk of the three categories in terms of their likely impact on the United States, the cost of quite limited engagements can still add up over time. They can also prompt later retaliatory action against American citizens and interests.

The combination of all three steps can be used to reach a net risk assessment of specific triggering contingencies and their potential implications for U.S. military engagement. Moreover, using a standard risk matrix that maps estimates of likelihood and impact, the *relative* risk of plausible contingencies can be evaluated, as illustrated in table 2.2.

CONVEYING PREVENTIVE FORESIGHT TO POLICY MAKERS

Much like early warning information, the insights gained from preventive foresight will be largely worthless if they are not conveyed to relevant policy makers in a compelling, persuasive, and timely manner. Several methods and useful insights gained from the burgeoning field of risk communication can be employed to increase the persuasiveness of the assessment.

The first method is to ensure that there are established conduits or transmission channels for relaying foresight analysis to decision makers who are empowered to make use of it. Ad hoc or irregular processes that are activated only when deemed necessary or that do not involve the relevant people are clearly deficient. This requirement was recognized, for example, in the creation of the Atrocities Prevention Board in 2011, which established clear procedures for relaying atrocity warning information to senior U.S. officials on a routinized basis as well as in emergency situations. The transmission of foresight, moreover, should not be one-directional; it must allow for interactions between the producers and the recipients, including the ability to request "deeper dives" into the reasoning behind specific assessments. When it comes to delivering preventive foresight information, the "messenger" and the "medium" both matter. This does not necessarily require that the individual delivering the assessment be someone of senior standing, though this is arguably preferable, but that its provenance be respected as credible and authoritative. A basic appreciation of how the assessment was produced, its logic and reasoning, as well as, moreover, the level of confidence attached to its conclusions, are essential. Care should also be given to how the assessment should be presented. As a considerable amount of research on the communication of public warnings has demonstrated, the receptivity of individuals to oral and written information can be enhanced in a variety of ways by tailoring it to specific audiences. Some officials, for example, will assimilate graphic information better than written text while others prefer data-intensive material.

Unless the magnitude of the risk is understood by the recipients of preventive foresight, these techniques to improve communication will be largely wasted. Policy makers need to appreciate the *significance* of the information they receive. Affixing easily understood labels to different types of contingencies that convey in a quick and compelling manner the level of risk can help in this regard. This is more or less the purpose of categorizing hurricanes and other extreme weather events to help the general public appreciate the potential harm and react accordingly. Something similar for conveying to policy makers preventive foresight assessments and in partic-

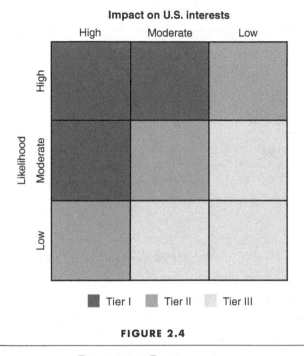

Impact on U.S. interests

FIGURE 2.4

Prioritizing Contingencies

Source: Center for Preventive Action, "Preventive Priorities Surveys," http://cfr.org/project
/preventive-priorities-survey.

ular the risk associated with discrete contingencies can be derived from
the matrix in table 2.2. Contingencies that fit inside specific "boxes" on the
risk matrix can be classified according to agreed rules for determining
relative significance and thus priority. Figure 2.4 indicates one common
way to organize contingencies into three levels or "tiers" of risk on the basis of aggregated estimates of their relative likelihood and impact.

Applying this approach to the preventive foresight risk matrix discussed
above would organize the range of contingencies into tiers of priority, as
illustrated in table 2.3. A very similar schema is used, for example, by the
United Kingdom for regular national security risk assessments that inform
its strategic defense reviews.[44]

TABLE 2.3 CLASSIFICATION OF PRIORITIES

	HIGH	MODERATE	LOW
Category 1	Tier I	Tier I	Tier II
Category 2	Tier I	Tier II	Tier III
Category 3	Tier II	Tier III	Tier III

Tier I: High/Category 1; Medium/Category 1; High/Category 2.
Tier II: High/Category 3; Medium/Category 2; Low/Category 1.
Tier III: Medium/Category 3; Low/Categories 2 and 3.

* * *

Ultimately, however, having a well-designed and functioning system to produce and convey preventive foresight is a necessary but insufficient ingredient to effective preventive engagement. Thinking ahead can sensitize policy makers to the likelihood of changing or emerging risks and make them more predisposed to take prudent preventive or preparatory measures—in other words, to act ahead—but many impediments can still inhibit policy makers from doing so. How to overcome these is the topic of chapter 3.

3

ACTING AHEAD

From Reaction to Prevention

It is necessary not only to pay attention to immediate crises, but to foresee those that will come and to make every effort to prevent them. For if you see them coming well in advance, then you can easily take appropriate action to remedy them, but if you wait until they are right on top of you, then the prescription will no longer take effect, because the disease is too far advanced. In this matter it is as the doctor's say of consumption: In the beginning the disease is easy to cure, difficult to diagnose; but, after a while, if it has not been diagnosed and treated early, it becomes easy to diagnose but hard to cure. So, too, in politics, for if you foresee problems while they are off (which only a prudent man is able to do) they can easily be dealt with; but when, because you have failed to see them coming, you allow them to grow to the point that anyone can recognize them, then it is too late to do anything.

—NICCOLÒ MACHIAVELLI

Preventing conflict involves creating conditions that make conflict less likely. Like a doctor practicing preventive medicine, we want, if possible to prevent conditions that provoke conflict from occurring, or at least heal them before they are serious.

—WILLIAM J. PERRY

N LATE NOVEMBER 2001, Secretary of Defense Donald Rumsfeld sent one of his infamous "snowflake" memos to his deputy, Paul Wolfowitz, asking him to draw up "a list of things that could go wrong, a separate list of things that could go right, and what we ought to do about each."[1] Quite what had motivated Rumsfeld to send this directive at that moment is unclear, but with the initial military phase of the campaign in Afghanistan coming to an end, this was probably the first opportunity since the 9/11 attacks for him to catch his breath and think about what new challenges might lie ahead. Although it would take some additional prodding from Rumsfeld, Wolfowitz eventually responded with what he called "a list of surprises we should perhaps be anticipating."[2] Several of these—"Afghanistan starts to turn bad next spring," "Terrorist attack on a major ally," "North Korea missile launch," and "Russian move into Georgia"—would eventually come to pass. There is no evidence, however, that Wolfowitz ever provided Rumsfeld with the specific policy recommendations he had requested or, more important, that the United States ever took precautionary steps to hedge against the "things that could go wrong."[3]

The exchange between Rumsfeld and Wolfowitz underscores the basic point that even the most prescient analysis is worthless if it fails to affect policy in a meaningful way. Put differently, there is no value in thinking ahead if one is not prepared to act ahead: preventive foresight has to be followed by a preventive response. In some cases this can be explained, as was discussed in chapter 2, with policy makers either disbelieving or rejecting early warning information. In many others, however, they actually accept and understand the nature of the threat but still do little if anything in response. The common excuse for this is the absence of political will; though the term is used regularly, it is neither very illuminating nor helpful.[4] The implication is that it either exists or it does not, and that policy making will either benefit or suffer either way. As former Australian foreign minister Gareth Evans has argued:

> The difficulty with most discussions of political will is that we spend more time lamenting its absence than analyzing what it means. We tend to talk about it as a single missing ingredient—the gelatin without which the dish won't set. But the trouble with this metaphor or any other way of thinking about "political will" as a simple, single factor in the equation is that it understates the sheer complexity of what is involved. To mobilize political will doesn't mean just finding that elusive packet of gelatin,

but rather working your way through a whole cupboard-full of further ingredients.[5]

This chapter will discuss how to make policy makers more responsive to information they receive about incipient dangers. As argued above, being more appreciative of risks rather than merely reactive to threats is an important step, but this is only part of the answer. To understand what else is needed, it is important first to understand better the nature of the challenge that policy makers must overcome to act more preventively. Being predisposed to act ahead, moreover, is not the same as knowing *how* to act ahead. The final section of the chapter, therefore, will lay out what preventive engagement entails in generic policy terms.

THE CHALLENGE OF ACTING AHEAD

Various factors can impede the willingness of policy makers to take precautionary measures in response to information advising them of latent or emerging risks. These are not mutually exclusive and are more often than not mutually reinforcing.

DAILY DISTRACTIONS

Probably one of the most common laments of policy makers is that "the urgent always crowds out the important."[6] At any given moment, senior decision makers are typically juggling multiple demands on their time, whether it is the need to follow through on already agreed-upon initiatives or manage new, unexpected events. Either way, the requirement to attend to the real and the immediate—"the fierce urgency of now"—is hard to put aside, if only temporarily, to focus on something that is hypothetical and distant, whatever the perceived risks may be. The disinclination of a policy maker to act will be even stronger, of course, if the interests that are putatively at risk in the future appear less or no more important than what is seemingly at stake in the present. Attention and resources are finite, and choices have to be made, usually in favor of managing immediate "known knowns" rather than uncertain future ones.

This challenge is hardly new—recall Henry Kissinger's famous quip, "There cannot be a crisis next week. My schedule is already full"—but the post–Cold War world with its more interconnected and faster moving events has arguably increased the demands on U.S. policy makers and made it even harder to think about much less plan for the future.[7] In the months after the fall of the Berlin Wall, Brent Scowcroft, national security adviser to President George H. W. Bush, later admitted that "we were just trying to keep up with things."[8] Condoleezza Rice, former secretary of state in the administration of George W. Bush, acknowledged much the same pressure after 9/11: "We were essentially just reacting. It took some time before we could stop, catch our breath, and make a critical reappraisal of what we were doing."[9] And likewise for the Obama administration, which had to manage the 2008 global financial crisis immediately upon taking office, followed soon after by a seemingly never-ending series of pressing problems regarding Afghanistan, Iraq, the Arab rebellions, the Ebola outbreak, the rise of ISIS, and Russian intervention in Ukraine.

POOR INCENTIVES

Besides wishful thinking whereby policy makers convince themselves—sometimes with reasonable logic—that a potentially harmful development is not likely to occur, a calculated disregard for what might happen in the future can also play its part.[10] For elected officials in particular, what happens after they are no longer in positions of responsibility or seeking an additional term of office will always be of secondary importance to managing problems in the present for which they can be held accountable. Warnings that come at the end of political terms are not likely to be treated with the same degree of urgency as those at the beginning. More often than not, looming problems get "kicked down the road."

It does not help, moreover, that there are few, if any, rewards—political or otherwise—for policy makers who avert something that will be difficult to prove would have happened had they not taken early action. Proving the counterfactual is next to impossible, which is hardly a strong incentive for politicians seeking public approval or bureaucrats wanting to advance their careers. In contrast is the management of clear and present dangers, where gaining credit for having "saved the day" presents an immediate and gratifying motivation to act. Again, to cite Kissinger, "it is the nature of successful policies that posterity forgets how easily things might have been otherwise."[11] As a result, for elected politicians who are dependent on public support, the inclination is to wait until there is a strong "demand signal" to act—without which they will have neither a clear mandate nor the requisite resources at their disposal.

The incentives to act can be further undermined if what is feared is also perceived to be largely inevitable or beyond the ability of anyone to avert. Policy makers can convince themselves that there is not much that can be done or that it is not obvious what the right response should be. In such circumstances, it is easier for them to defer making a decision until there is not just greater clarity about the direction of events but also what to do when that moment arrives.

PERCEIVED DISINCENTIVES

Even when policy makers appreciate what is at stake and are predisposed to act, countervailing concerns can dissuade them from doing so. As numerous studies of decision making have shown, individuals are typically loss averse—that is, they place a greater value on avoiding certain losses than they do in achieving potentially greater gains. The sobering implication for preventive action is that decision makers are reluctant to incur an initial expense for the larger benefit of avoiding greater, if less certain, costs.[12] This reluctance to invest in preventive action can be rationalized not only as an aversion to incurring an upfront and possibly unnecessary expense but also in terms of foreclosing future policy options. Diplomats, for example, are notorious for preferring to let events "mature" or "ripen" to not only avoid taking potentially fruitless and even self-constraining actions but also to exploit the opportunities that they feel could arise to their advantage in a crisis.

The initial price to pay will clearly loom much larger in instances where the threat or incipient risk does not clearly rank very high in terms of the "national interest." As Alexander George and Jane Holl note, "In many ethnic and religious conflicts, humanitarian crises, or severe human rights abuses *timely and accurate warning may not be the problem at all.* Rather, for one reason or another . . . no serious response is likely to be taken solely on the basis of early warning simply because a simmering situation that threatens to boil over may not be deemed important enough to warrant the type and scale of effort deemed necessary to prevent the hypothetical catastrophe."[13] The disinclination to act because limited interests are believed to be at stake can be reinforced by the expected costs of the associated preventive measures. There may be a reluctance to act, as George and Holl observe, "not because warning is *not* taken seriously, but rather because decision-makers take it very seriously but are nonetheless deterred by the prospects of a 'slippery slope,' that is, inexorable and potentially intractable involvement in an already nasty problem."[14] The fear of mission creep, eventual entrapment, and making the situation worse through actions taken with incomplete information about their likely efficacy can have the same effect. Here another well-known cognitive trap—*hindsight bias*—can come into play. Judgments about what happened in comparable situations in the past will understandably affect how decision makers react to new situations calling for a response. These judgments are typically arrived at intuitively rather than on the basis of systematic evaluation.[15]

Delaying action can, however, result in making the policy dilemma more acute. Accounts of past crises frequently reveal how policy makers have regularly found themselves in situations where the options presented to them are viewed as "all bad" or as "problems from hell" in that the choices have effectively narrowed to either embarking on something potentially very risky and costly or, alternatively, doing nothing at all, with conceivably equally bad (if not worse) outcomes.

Such calculations have vexed U.S. decision makers repeatedly in the post–Cold War era—notably, at the outset of the civil war in the former Yugoslavia, in the genocide in Darfur, and more recently with regard to the conflict in Syria.

OPERATIONAL IMPEDIMENTS

Besides the perceived costs of taking action, other obstacles or concerns can help dissuade policy makers from doing what they believe to be necessary or prudent. These range from insufficient resources (either because they do not exist or are committed elsewhere) to various political restrictions—notably, the need to respect national sovereignty when addressing internal conflicts. The challenge of mobilizing international actors into "coalitions of the willing" when their interests and level of commitment will likely vary also takes a huge amount of patience and energy.

STRATEGIES FOR PREVENTIVE ACTION

These are clearly all formidable obstacles to acting ahead that cannot be wished away. They can be lessened, however—if not overcome at all times—with a variety of measures to encourage and facilitate preventive action.

INCULCATING PREVENTIVE ACTION

Without a clear "demand signal" from senior officials to subordinates that they not only value but will also reward precautionary thinking and action to manage emerging problems, the operational posture of any organization is likely to remain reactive. Declaratory commitments in support of preventive action and new operating procedures that encourage risk management can over time bring about a normative shift toward a more proactive operational posture. Some organizations have also adopted what is often referred to as the precautionary principle to be their default operating norm to manage risk.[16] This principle is designed to overcome the natural hesitancy that organizations experience when facing uncertain problems. As Jessica Stern and Jonathan B. Wiener explain,

> The precautionary principle is particularly aimed at overcoming the burden of proving that a risk is real or imminent, and authorizing protective

government action even when the risk is quite uncertain but could turn out to be very harmful. It is intended to enable and impel governments to address more risks that may be false negatives (problems initially but erroneously thought to be absent or small that later turn out to be real and serious) and to be less hesitant about regulating those that turn out to be false positives (problems initially but erroneously thought to be serious that later turn out to be absent or small).[17]

The general principle was cited, for example, in the UN's 1992 Rio Declaration on Environment and Development, which states, "Where there are threats of serious and irreversible damage, lack of full scientific certainty shall not be used as a reason for postponing cost-effective measure to prevent environmental degradation."[18] The European Union has also explicitly adopted this principle for health and environmental policy making.[19]

This approach to managing risk is more or less what public health officials advocate in promoting healthy lifestyles as a general precautionary measure while more tailored actions are recommended for those considered at higher risk of a specific ailment because of their family history, age, occupation, etc., even if they have yet to exhibit outward signs of ill health. The need for precautionary measures is thus decoupled from the triggering requirement of a robust diagnosis (early warning).

INSTITUTIONALIZING PREVENTIVE ACTION

Fostering a precautionary culture within an organization can be reinforced with dedicated agencies and personnel to advocate and support such action. As Gareth Evans has argued, "There is a great deal to be said, in any organizational setting, actually to have an organization . . . within the system whose responsibility is to think about prevention, and devise and recommend up the decision-making food chain appropriate policy responses."[20] Ultimately, a planning operation of the appropriate level of institutional standing attracts quality personnel to staff it. Dedicated agencies can also be empowered to carry out such planning through formal obligations. This is essentially the mechanism by which the U.S. Department of Defense regularly reviews and updates its planning for numerous military contingencies. The Department of Homeland Security is also now required to do the same for a range of potential national emergencies. While both these planning efforts are precautionary in the sense that they improve preparedness to manage specific contingencies, they do not constitute true preventive planning to lessen their likelihood. It is not hard to imagine, however, a similar process in which broader interagency policy planning could be regularly mandated on the basis of the kind of horizon scanning/foresight analysis discussed in chapter 2. Such planning, moreover, could also be automatically triggered on a more ad hoc basis should an emerging concern be judged to pose a specific level of risk.[21] For example, contingencies assessed as Tier I and Tier II concerns on the risk matrix outlined in chapter 2 would require immediate and regular review at a specified level of decision making.

MOTIVATING PREVENTIVE ACTION

Policy makers can be incentivized to act ahead by making them more sensitive to not just the likelihood of plausible contingencies occurring but also their potential implications. For example, the warnings about Iraq's potential invasion of Kuwait in 1990 were not accompanied by an assessment of the likelihood that the United States might feel compelled to come to the assistance of Kuwait and Saudi Arabia once they were attacked. Similarly, the risk of the United States eventually becoming embroiled in the breakup of Yugoslavia was seemingly never appraised and thus was not a consideration in how policy makers reacted to the initial warnings. Furthermore, despite all the warnings of a terrorist attack prior to 9/11 there appears to have been no high-level discussion of how the United States might react in such an eventuality. The categorization of risks outlined in chapter 2 can help provide an initial indication of what is at stake in any given contingency and prompt a deeper and more comprehensive assessment.

GUIDING PREVENTIVE ACTION

Providing policy makers with timely advice about the feasibility of different preventive options (their probability of success and likely costs), along with—just as crucially—the potential risks of doing nothing, can help them overcome the potential disincentives to act.[22] In particular, it is important that the range of policy choices not become artificially limited out of ignorance of the possibilities or, alternatively, because of the self-interested preferences of some of the parties involved. Put differently, when there is a way, it will be easier to generate the will.

ENABLING PREVENTIVE ACTION

The inclination to act will always be influenced by the availability of resources with which to implement the potential policy options. These resources include contingency funds that can be drawn upon and used in a flexible manner on short notice and the deployment of diplomatic assets with trained and experience personnel to carry out special preventive missions. Being able to call upon the resources of other interested actors in an equally timely fashion is important for the same reasons. Besides sharing the associated costs, their involvement could also improve the chance for success in a variety of ways as will be discussed in chapter 7.

All these strategies can help policy makers overcome the various obstacles to acting ahead. They still need to know, however, what this means in practical terms and how to fashion an effective program of preventive action.

THE PRACTICE OF PREVENTIVE ACTION

Despite regularly stated pronouncements about the desirability of avoiding potentially costly crises and conflicts, no generally accepted set of operational practices exists to inform policy planning and ultimately help policy makers choose what course of action to take. To be clear, policy makers will almost certainly be aware of broad approaches to managing crises and conflict situations because of their formal education, direct experiences in previous policy-making positions, or the received wisdom of colleagues. This understanding will likely include general beliefs about the efficacy of coercive versus cooperative techniques (or some combination thereof) in bargaining and dispute resolution. The former includes most obviously the use of sanctions and the threat of military force to deter and dissuade potential adversaries, whereas the latter typically involves the use of diplomacy to mediate and resolve differences through peaceful persuasion and sometimes positive inducements. Policy makers will likely also be generally aware of the range of diplomatic, military, and economic "tools" at their disposal.

Knowledge of what is inside the proverbial toolbox is useful but not sufficient, however, for the purpose of comprehensive and detailed policy formulation. As Lawrence Woocher argues, such awareness is undoubtedly helpful in highlighting

an array of specific instruments that may be available to different actors to help reduce the risk of violent conflict. But we should recall that to build a piece of furniture, a full toolbox must be paired with a blueprint describing when to use a hammer, a saw, or a screwdriver, plus knowledge about how to use each of these tools effectively. Likewise, the conflict prevention toolbox is of limited utility without knowledge about when and how to use different tools. More fundamentally, however, the toolbox metaphor fails to capture the complex, dynamic, and political nature of conflict and its prevention. Unlike wood, potential combatants are strategic political actors, anticipating and responding to others' actions in hard to predict ways, in contexts where small changes can have disproportionately large consequences, all the while balancing the utility of violence against their interests and other options—often making mistakes and miscalculations.

Moving from toolbox to strategy requires asking critical questions such as:

- What mix of diplomatic/political, economic/social, legal/constitutional, and military/security tools are most effective in different types of situations?
- In what circumstances are cooperative vs. coercive measures most effective? How should these be sequenced?

- How can structural and operational prevention strategies be made complementary?
- How much more effective are multilateral preventive strategies than unilateral ones, if at all?

The empirical literature offers surprisingly little that would help decision makers or their advisers respond to these and similar policy-relevant questions.[23]

The lack of a well-developed praxis for preventive action in foreign policy should not be surprising given how little effort is given in general to the professional training and career development of civilian policy makers in the United States—certainly in comparison to their military counterparts. Many are short-term political appointees and come to their jobs with no prior experience of holding government positions of responsibility. While they will receive some instruction relating to working practices, such as essential security and communication procedures, most will be unfamiliar with not only how the U.S. government actually works—the complex maze of regulations, budgetary authorities, and organizational responsibilities that govern the system—but also basic policy formulation and planning techniques.[24] Unless imparted informally, useful information on what might have worked or did not work in the past that could be relevant in addressing comparable problems or situations in the present will not be accessible for the simple reason that such knowledge is not systematically captured and retained as an organizational imperative.[25] This problem is compounded by the regular turnover of senior policy makers and the rotation of midcareer officials to other positions where their acquired operational knowledge may have little or no relevance. In contrast, the U.S. armed forces devote considerable effort to training, professional development, and the regular refinement of operational doctrine and plans based on learned experience. The result is that the United States has a well-developed doctrine for fighting the nation's wars but nothing remotely comparable for the task of preventing them.

The framework for such a doctrine can be found in the approach now commonly used by public health practitioners to manage the risk of disease and certain ailments. Public health officials long ago established the practice of employing empirically based and carefully sequenced interventions to inhibit the emergence, onset, and progression of specific medical problems. As mentioned in chapter 1, these are commonly classified as "primary," "secondary," and "tertiary" forms of preventive action that correspond with what are relatively discrete stages in the evolution of any health concern.[26] As a strategic framework, the public health model has many compelling features, not the least of which is its holistic and multidimensional approach to tackling disease. For this reason, law enforcement officials have increasingly adopted the public health model as a comprehensive approach to crime prevention that addresses not just the "symptoms" of crime through traditional policing but also its root causes and other contributing factors through various social and economic initiatives.[27]

It is generally accepted that crime results from the conjunction of three factors: first, a desire or motive on the part of an individual or group to engage in unlawful activity; second, the means or skills needed to carry such activity out; and third, a perceived opportunity to do so. Crime prevention strategies have accordingly been developed to limit, if not wholly eliminate, one or more of these factors. As a result, criminologists often distinguish between different types of crime prevention strategies:[28]

- Developmental prevention refers to efforts designed to affect the early development of individuals to lessen their later inclination to engage in criminal behavior. This process typically involves reducing known risk factors while also enhancing known protective factors in how individuals develop. It is thus a form of primary prevention.
- Situational prevention typically refers to efforts to reduce both the means and opportunities of those already predisposed to commit crime. These efforts can range from the general role of policing in deterring crime to very specific measures that identify, manipulate, and control the situational or environmental factors associated with certain types of crime. The goals are to lower the risk associated with offending, lower the expected rewards of offending, and generally make crime less attractive. It can thus be considered a form of secondary prevention.
- Community prevention, in contrast, refers to interventions designed to change the context of potential crime in terms of social conditions and

institutions—notably, families, peers, norms, and workplaces. As such, it straddles both primary and secondary types of prevention.

It is also worth mentioning here that law enforcement officials increasingly rely on what are essentially epidemiological research methods and early warning techniques modeled on those of the public health sector to direct and orchestrate police assets to where they are needed most to prevent crime. These tactics have been widely credited with having contributed to the remarkable decline in serious crime in the United States since the early 1990s following three decades of steady growth.[29]

Adapting the approach used by public health and law enforcement officials to lessen the risk of U.S. military engagement does not require a huge leap in imagination.[30] As was noted in chapter 2, the various contingencies most likely to trigger military action by the United States derive from various types of political unrest and conflict that are perceived to threaten U.S. interests in one way or another. Lessening the possible onset and escalation of those sources of political unrest and conflict can be approached in much the same way that infectious disease or violent crime is managed. More specifically, the same three basic types of policy intervention can be adapted for the purpose of conflict risk reduction, crisis prevention, and conflict mitigation, as will be discussed in the next section.[31]

THREE TYPES OF PREVENTIVE ACTION

CONFLICT RISK REDUCTION

The first type of preventive action, *risk reduction*, broadly involves eliminating or minimizing factors known to be associated with political instability and violent conflict *before* they manifest themselves and begin to exert a potentially pernicious effect.[32] Risk reduction measures can be designed to have broad—sometimes referred to as systemic—effects or, alternatively, be configured to address more specific contingencies or particular regions of concern. As with their health care equivalent—promoting nutritious diets, regular exercise, and other prudent lifestyle choices—risk reduction measures are pursued as much to reap their intrinsic benefits as they are to lower the overall risk of poor health—or, in this case, instability and conflict. They thus do not require—and this is important to note—specific warning signs of growing risk to trigger preventive action. The following measures are widely considered to be beneficial to lowering the risk of violent conflict both between states and within them. As will also become clear, they are in many respects mutually reinforcing.

Rules and Institutions

The most fundamental—and thus most important—conflict risk reduction measure is the promotion of rules and institutions that in one form or another foster societal order. As Douglas C. North, John Joseph Wallis, and Barry R. Weingast note, "All societies face the problem of violence. Regardless of whether our genetic makeup predisposes humans to be violent, the possibility that some individuals will be violent poses a central problem for any group. No society solves the problem of violence by eliminating violence; at best it can be contained and managed."[33] The answer to the disruptive challenge of conflict is almost always the creation of social norms and more explicit rules of behavior to regulate the circumstances under which resorting to violence is permissible and when it is not.[34] Although the collective benefits of social rules may in some cases be sufficient to ensure that they are observed voluntarily, some kind of sanction for noncompliance, along with a reliable mechanism for its delivery, is typically required to ensure that social rules are respected and that order is maintained. The sanction, moreover, must be sufficiently costly and credible in terms of its delivery to encourage enough people to obey the rules lest they simply be ignored and anarchy ensue. Monopolizing coercive power within social groups—that is, reserving to specific individuals and institutions the exclusive right and means to use force—for the purpose of maintaining order became the logical response to this problem. This was accomplished through a process that was part voluntary and part imposed as individuals and subgroups saw personal advantage in controlling coercive power. Rules that were initially designed to minimize interpersonal violence thus progressively expanded to include those designed to protect the leaders or rulers of a social group from internal challenges to their authority and, moreover, increase their capacity to respond to threats from other social groups.

As others have explained more fully, nation-states eventually evolved to perform this function in various ways—principally, by reducing the incentives for using force to settle personal disputes (through policing, third party conflict resolution mechanisms, and the provision of services that meet basic needs), restricting the physical means and opportunities to engage in violent acts (by monopolizing coercive power and deterring rebellion via credible penalties), and controlling their borders from potentially destabilizing threats of various kinds.[35] As instruments of violence reduction in human affairs, states have proven to be highly effective; on this the historical record is clear.[36]

States, of course, can also be a source of international insecurity and conflict. Another set of rules and institutions thus had to be developed to promote order among states. The most important are the established norms of state sovereignty—particularly the proscriptions on the use of force and interference in the internal affairs of states, which are enshrined most explicitly in the United Nations Charter.[37] The UN (and in particular its Security Council) in turn serves as the principal international body for upholding these rules and has on numerous occasions acted to punish transgressors through sanctions and other penalties. To many, these actions and other normative changes have contributed to the delegitimization of interstate aggression—certainly for the purposes of acquiring territory and power.[38] At the very least, flagrant breaches of this norm are now virtually guaranteed to incur general international opprobrium and most likely sanctions of one kind or another. The UN has also helped to institute another set of norms designed to set standards on how states treat their citizens and respect their basic human rights, and these are also generally considered to be beneficial in helping to reduce intrastate violence.

Finally, the UN and international institutions more generally help to promote global order in other important ways.[39] By providing an institutional platform for functional cooperation and peaceful dispute resolution (as well as conduits for sharing information), international organizations help to build trust and cooperation on broader political issues. The net benefit that accrues from such cooperation, particularly as the density of institutional connections grows, also lessens the likelihood that states will engage in aggressive behavior since the likely costs will outweigh the putative advantages. International organizations can also limit the freedom of action of states to threaten and attack others. Besides economic-related constraints, disarmament and arms control regimes often have complex verification and consultative mechanisms that are clearly designed with this purpose in mind. Judging from various studies designed to test the impact of international institutions empirically, the results vary according to the type of international organizations and the density of such connections.[40]

Strategic Stability Measures

These basic international rules and institutions arguably could never evolve or survive without additional measures to promote strategic stability among the major centers of power and influence within the international system. They simply would not be respected and supported to the degree required to ensure broad adherence. Active balancing by the major powers of each other's military capabilities to deter hostile acts and self aggrandizement—whether pursued independently or in partnership with other states through alliance relationships—is often viewed as the primary prescription for strategic stability and, by extension, international peace. Such balancing, however, brings its own risks in deepening or exacerbating the very insecurities and antagonisms that it is designed to mitigate. Besides leading to potentially expensive arms racing it can, as numerous cases have shown, also lead to dangerous misunderstandings and risky interactions in times of crisis.

For these reasons, major states have often reached both formal and informal arrangements to moderate their relations in the interests of preserving peace. The Concert of Europe, established by Great Britain, Russia, France, Austria, and Prussia in the aftermath of the Napoleonic Wars in 1815 and extending until the outbreak of the Crimean War in 1854, is held up as an exemplar of an informal great power arrangement that kept the peace in Europe through a combination of the nations' mutual respect for one another's spheres of influence and a collective commitment to resolve crises that threatened to destabilize the continent. The concert did not preclude great power politics and geopolitical jockeying, but it did for several decades prevent such rivalry from escalating into outright conflict. Something similar to the concert has been proposed in various forms since then; President Franklin Delano Roosevelt's conception of the Four Policemen—the United States, Soviet Union, Great Britain, and China—collectively maintaining global order in the aftermath of World War II, and French president Charles de Gaulle's call in the 1950s for a British, French, and U.S. "directorate" to manage Western affairs during the Cold War—albeit within the UN and NATO, respectively—undoubtedly had the Concert of Europe in mind.

These ideas never came to fruition, or at least not in the way envisaged,[41] but it is now generally accepted that the Soviet Union and the United States prevented the Cold War from turning "hot" in large measure by deliberately establishing informal rules of the road to stabilize their otherwise adversarial relationship and ultimately promote peaceful coexistence. As John Mearsheimer has argued,

> During the first fifteen years of the Cold War, the rules of the road for the conflict were not yet established, giving rise to several serious crises. However, over time each side gained a clear sense of how far it could push the other, and what the other would not tolerate. A set of rules came to be agreed upon: an understanding on the division of rights in Austria, Berlin, and elsewhere in Europe; a proscription on secret unilateral re-deployment of large nuclear forces to areas contiguous to the opponent; mutual toleration of reconnaissance satellites; agreement on rules of peacetime engagement between naval forces; and so forth. The absence of serious crises during 1963–90 was due in part to the growth of such agreements on the rights of both sides, and the rules of conduct.[42]

The informal rules were also bolstered by formal ones, particularly as they related to strategic weapons capable of upsetting the underlying equilibrium. Thus, by the late 1960s both sides accepted the logic of mutual assured vulnerability to nuclear destruction as the basis for strategic stability, leading in turn to formal limits on offensive nuclear weaponry and the virtual proscription of defensive systems that could negate their potency.

Alliances also appear to have had a positive effect on promoting strategic stability during the Cold War—contrary to other periods when they have more often than not increased the likelihood of war rather than decreased it.[43] For the U.S.-led Cold War alliances, at least, their positive impact can be attributed not only to their deterrent effect on potential Soviet aggression (backed up by the sobering prospect of nuclear weapons use) but also to their constraining effect on the behavior of other alliance members. Certainly in the initial stages of the Cold War, the reassuring presence of U.S. forces stationed in Germany and Japan was just as important—and arguably more so to neighboring states that had been victims of Nazi and Japanese aggression—as their role as a trip wire for American military involvement. There is also strong evidence that U.S. security guarantees appear to have dampened the inclination of several states to develop nuclear weapons during this period that would likely have upset regional stability.[44] Finally, the inherently defensive nature of U.S. Cold War alliances—as distinct from the outward orientation or purpose of many previous alliances—may also help to explain their positive stabilizing role.[45] It is revealing, moreover, that in the aftermath of the Cold War, when the ostensible purpose of the alliances had ceased to exist, there were no defections—only requests to join.

Democratic Governance

A third set of risk reduction measures concerns the international promotion of democratic forms of governance. As many have observed, violent conflict between democracies is exceedingly rare and major war virtually nonexistent. By one calculation, "two highly democratic countries are some 80 percent less likely to get into a violent dispute with each other than are two countries—otherwise similar—that are ruled by strong dictatorships. In medical research such a reduction in risk would be a very big deal."[46] The important caveat here—as many have pointed out—is that democracies are not inherently peaceful, since in numerous cases they have attacked or engaged in war with non-democratic states.[47] Great powers, whether democratic or authoritarian, are also more likely to become involved in violent conflicts than are other states.[48] Finally, it should not be overlooked that democracies and authoritarian states can forge productive peaceful partnerships.[49] Logically, however, the progressive expansion of democracy should bring about, if not immediately, a commensurate reduction in the risk of violent interstate conflict.

What accounts for the positive relationship between democracy and international peace is a matter of some debate. The pacific nature of democratic states—at least toward one another—is variously attributed to their structural constraints on the latitude of elected officials to engage in war making. In addition, one must consider their commitment to consensual dispute resolution and the larger normative effect this has on shaping international relations; their mutual transparency, which helps reduce international mistrust and thus insecurity; their support for transnational civil society organizations that can become important constituencies for peace; and their relative openness to international trade and investment, which makes them more interdependent and less inclined to risk the commercial benefits that come with prolonged peace.[50] Some combination of all of these causal linkages seems likely.

Democratic governance is also generally considered to be advantageous to promoting peaceful societies. By permitting regular opportunities to change governments through free, fair, and inclusive elections, established democracies are on the whole more stable and peaceful than autocracies and, especially, anocracies (hybrid regimes that are neither fully democratic nor fully autocratic), presumably because they reduce the motivation for violent change.[51] States that respect basic human rights (notably, the freedoms of speech, assembly, religion, and fair trial) and do not engage in systematic discrimination of women, minorities, or ethnic groups (whether political or economic) are likewise less susceptible to violent conflict.[52] Ensuring that women are fully represented and, moreover, engaged in political decision making at the highest levels is likewise generally accepted as the foundation for more peaceful and vibrant societies.[53] Such states enjoy greater legitimacy, and thus the support of their citizenry.

How best to promote democratic governance is an even more contentious issue, though there is broad consensus that it should not be externally imposed (except in cases where necessary, to restore effective governance) and that a one-size-fits-all approach is to be avoided.[54] Some advocate a top-down strategy that emphasizes the need to build the necessary institutions and processes common to all democratic states—constitutions and bills of rights; regular, free, and fair elections; and effective party systems—while others believe in a bottom-up approach that emphasizes the need to nurture a vibrant civil society, including a free media, and stimulates business interests that understand and appreciate the economic advantages of democracies. Logically, the two methods should not be seen as mutually exclusive but instead as complementary. Placing more emphasis on one rather than the other approach should only occur after an assessment of local conditions. The top-down approach of promoting democratic forms of governance is likely to be more appropriate when the target country is receptive to assistance, whereas the bottom-up approach represents a longer-term, indirect approach for promoting the reform of authoritarian or semi-authoritarian regimes that are not seemingly conducive to change.

The transition to democratic governance from autocratic rule can be hazardous, however. Partial democracies with high degrees of political factionalism are particularly at risk of instability. As one study argues, it is therefore essential "to seek policies and institutions that blunt or discourage factionalism when opening up political participation and competition, if reforms are to produce stable regimes rather than greatly increase the risks of instability."[55] Similarly, given the high levels of recidivism in societies emerging from violent conflict, the inclusiveness of the political settlement ending the dispute, and other societal reconciliation efforts, are viewed as critical to producing a stable peace.[56]

Economic Interdependence

Promoting economic interdependence between states represents another broadly acknowledged measure for lowering the risk of interstate conflict. Numerous studies have demonstrated a robust positive relationship between increased levels of international trade and a reduction in violent international conflict.[57] Similar benefits have been observed, furthermore, with foreign direct investment.[58] Some believe, in fact, that promoting trade and investment is considered a better overall risk reduction strategy than democracy promotion.[59] Much like the debate over the effects of democratization, different arguments have been advanced as to the nature of the pacifying mechanism at work. Some feel that economic interdependence and the broader effects of a globalized marketplace have rendered irrelevant whatever economic gains could be achieved from territorial conquest. Moreover, as the benefits of international trade and investment have grown, business interests have become increasingly powerful advocates for peace.[60] Others, however, focus on the negative incentives for war to argue that economic interdependence deters violent conflict by more or less guaranteeing that both sides will suffer substantial if not unacceptable costs.

Economic Development and State Capacity Building

Finally, another set of risk reduction factors falls under the general rubric of economic development and state capacity building. Economically developed states are at a much lower risk of experiencing armed conflict, as figure 3.1 illustrates.

Simply stated, "As national per capita incomes rise, the risk of war declines."[61] A straightforward explanation for this is that as general well-being improves, grievances born of economic deprivation diminish or never arise. The logic of this argument is compelling and certainly drives targeted efforts to provide economic opportunities—usually in the form of gainful employment—to segments of the population known to be especially at risk of violent behavior (males between the ages of sixteen and twenty-five).[62] This is especially evident in societies experiencing so-called youth bulges or undergoing rapid demobilization after a civil war.[63] Others, however, contend that the correlation between economic development and a diminished likelihood of civil conflict has more to do with improving the capacity of states through tax revenues to maintain public order, control their territory, deter insurgency, or simply "buy off" dissent.[64]

There is broad consensus that what makes some countries more successful than others in generating economic growth and national prosperity is the creation of what are variously called *open-access* economies, *depatrimonialized* polities, and *nonextractive* institutions.[65] These terms mean more or less the same thing; in essence, these are economies that are broadly inclusive and rule-based so as to limit the influence of informal arrangements

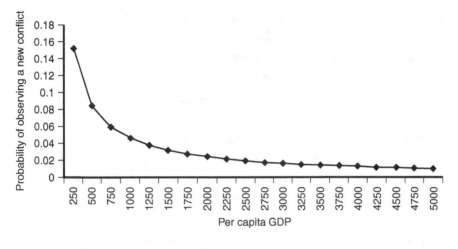

FIGURE 3.1

GDP (per Capita) and the Risk of Armed Conflict

Source: Macartan Humphreys, *Economics and Violent Conflict* (Cambridge, Mass.: Harvard University Press, 2003), http://www.unicef.org/socialpolicy/files/Economics_and_Violent _Conflict.pdf.

that confer advantages to certain groups or elites. Political liberalization is not essential to national "takeoff," as numerous cases demonstrate, but sustaining economic growth indefinitely without it has yet to be proven. Investments in critical infrastructure and human capital are certainly important too, but are wasted without the necessary structural conditions.

Economic development does rely heavily on building functioning state institutions and infrastructure that provide essential public goods and services—most of all, public order and security. Accomplishing in the short term what has typically taken many decades if not centuries of effort presents a major challenge to the task of contemporary state building.[66] The long-standing technocratic approach of using foreign aid and technical assistance to build effective institutions in weak and fragile states has had mixed results. Even the success stories of state building have still taken on average several decades to produce the desired effect in improving overall standards of performance.[67] In general, progress has appeared to hinge on such factors as the preexisting level of development, prior experience with democracy, the size of the states and their ethnic homogeneity, and—most of all—whether the interests and thus priorities of the recipient states are properly aligned with those of the donors. Too often the personal interests and narrow political agendas of those receiving international largesse have run counter to broader state-building goals.

The conventional wisdom on state building has consequently shifted to emphasizing the importance of inclusive political settlements or "inclusive-enough coalitions" of political factions and other competing interests as a necessary precondition for durable state building.[68] Without broad-based political support, the core institutions of the state will enjoy neither the legitimacy that comes with their formal status nor—more important—being seen as effective service providers by the state's citizens. When uncertainties exist about political stability, "outsourcing" certain key government functions to external organizations or states, or nurturing their capacity incrementally, are also seen as attractive approaches.[69]

CRISIS PREVENTION

The second type of preventive action, *crisis prevention*, entails averting the onset of a dangerous contingency when the risk factors are already present and, by outward appearance, likely to intensify. Just as in health care, various timely interventions can be employed to lower the likelihood that the underlying disagreements or tensions will escalate into a dangerous incident or crisis. Since crises do not arise spontaneously but rather derive from the conscious acts of humans, preventive action at this stage is focused, much like crime prevention, on influencing the decision calculus of the relevant parties involved—in particular, their motivations to initiate actions that might trigger a crisis, the means at their disposal, and the opportunities they perceive to be available. Depending on the nature of the conflict, a variety of preventive measures can be targeted at each of these variables.

Taking interstate conflict first, the most dangerous crises arise in broad terms as a consequence of three sources of friction: insecurity about the hostile intentions of other states, including the use of proxy forces; contending territorial claims and competition over valued resources; and the cross-border spillover effects of civil conflict and general state weakness, including the actions of harmful transnational actors that exploit such conditions. The potency of these sources of interstate conflict can in turn be affected by less tangible considerations having to do with national honor and standing.[70]

The most fundamental form of crisis prevention is obviously that which resolves or at least ameliorates these sources of tension. Where tension derives from basic mistrust and particularly clear perceptions of hostile intent, only a fundamental transformation in the character of the bilateral relationship as a result of political change in one or both of the states involved is likely to be truly satisfactory. This could take many years if not decades to occur, however, and thus other trust-building measures become relevant. These include promoting regular high-level political exchanges, information sharing to promote mutual transparency, and tangible cooperative projects.

Where the source of tension derives from a territorial or resource dispute, international arbitration can be employed to lessen the risk of escalation and overt hostilities. The International Court of Justice in The Hague is the most prominent and has addressed numerous territorial disputes to the apparent satisfaction of the claimants. These include agreements between El Salvador and Honduras in 1992, Libya and Chad in 1994, Bahrain and Qatar in 2001, Nigeria and Cameroon in 2002, Singapore and Malaysia in 2008, Romania and Ukraine in 2009, and Nicaragua and Colombia in 2012.[71] In many instances, the UN and representatives of relevant regional organizations have facilitated discussions between contestants of disputed territories.[72] Such agreements are nonbinding, however, as China's rejection of the 2016 ruling on the South China Sea territorial dispute illustrates.[73]

In cases where arbitration is pending or not considered feasible, the issue of sovereignty can be temporarily shelved without having to suspend potential commercial activities in the disputed area, which can also be beneficial in relieving tensions. Joint economic use and access can accomplish this and also lessen the likelihood of conflict. Examples include the joint management of the Inguri Dam power plant on the border between Georgia and the disputed region of Abkhazia; the agreement between Japan and

China to develop natural gas deposits in the East China Sea; and the similar agreement between China and Vietnam for the South China Sea.[74] Where countries have sovereignty over or access to common resources such as rivers, aquifers, and fish stocks, disputes have been resolved or at least minimized through joint management agreements. Numerous cases exist, including regulatory agreements for the Euphrates, Indus, Yarmuk, and Jordan Rivers and fishing arrangements in the Arctic.[75]

Efforts at resolving or ameliorating the source of an international dispute can be complemented by preventive measures that limit the means or opportunity for either party to use force. These include formal and informal constraints on the military capabilities of the disputants (qualitatively and quantitatively) to reduce the freedom of action to engage in offensive actions that might encourage preemptive behavior on either side in a crisis. Agreement can also be reached to desist from deploying or exercising military forces in sensitive areas. Creating demilitarized buffer zones between opposing forces, inviting neutral observers or peacekeeping forces to monitor and patrol such zones, developing specific rules of the road to guide the interaction of forces in close proximity with one another, and establishing dedicated crisis communication channels and dispute resolution mechanisms to manage dangerous incidents that may occur are additional measures. Again, there are many examples of these arrangements working to prevent misunderstanding and unintended escalation.[76]

Finally, where there is not a mutual commitment to manage a militarized dispute, recourse to deterrent measures is the standard option of averting conflict. This is traditionally accomplished by enhancing defensive preparations, minimizing military vulnerabilities, and credibly threatening costly retaliatory actions in the event that force is used. Security guarantees, arms transfers, military assistance of various kinds, economic sanctions, and shows of force all fit into this category. The challenge with such measures, however, is signaling not only the credibility of intentions but also their essentially defensive purpose; otherwise, the risk of conflict can actually grow.

A similar set of crisis prevention strategies can be employed to minimize the risk of internal conflict; in essence, to try to resolve the structural drivers of the conflict and, where this is not feasible, anticipate and manage potential triggering events to avert the outbreak of violence. Although intrastate violence manifests itself in many forms with often convoluted etiologies, the focus here will be on three broad types.[77] The first is *armed rebellion*, where the motives are essentially political: to overthrow or otherwise change the leadership and prevailing governing order of a state or to seek political independence from it. Such motives could be driven in whole or part by personal yearnings for power and wealth, or they may derive from broader bottom-up grievances against the central authorities that may also have economic as well as ethnosectarian dimensions. At least one of the parties in such conflicts, therefore, is the state.

The second category is *communal violence* between factions or groups within a state—usually along ethnic or religious lines. Here the conflict typically derives from what are sometimes defined as horizontal inequalities, where one of the groups feels insecure or disadvantaged in some fundamental way.[78] Security dilemma dynamics similar to those at the interstate level can manifest themselves in these situations. Such conflicts need not necessarily involve the state as one of the initial disputants, though such involvement may become implicated, if only to maintain order. While the disputants may not have political agendas, communal disputes can clearly evolve in that direction. Finally, the third type of intrastate conflicts are essentially one-sided in that they derive from the deliberate efforts of the state to oppress and even eliminate a subgroup for a variety of reasons. These conflicts are sometimes classified as acts of politicide or genocide.

Specific triggering events can cause these different types of intrastate conflict to erupt violently. Where tensions stem from who governs the country, events like elections, coups, assassinations, and other unexpected leadership transitions can all provide the spark. Violent acts of repression by state authorities in response to nonviolent protests or high-profile acts of defiance can have the same effect. Communal violence, on the other hand, can be ignited by either deliberately provocative acts on religious and culturally significant anniversaries and at sensitive historical sites or by random incidents involving lower-level community or religious leaders that escalate in unpredictable ways. Community leaders, for example, will sometimes use religion and ethnicity to incite violent acts. Finally, what are sometimes called endogenous shocks may also exacerbate underlying tensions or present new opportunities to use violent means. Major changes in commodity prices, natural disasters, and turmoil in a neighboring country have all been known to have a destabilizing effect on domestic order within the affected state.

The expression of grievances and other conflicts within societies is unavoidable and in some instances actually desirable as drivers of positive change. Even low levels of violence associated with such disputes might—in the grand scheme of things—be considered an acceptable, if still regrettable, price to pay if it leads to an overall improvement in the quality of life for the average citizen. Thus, while it hardly needs to be emphasized, the desirability of preventive action in any given situation must rest on an assessment of the overall risks and benefits of letting events take their course.

Established principles of sovereignty clearly constrain how much external parties can engage in crisis prevention regarding internal disputes, but they certainly do not preclude it. Concerned states—whether neighbors or more distant powers—can clearly use whatever political, military, or economic leverage they have to affect the behavior of the relevant parties. They can also influence in essence what comes in and goes out of the affected state—people, money, arms, trade, etc.—and this can have a bearing on how an internal conflict might evolve. Where access is limited or bilateral efforts have been rebuffed, international organizations often have the best chance of engaging in early preventive engagement. Even so, unless the warning signs are compelling, mobilizing the attention and resources of the UN or relevant regional organizations can still be difficult given other, more immediate demands, not to mention the general reluctance to pressure member states about their domestic affairs. Some states can also rely on powerful patrons to block the attention of international organizations.

Where there are external points of entry into a brewing civil conflict, an established menu of positive and negative inducements can be employed to influence the behavior of the relevant parties and the conflict's ultimate trajectory. With state actors and the business community, the principal economic levers are either the offer or withdrawal of foreign aid, capital investment, technical support, or trade and banking opportunities in the form of targeted sanctions. Political inducements include either diplomatic recognition or censure, membership in or banishment from international organizations, and the threat of legal prosecution. And in the security realm, the main levers are the provision or retraction of military assistance, arms supplies, intelligence support, and security guarantees.

Depending on the nature and source of the internal conflict, these instruments of leverage can be applied to encourage various initiatives designed to resolve or ameliorate the dispute. Where legitimate political grievances fuel challenges to the central authorities, various power-devolving and power-sharing arrangements have worked for approximately half the instances where they have been tried, though often only after much conflict and bloodshed. Examples include Mozambique, Zimbabwe, Madagascar, Ethiopia, Nigeria, Lebanon, and Bosnia, though for all these cases their ultimate success is still in some doubt.[79] A somewhat different approach is to promote and support the development of indigenous conflict management capacities at different levels within a state. Such initiatives are sometimes referred to as "national infrastructures for peace" that involve integrating many different initiatives and mechanisms designed to promote education, dialogue, and mediation at multiple levels. This approach has been used by several countries with reportedly positive results in countries as varied as Guyana, Ghana, Bolivia, Kenya, and Nepal, among others.[80] National institutions and networks for dialogue and mediation are seen as enjoying greater legitimacy and sustainability though outside assistance, though regular prodding is still necessary.[81]

Aid and investment can also be targeted to boost economic opportunity and employment in areas that, for whatever reason, have been disadvantaged; this can help buttress political reconciliation and reform. Where resentment over corruption—particularly at the national level—is the principal concern, more transparent and accountable public finance and banking systems can be developed, again with the help of external advisers. Special arrangements can also be implemented to prevent economic resources being plundered for personal or political gain or to underwrite armed rebellion. Various schemes of this kind have been promoted and in some cases adopted by states, sometimes with assistance from international organizations. For example, in 2000 Chad agreed to cede control of revenue from the recent discovery of oil if the World Bank financed a $3.5 billion

Chad-Cameroon oil pipeline project. The World Bank ended the agreement in 2008, however, because Chad had failed to meet its commitments to allocate funds to development and poverty alleviation projects. Ironically, Chad had repeatedly argued that it needed to use revenue for security due to an internal rebellion and spillover from the conflict in the Darfur region of Sudan.[82] Though the Chad experiment has not yet been repeated, states have agreed to cede control over revenues received from the extraction of natural resources. Botswana, Azerbaijan, Chile, Oman, Venezuela, Gabon, Norway, Kuwait, Chad, São Tomé and Principe, Tuvalu, and Nigeria have deposited resource revenues into state-owned investment accounts that are held and managed overseas; these so-called natural resource funds have apparently worked in some places and not others, principally due to the laxity of rules governing when funds can be withdrawn.[83] More focused efforts to restrict the use of so-called blood diamonds with the Kimberley Process and the Extractive Industries Transparency Initiative (EITI) begun in 2000 also appear to have had a positive effect.[84]

Where ethnic groups have been politically and economically disadvantaged, outside pressure can be applied to redress the legal and educational basis of such discrimination. Perhaps the most successful example was the role of the Organization for Security and Co-operation in Europe's high commissioner for minorities, who through deliberate but discreet cajoling—often referred to as quiet diplomacy—encouraged several eastern European states to reform their domestic laws.[85] The European Union also used the promise of accession to influence states from the former Yugoslavia to introduce national legislation protecting minority rights.[86]

Where sectarian tensions exist, a further set of preventive measures can be employed. In addition to redressing possible discriminatory laws and practices that may lie at the heart of the tensions, educational initiatives to promote religious tolerance and interfaith dialogues to address specific issues can be used.[87] Religious leaders can likewise be encouraged through sermons and edicts to delegitimize the use of violence in the name of their faiths. Measures to outlaw so-called hate speech and other deliberately inflammatory forms of public incitement also fall into this category.[88]

These efforts to resolve the underlying conflict may prove unsuccessful or, when they do make a difference, progress can be slow. In any case, preventing eruptions of violence around known flash points or fault lines in an existing or emerging conflict represents a desirable goal. It is now commonly acknowledged, for example, that the period leading up to and immediately following an election or referendum is particularly vulnerable to unrest and violence.[89] Intimidation and fraud, as well as protests over election results, can frequently mar elections and lead to political instability. In anticipation of violence that often erupts around election time, a variety of strategies and best practices have been developed by national aid agencies, international organizations, and nongovernmental organizations (NGOs) to minimize the risk.[90] These range from measures to reduce corruption (related to the transparency of campaign financing and voter registration) to minimizing intimidation and violence during and immediately following polling including curtailing, if not prohibiting, "hate speech."

How the international community learned from its failure to anticipate and respond to the outbreak of violence in the 2007 Kenyan elections and thus avert violence in the 2013 elections provides a good example of what can be accomplished.[91] Other cases include Guyana in 2006 and Ghana in 2008, following earlier electoral violence in those nations.[92] Related efforts to promote press freedom and bolster the role of civil society in conflict afflicted states have also achieved modest success in Burundi, Bangladesh, and Myanmar.

Coups, assassinations (successful or unsuccessful), or the sudden death or incapacitation of political leaders have also been known to trigger civil strife. Timely political intervention to defuse such crises and head off the escalation of violence is possible, however. In this respect, the UN's political missions and special envoys have in recent years increasingly emphasized early conflict prevention rather than just postconflict peace implementation with evident success on numerous occasions.[93] These include in Guinea following a coup in 2009, in Kyrgyzstan following ethnic riots in 2010, and in Libya following the ouster of Muammar al-Gaddhafi in 2011.[94] The UN and some regional organizations are also increasingly asked to conduct special investigations that defuse potentially explosive situations. Examples include the UN-led investigation into the assassination of Lebanese prime minister Rafiq al-Hariri in 2005, a joint UN–Economic Community of

West African States (ECOWAS) fact-finding inquiry into the death of Ghanaian migrants in the Gambia in 2007, a 2009 investigation into human rights violations at the end of the Sri Lankan civil war, and an independent panel of inquiry into the Israeli raid on a flotilla of ships carrying aid to Gaza in 2010. More recently, the UN has initiated inquiries into various human rights abuses in Burundi, Syria, and South Sudan.

How armed forces and other security services react to political disturbances and public disorder in general can also determine whether flash points turn into sustained violence. Again, external actors (through various bilateral and multilateral military education and training programs) and the regular professional contacts of attachés can help the armed forces of an at-risk state prepare for and react in ways that minimize violence. The United States, with the most extensive network of foreign military assistance and exchange programs in the world, has extensive experience in this kind of preventive engagement. On numerous occasions, albeit sometimes under serendipitous circumstances, U.S. military officers have played a positive role in preventing such crises from deteriorating into widespread violence. This happened during the crisis in East Timor in 1999, in the Philippines in 2001, and in Egypt in 2011.[95]

For managing potentially destabilizing endogenous shocks, several international bodies issue famine and public health warnings to mobilize emergency relief efforts and help local communities prepare for the worst. In the event disaster strikes, the provision of emergency economic assistance and humanitarian aid is the standard approach. Both the World Bank and the International Monetary Fund have in recent years used such mechanisms as contingent emergency loans and rapid credit lines with more limited conditionality to avert economic crises.[96] The UN's World Food Program has also created a system to warn of potential food shortages.

CONFLICT MITIGATION

The third type of preventive action—*conflict mitigation*—entails actively managing the eruption of violence so as to halt and reverse further escalation if not resolve the underlying source. Emergency care would be the medical equivalent. Halting and reversing the momentum of a conflict that has already degenerated into violence represents a tougher challenge to crisis prevention efforts. Once blood has been spilled (literally), the willingness to compromise by one or both sides of a conflict typically diminishes. New motives to use or continue to use force—the desire to reverse an initial loss, settle scores, or "lock in" a gain, to name just some—can make efforts to de-escalate a crisis very difficult. On the other hand, common impediments to earlier preventive action, whether they derive from disbelief that the situation will deteriorate or organizational inertia, are somewhat easier to override as the imperatives to act are now clearer. International organizations or "coalitions of the willing" can also be mobilized to take measures that earlier may have appeared to many as intrusive and illegitimate. Direct pleas for assistance from affected states and humanitarian concerns help in this respect.

In practice, conflict mitigation is broadly similar to crisis prevention in that positive and negative inducements are typically employed to influence the calculus of the principal actors in ways that de-escalate the violence. Other affected and potentially influential parties, such as neighboring states, regional bodies, NGOs, and private sector players, can also be engaged and harnessed as part of a general de-escalation strategy. Depending on the situation, the chosen strategy can be exclusively coercive or consensual in nature or, alternatively, some combination of the two—"carrots and sticks," in the vernacular. Attempts to de-escalate a conflict may ultimately fail, at least in the short term, and thus the goal may at best be to contain the conflict and minimize the level of human suffering until a more propitious moment arrives to resolve it.

Coercive de-escalation measures entail a range of possible actions, from economic sanctions (trade embargoes, banking and insurance restrictions, foreign aid cutoffs) to political penalties (public condemnations, expelling and banning diplomats, ejecting states from organizations) to threats of legal prosecution (war crimes, crimes against humanity) to various uses of force (military threats, blocking deployments, training and equipping opposition groups, and limited strikes). If such measures fail, military intervention represents the ultimate coercive instrument, as was the case in expelling Iraqi forces from Kuwait in 1991, during the Balkans in the mid-1990s, and more recently, to prevent mass atrocities in Benghazi, Libya, in 2011. Consensual de-escalation can involve offering various inducements and rewards for compliant behavior (e.g., economic assistance, diplomatic recognition, military support, security guarantees, and domestic power sharing). Depending on the circumstances, both types of measures can be applied in a broad fashion against specific states and nonstate entities or targeted in a more discriminatory fashion against their leadership, supporters, and sources of funding.

Since every situation is different, there is no tried and trusted formula that will determine the success of conflict mitigation efforts. Some general factors or variables are clearly important, however, including the nature of the target (whether it's a state or nonstate actor), how powerful they are, whether they enjoy the backing of a great power (especially a permanent member of the UN Security Council), their level of economic development, their dependency on external trade and communications, and their geographic location and demography. Also having a bearing on which conflict mitigation strategies to use is the level of international support, particularly in the immediate vicinity of the target state/actor; whether broader strategic and reputational issues are at stake; and how much has already been invested in trying to prevent the conflict before it escalated. Finally, as a general rule, deterring others from taking certain actions is easier than compelling them to reverse course.

The United States already has considerable experience in conflict mitigation efforts, with some notable successes. Examples include multiple efforts to diffuse ongoing conflicts between India and Pakistan over Kashmir and between North and South Korea; conflicts between Armenia and Azerbaijan in 1994, Russia and Georgia in 2008, Eritrea and Djibouti in 2008, and more recent diplomatic interventions to avert conflict between Sudan and the newly created state of South Sudan as well as between China and the Philippines over territorial disputes in the South China Sea.[97] The United States has also acted in concert with others to defuse various intrastate conflicts that have flared up periodically, although not all efforts have contributed to preventing or mitigating violence successfully. Burundi in 2003, Kenya in 2008, Central African Republic in 2014, and in the Democratic Republic of Congo since 2016 are a few examples.[98]

The UN can also point to several successful mediating efforts in defusing disputes between Turkmenistan and Azerbaijan, Nigeria and Cameroon, and Gabon and Equatorial Guinea.[99] It has also increasingly used its "good offices," special envoys, fact-finding missions, and various mediation mechanisms to manage intrastate conflicts; many believe that these have had good effect in numerous such conflicts over the last decade, including those in Niger, Guinea, Ghana, South Sudan, Kenya, Madagascar, Kyrgyzstan, Nepal, and Iraq (Kirkuk).[100]

* * *

These three categories of preventive action can clearly be used to develop more detailed policy templates manage to commonly recurring contingencies. One can imagine, for example, templates being developed for a range of potential interstate crises that might involve territorial or resource-related disputes where there are already militarized borders with forces in confrontational postures. Equivalent templates can be developed for intrastate disputes. Obvious candidates would be the threat of coups and political succession disputes, including electoral violence, popular uprisings, religious and ethnic tensions, and resource-related conflicts. Similar crisis management templates can be developed for other commonly recurring incidents, such as border clashes, a terrorist incident, a hostage taking, or humanitarian contingencies.

PART TWO

A U.S. STRATEGY OF
PREVENTIVE ENGAGEMENT

SING THE APPROACH laid out in part 1, the United States can actively manage the risks of a more disorderly world through a multilevel strategy of preventive engagement. Each level corresponds to the three principal types of preventive action—long-term risk reduction, medium-term crisis prevention, and short-term conflict mitigation. Though conceptually distinct, the three levels are intended to complement and reinforce one another in practice. Thus, long-term risk reduction should over time help to reduce the number of plausible crises that the United States would need to be concerned about in the medium term as well as, ultimately, those it may have to manage in the short term. Besides this "trickle-down" effect, there are also "trickle-up" benefits. Preventing ongoing conflicts from escalating further will reduce the likelihood of new crises emerging in the medium term while helping to reinforce longer term initiatives.

Preventive engagement can thus be conceived as a three-level "game." Ensuring that each level is "played" in a complementary fashion requires regular oversight and discipline. Priorities have to be set and followed at each level to avoid costly distractions and the dissipation of effort. At the same time, policy makers have to be cognizant of how actions taken on one level could harm or undermine initiatives being pursued on another. These requirements will become evident in the chapters that follow.

4

RISK REDUCTION

The Long Game

Risk is like fire: If controlled it will help you; if uncontrolled it will rise up and destroy you.

—THEODORE ROOSEVELT

The task facing American statesmen over the next decades . . . is to recognize that broad trends are under way, and that there is a need to "manage" affairs so that the relative erosion of the United States' position takes place slowly and smoothly, and is not accelerated by policies which bring merely short term advantage but longer term disadvantage.

—PAUL KENNEDY

O F THE THREE components of a U.S. strategy of preventive engagement, long-term risk reduction would appear to represent the toughest challenge. Although policy makers will routinely extoll the virtues of "taking the long view" and "playing the long game," these are easier to preach than to practice. Given the press of daily events, it is hard enough to give much thought to what might be brewing just over the horizon, much less consider how the long-term future could pan out for better or worse. Moreover, the notion that much can be done in any case to "shape" or "bend" the course of events to lessen the risk of the United States being drawn into costly military conflicts will likely strike many as a fool's errand and even the height of conceit. History's unpredictable twists and turns, after all, routinely make a mockery of not only our most confident assumptions but also our best laid plans.

Long-term risk reduction, however, is not the hopeless endeavor that it might seem. For a start, it does not rely on accurately predicting the future, something that is clearly impossible. Rather, it is based on the premise that while the world could evolve in many conceivable ways, some are more plausible than others. Within the realm of the plausible, moreover, it is possible to assess which of the alternate "futures" are likely to be more dangerous and threatening to the United States and thus pose a greater or lesser risk of it becoming involved in costly military engagements. As was argued in chapter 2, such foresight will not only sensitize policy makers to the dangers ahead but also motivate them to do things that improve the odds that the world moves in a more benign and—for the United States, at least—less risky direction.

What America can do and encourage others to do in this respect should also not be viewed as either outlandish or quixotic. Indeed, as will become clear in this chapter, the United States has in many respects been pursuing elements of a long-term risk reduction strategy for decades with demonstrable benefits for its own security and international order more generally. Such efforts are faltering, however, in part because their value for conflict risk reduction is either unappreciated or underrated. This needs to be rectified.

This chapter will make the case for an invigorated U.S. risk reduction effort. It begins with a brief horizon scan of the future, out to 2050, to assess how the risk of U.S. military engagement could change for better or worse over this period. Which of the potential risks clearly deserve more priority than others for U.S. policy makers will then be discussed. This leads to a detailed examination of the specific risk reduction measures that the United States should pursue over the long term.

THE LONG VIEW: THREE FUTURES

Using the cone of plausibility foresight methodology outlined in chapter 2, it is possible to imagine three alternative trajectories for the future, with each having different levels of risk for the United States. These consist of a standard baseline scenario in which current political, demographic, economic, technological, and environmental trends are more or less projected forward. Two variants are added to this baseline: one that imagines the world growing progressively more peaceful and the other more disorderly and prone to conflict. These three futures clearly do not exhaust the conceivable scenarios, but they do serve to capture the most important long-term risks to the United States.

BASELINE SCENARIO: MORE OF THE SAME

The baseline projection assumes that the nation-state will remain the primary political unit of global politics. The number of state members of the United Nations has steadily grown from the original 51 in 1945 to 193 today. While the pace of state formation has slowed considerably since the era of decolonization and the period immediately following the Cold War, further additions seem plausible in the future given the presence of secessionist movements in several countries and the potential breakup of some currently experiencing internal strife. At the same time, a significant contraction in the number of states, for whatever reason, seems very unlikely. Less certain is the future political character of states. As indicated in figure 4.1, the number of democracies in the world had until recently been steadily growing, but this trend has now stalled and by some estimates even gone into reverse. The baseline scenario assumes, however, that there will neither be a great recession nor a significant expansion—a new wave—of democratization.

On the basis of current birth rates and estimates of life expectancy, the world's population will continue to grow, reaching close to 10 billion people by the middle of the century, up from around 7.2 billion today. Thereafter, the trend lines are less certain and, depending on what assumptions are made about fertility and mortality, the world's population may level off, fall below current levels, or grow to over 16 billion by 2100, according to some UN projections. By 2028 India is expected to overtake China as the most populous country. The United States will likely stay in third place through the middle of the century, followed by Indonesia, Nigeria, Pakistan, Brazil, Bangladesh, Russia, and Mexico. Most of the population growth in this period will occur in developing countries, with sub-Saharan Africa witnessing the biggest increase. By 2050, over 60 percent of the

95

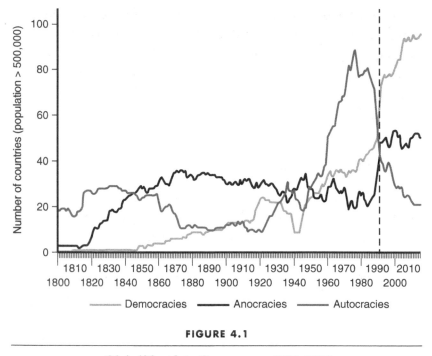

FIGURE 4.1

Global Trends in Governance, 1800–2015

Source: Center for Systemic Peace © 2016.

world will live in Africa and Asia. Meanwhile, the developed world (except the United States) will see only modest growth as its populations age; indeed, some countries in Europe, as well as Japan, will experience significant declines unless fertility rates change significantly or considerable immigration occurs. The current trend toward urbanization is also expected to continue: today, close to half of the world's population lives in urban areas; by 2030 that will climb to nearly 60 percent.

Given these population projections, global economic output can also be expected to grow, helped along by the likely expansion of international trade and various production-enhancing technologies. This has certainly been the long-standing trend, as indicated in figure 4.2, though much like the extension of democratic governance, there could be periods where both global output and trade are stagnant and even decline temporarily—as has happened in the past.

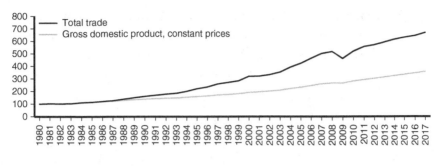

FIGURE 4.2

World GDP and Global Trade (1980 = 100)

Source: International Monetary Fund, World Economic Outlook Database, April 2017.

By all indications, moreover, the global economic "center of gravity" will continue to move eastward as the economies of South and East Asia grow in size and account for a larger share of global output.[1] By 2032, if not earlier, the overall size of China's economy will exceed the United States, though in terms of per capita gross domestic product (GDP), the United States will remain the richer country for many years thereafter. Using a broader-based index of national power developed by the U.S. government that aggregates population size, GDP, military spending, investment in technology, and the quality of health, education, and governance, China is expected to surpass the United States in global rankings sometime after 2043. Such projections, of course, rest on the assumption that the Chinese economy continues to expand (albeit at slower rates of growth) and does not go into serious recession—what is sometimes called a hard landing.

As these macrodemographic and macroeconomic trends gather momentum, power will continue to grow more diffuse in the world. Several countries not traditionally classified as part of the West could become bona fide regional powers—notably Brazil, South Africa, Nigeria, Indonesia, Mexico, Turkey, and most probably Iran, though such estimates have in recent years been adjusted downward as some of these countries have experienced significant economic and political difficulties. Many other countries in the developing world will also likely undergo considerable growth because of their comparatively youthful populations. Meanwhile, the economies of

Europe, Japan, and Russia will most likely continue their slow decline relative to the emerging powers of the world. Their trajectory will rest in large part on how they exploit new technological advances in such areas as robotics, bioengineering, and three-dimensional printing, as well as their openness to immigration for the purpose of rejuvenating their workforces.

The anticipated increases in global population and economic growth will inevitably increase the demand for various natural resources (especially food, water, and energy) while also placing the world's atmosphere, biological organisms, and principal ecosystems (forests and oceans) under increasing stress.[2] Food and water shortages are likely to occur in many areas of the world as a consequence of the combined effects of rising demand, environmental degradation, and climate change from continued human development. How acute such shortages could become, and what impact climate change will have on human development, is difficult to gauge with any precision; much will depend on how the world adapts and, in particular, develops various technological innovations that might mitigate these pressures—as has occurred, for example, with the advent of hydraulic fracturing (fracking) on projections regarding the global energy supply—or alters environmental change through geoengineering. These developments—with potential policy interventions that affect the rate of greenhouse gas emissions and climate change—are critical factors.

Besides these broad trends, there is also general agreement that the world will see continued growth in what is often referred to as individual empowerment. This includes the ability of people to exploit expanding educational opportunities for personal gain, as well as to obtain greater access to information, health care, technology, capital, communications, and transportation. Some assessments of the future go so far as to argue that individual empowerment is the most important of the macrotrends shaping the future, since it affects, one way or another, all of the others.[3]

Taken together, these trends are likely to create a more dangerous strategic environment for the United States, though the risk of specific kinds of conflict will vary. Thus the likelihood of military conflict with China or Russia will increase but will, overall, remain low. Neither China nor Russia has any compelling need to challenge the status quo (certainly not in any fundamental way) and in the process risk major war with the United States. Although rising powers have challenged the predominant world power in the past, this seems neither inevitable in the case of China (as some scholars maintain it is) nor likely from today's vantage point. China's trajectory toward global primacy looks far from certain, and the need to ensure that it continues to prosper economically while remaining under Communist Party rule is likely to preoccupy its leadership.[4] Meanwhile, Russia faces a much harder economic and political challenge as a declining major power over this same period.

Nevertheless, U.S.-China and U.S.-Russia relations can be expected to grow more distrustful and at times confrontational as both powers challenge America's predominant influence within various global institutions and engage in activities intended to increase control of areas considered to be their traditional or natural spheres of influence. This is already leading to more overt balancing behavior by the United States toward China in East Asia and the Western Pacific through a basket of military and economic initiatives known as the U.S. pivot or rebalancing strategy and toward Russia in eastern Europe as part of a NATO-wide strategy. Each of the three powers is developing new strategic capabilities, reorienting its operational posture, and adjusting its military deployments with the possibility of major conflict in mind. Furthermore, a largely hidden but increasingly vigorous assault against the United States using cyberwarfare tactics is also being conducted. Both trends can be expected to continue.

At the same time, China and Russia are actively jockeying for influence in areas well beyond their immediate periphery—including Africa, Latin America, and the Middle East—and this is also stoking concern in the United States. Though driven mostly by commercial considerations, such actions could increasingly devolve into active opposition to U.S. regional interests, as has happened with Russian military support for the regime of Bashar al-Assad in Syria.

Under the baseline scenario, the risk of the United States becoming embroiled in a major regional war can be expected to grow. The Korean Peninsula is becoming more unstable as North Korea develops nuclear weapons and long-range ballistic missiles capable of threatening U.S. allies and most likely U.S. territory in the next five to ten years. Another major Korean war could be ignited by any number of plausible causes, including a collapse of the ruling Kim family regime. The Middle East and North Africa are also likely to become more unstable in the foreseeable future, with many areas wracked by chronic violence as nonstate actors, some of them proxy forces for regional powers, challenge the authority and control of existing regimes. The biggest long-term concern, however, is that the underlying Shia-Sunni sectarian schism in the region will be transformed into a more open military confrontation between several Persian Gulf states led by Saudi Arabia, along with perhaps Turkey on the one hand and principally Iran and potentially Iraq on the other. This conflict could play out along the fault lines of the sectarian divide, as well as in areas where neither sect predominates but where it has ties or interests at stake. The likelihood that the main protagonists will acquire nuclear weapons or other weapons of mass destruction, along with associated long-range delivery systems, will almost certainly grow as well, thereby further adding to the level of insecurity and latent risk of a major interstate war. Again, several quite plausible scenarios could unfold in a way that leads to the United States once again being engaged in major military operations in the Middle East.

Outside eastern Europe, Northeast Asia, the Middle East, and North Africa, the likelihood of the United States becoming involved in a major regional war seems low. In South Asia, the risk of renewed fighting between India and Pakistan certainly exists and could very easily increase in the coming years, but the United States is unlikely to become directly involved beyond diplomatic interventions given it has made no formal defense guarantees to either country. Elsewhere, especially in Africa and Latin America, the risk is even lower and is expected to stay that way. In all these areas, however, the risk of the United States engaging in limited military operations will likely remain, primarily to counter the threat from terrorist groups and to carry out or support peacekeeping and humanitarian relief operations that will arise from time to time.

A NEGATIVE VARIANT: REGRESSIVE GLOBALIZATION

Many of the worrying trends identified in the baseline projection could intensify and produce an alternative scenario, referred to here as regressive globalization. In sum, the forces that have propelled greater global integration and interdependence for the last thirty years would stall and go into reverse, leading to an increasingly fragmented and disorderly world. This could unfold as a result of several developments or "shocks" that occur simultaneously or in quick succession to one another.

The first would be a major crisis or series of crises that resulted in the armed forces of the United States and China or Russia facing off against each other and conceivably even exchanging fire. Several extant territorial disputes and potential flash points could provide the precipitating context for such a confrontation. While the risk of general war would likely restrain further escalation, the net effect of such a serious crisis would be to propel the major powers involved toward adopting more overtly confrontational postures, much like the Cold War evolved.[5] Other states would almost certainly be drawn into taking sides or declaring themselves to be non-aligned in the process, again in similar fashion to the Cold War. China and Russia could conceivably become more closely aligned strategically, if not formal allies, as a consequence. India could also be drawn into this larger strategic realignment, most likely alongside the United States. Sino-Indian relations have at times been tense over various territorial disputes and because of China's military support to Pakistan. India also hosts the Dalai Lama, the spiritual leader of Tibet (whose people aspire to be independent from China), and that is another source of friction.

The reemergence of confrontational relations between the major powers would have profound consequences globally. Several important strategic arms control regimes could likely unravel, while new areas of competition—notably, cyberspace and outer space—would become more actively contested. Cooperation at the United Nations (and in particular its Security Council) would once again become stymied if not absolutely paralyzed, thereby undermining its effectiveness in managing a host of global and regional problems. This would further tarnish the general legitimacy of the UN with potentially fatal consequences for its long-term survival.

A severe economic recession could provide another inflection point toward regressive globalization. Unlike the 2008 financial crisis, which is generally considered to have been managed effectively by the G20 nations, the world may not be so fortunate should there be another severe economic downturn. Populist and protectionist sentiments have grown considerably since then, as indicated by the growing opposition to new regional trade agreements, the backlash against immigration in the European Union, particularly the UK Brexit vote, and support for right-wing nationalist politicians in many countries. It cannot be confidently assumed, therefore, that effective multilateral cooperation would materialize once again, especially if the major players are also at loggerheads for other reasons. A prolonged recession that depressed the global demand for commodities and finished goods and that also precipitated capital flight, thus destabilizing markets, would likely do serious harm to the economies of many developing countries. Those already deemed fragile or vulnerable because of poor governance and corruption, religious and ethnic schisms, or demographic profile, among other risk factors, could experience serious instability. Armed non-state actors, whether politically or criminally motivated, would likely emerge to exploit the opportunities presented by weak and failing state institutions and, in the process, grow more powerful. Sub-Saharan Africa, parts of the Middle East and Central Asia, and even some countries in Central America would be most at risk.[6]

A failure of the main international institutions to respond to a severe economic crisis would also undermine their legitimacy as effective bodies. The current global regime regulating trade and financial flows could come under increasing strain and conceivably start to unravel as more and more countries sought unilateral or regional solutions to their plight. Rival economic blocs with mercantilist impulses could emerge as a consequence, further eroding the current global economic order. Tensions between the Global North and South could also grow more pronounced in the process, especially if the more prosperous and thus more resilient northern countries were perceived to be indifferent to the plight of the less advantaged. Furthermore, capital flight and migration would almost certainly increase and exacerbate the situation in the source countries—since it is often the best and the brightest that seek to leave—while adding to xenophobic and protectionist sentiments in the immigrant-receiving countries. Several emerging technological trends could accelerate the decoupling of the global economy by shifting the production of goods and services to local sources, thereby lessening the interdependencies that come with international supply chains.[7]

Various natural or man-made shocks could further contribute to international tensions, and with them could come a general stress on global institutions. The effects of climate change could become much more severe than anticipated, causing more frequent extreme weather events in some areas of the world as well as prolonged food and water shortages. Managing such crises could progressively exhaust the resources of both national and international aid agencies and eventually overwhelm them, causing deep resentment in the affected areas. Various health-related crises could have the same effect. The risk of political unrest and outward migration would likely grow as a consequence.

Under this variant to the baseline scenario, the risk to the United States could grow dramatically. The possibility of great power conflict, major regional war, and limited military engagements would all increase.

A POSITIVE VARIANT: PROGRESSIVE GLOBALIZATION

An alternative, more optimistic scenario to the baseline projection is also conceivable. This scenario envisages a world of deepening economic integration and international cooperation that brings with it a steady diminution of organized violence; tensions between the great powers would recede and interstate conflict would become increasingly unimaginable. The so-called Long Peace would in effect be extended indefinitely. While some areas of the world would continue to be wracked by conflict and instability, these would be managed by the UN, regional organizations, and "coalitions of the willing" involving one or more major powers. Overall, the level of risk to the United States would consequently be much lower than the baseline trajectory.

This optimistic scenario is unlikely to come about spontaneously, however. In this respect, several conceivable developments could serve as triggers of progressive globalization. Peaceful democratic change in China and Russia—whether sudden or gradual—is an obvious one. Such a transformation would have profound consequences globally, though on balance the systemic impact of China—a rising power—turning democratic would be greater. Although economic competition among the major powers would not disappear, the probability of the Long Peace coming to an end would diminish significantly, if not disappear altogether. Cooperation within the UN Security Council would almost certainly improve, and other multilateral mechanisms and regional organizations could also be expected to become more effective. The prospect of collective action on a host of regional and global problems—notably, nuclear proliferation, violent extremism, and climate change—would also increase.

Furthermore, the political transformation of China and Russia would likely provide a huge boost to prodemocracy movements in other regions of the world. A new wave of political liberalization—again, if carried out relatively peacefully—would in turn have a positive impact on international trade and investment. Earlier projections of the world's economy doubling by the 2030s and possibly again by 2050 would become more realistic as a consequence. Steady economic growth in the developing world, as noted earlier, has generally translated into improvements to state capacity and the quality of governance, and this has helped lower the overall level of armed conflict. The number of countries likely to have per capita GDP below US$5,000—which, as noted in chapter 2, are more susceptible to armed conflict—is also likely to diminish substantially and be almost exclusively confined to sub-Saharan Africa.

Besides the possibility of political change in Russia and China propelling progressive globalization, certain negative shocks could conceivably have the same effect. A worldwide pandemic, the use of nuclear weapons in a conflict or by a terrorist organization, or a major (natural or man-made) environmental catastrophe could elicit a level of international cooperation that spills over into other areas and develops a self-reinforcing momentum with lasting effects.

LONG-TERM PREVENTIVE PRIORITIES

Given the preceding assessment of how the world could plausibly evolve up to the middle of the century, the United States will in all likelihood remain the preeminent global power during this period. Thereafter, however, its prospects are less certain and will depend in large degree on which of three alternate scenarios transpires. Each clearly presents very different levels of risk to international order and, by extension, U.S. interests usually defined by various measures of national security and well-being. The expected costs associated with managing these risks, whether it be for protecting the homeland, ensuring access to overseas markets and materials, or restoring peace in conflict stricken countries, will likewise vary. The extent of such exertions in turn has a bearing on America's capacity to maintain its preeminent position; the greater the drain on its national resources, the greater the danger it will slip, all else being equal.

Across the three scenarios a clear hierarchy of long-term preventive priorities for the United States can be discerned.

The first is to prevent a fundamental deterioration in the U.S. relationship with China and/or Russia to the extent that either becomes overtly adversarial, which would return the United States to Cold War levels of national insecurity and once again endanger the planet's very survival. As suggested in the discussion of the regressive globalization scenario, the systemic effects of renewed major power confrontation would be enormous; it would likely paralyze the work of the United Nations and possibly even lead to its demise, increase international tensions in several regions of the world as the principal protagonists jockeyed for influence, and undermine the prospects for collective action on a host of global problems, not the least of which would be climate change and the proliferation of deadly technologies. The rules-based global economic order would likely also unravel as the world polarized around competing blocs.

The second long-term priority is to prevent the emergence of major regional rivalries that could increase the risk of significant and prolonged U.S. military intervention to restore international order and/or assist an endangered ally. Both the baseline and the regressive globalization scenarios project this risk to grow in the Middle East and Northeast Asia. Although a major regional war would not expose the U.S. homeland to the same level of risk as would exist in an adversarial relationship with another major power, the associated dangers and costs could still be substantial. Besides the potential expenses associated with direct U.S. military involvement in a future regional conflict, the security of the United States is unlikely to remain unthreatened. The ability to do harm from afar can be expected to grow with the global diffusion of various technologies, which some regional powers already possess and others will surely emulate. The potential use of unconventional proxy actors capable of taking the fight to the U.S. homeland cannot be discounted. And finally, the economic consequences of a major conflict are also likely to resonate well beyond the affected region given the interdependencies of a globalized economy.

The third long-term priority is to prevent the emergence of endemic instability and civil violence in large parts of the developing world that would threaten U.S. interests and increase the risk of regular, albeit more limited, military interventions. As mentioned earlier in this chapter, dangerous nonstate actors can exploit instability and ungoverned spaces to attack U.S. property and mount campaigns against the homeland. Serious humanitarian crises brought on or exacerbated by conflict can also have destabilizing spillover effects on neighboring areas that become difficult and costly to remedy. Other risks, such as pandemic health threats, can also grow under such circumstances. In sum, what may initially seem distant and inconsequential can evolve in harmful ways.

LONG-TERM RISK REDUCTION

The United States can tackle these long-term preventive priorities by pursuing seven broad policy initiatives that collectively reduce the risk of U.S. military engagement. All but one of these initiatives derive from what has apparently helped to promote global order in the past—specifically, the conflict risk reduction measures discussed in chapter 3. The single outlier concerns the management of global climate change, which has no precedent. While the seven initiatives do not absolutely preclude the possibility that events may transpire to push the future in an unwelcome direction, as just described, they make it less likely. As will become clear, the initiatives are in many respects mutually reinforcing and certainly wide ranging in that they contribute to each of the three long-term preventive priorities of the United States.

PROMOTE STRATEGIC STABILITY AMONG THE
MAJOR POWERS

Several strategies could in principle be adopted by the United States to lessen the likelihood of relations deteriorating in a dangerous way among the major powers. One is to actively seek an informal concert arrangement by which the four major powers (China, Russia, India, and the United States) agree to lessen points of friction and work together on emerging challenges to international order where they share a common interest. This sounds superficially appealing but, in practice, concert arrangements—certainly if the past is any precedent—would likely require the mutual recognition of de facto spheres of influence, with the most important usually being on the immediate periphery of each power. Since many U.S. allies are located close to China and Russia, the United States would face the prospect of having to relinquish its formal security commitments to these states or attenuating them in such a way as to render them virtually meaningless. The affected countries would either accept their fate and move closer to China and Russia or actively resist any such accommodation by seeking unilateral solutions to their new security predicament, including potentially developing a nuclear deterrent. Either way, the United States would lose the political and economic influence it had with its erstwhile allies while suffering serious damage to the credibility of its security commitments to those that remain under its protection. And without the U.S. security blanket, long dormant regional rivalries could also reemerge while the global nonproliferation regime could become fatally undermined.

Another option to promote major power stability would be to develop a common code of conduct based on a broad set of principles that could be explicitly defined or tacitly observed. This appears to be the intent of official Chinese declarations that call for a "new type of relationship for major countries in the twenty-first century." This suggestion was first proposed in a speech by then vice president Xi Jinping during his visit to Washington in February 2012. Xi called for "mutual understanding and strategic trust," respect for each other's "core interests," and "mutually beneficial cooperation" as the principal elements of future relations.[8] These themes have been reiterated and elaborated subsequently by senior Chinese officials, including the current president Xi, in numerous speeches and publications. Although focused primarily on moderating the U.S.-China relationship and avoiding the dangerous tensions and misunderstandings that have frequently arisen between established and rising powers, Chinese officials have also emphasized similar principles, if not the exact same formulation, in high-level meetings with Indian and Russian leaders.[9]

American officials have so far steered a middle ground in response to the Chinese proposal by being broadly supportive of its general intent without formally endorsing specific ideas that could be translated into policy. This is in part because the operational implications of what China proposes is still unclear, while there is an understandable reluctance to supporting something that could be construed more widely as either great power collusion at the expense of allies and partners in Asia or, worse, ceding to China more than is obtained in return.

Although there may be some value in the four powers agreeing formally to a general statement of principles or code of conduct to regulate their future relations, it is doubtful whether it would ever rise above the platitudinous or amount to anything more than what is already enshrined in numerous international declarations, not the least of which being the UN Charter, which calls on states to respect each other's sovereign independence, settle disputes peacefully, and not interfere in the internal affairs of other states.[10] In short, a more meaningful arrangement is required that would foster a stable and durable strategic relationship. This will necessitate both restraint and reassurance in several critical areas.

The first and most fundamental is desisting from activities that undermine confidence in the national security of each major power and that could imply at least potential hostile intent. For each of the major powers, confidence in its national security—certainly from coercion or attack from another—rests ultimately on the credibility of its strategic nuclear deterrent force to assuredly inflict unacceptable costs on an adversary even in the eventuality it had been attacked first. Active strategic reassurance requires not only unambiguously signaling a basic acceptance of this condition of mutual vulnerability but also, and more important, refraining from activities that might reasonably suggest a contrary motive. The latter includes the development of highly effective offensive weapons systems that could directly destroy or indirectly incapacitate the deterrent force of a major power, and/or highly effective defensive systems that could render an aggressor more or less immune from assured retribution. Strategic stability pertains, in other words, when no major power—or, more crucially, *combination of powers*—could strike another in the belief that it or they could avoid incurring massive destruction in return. Stated differently, no power—especially in crisis situations—should ever feel motivated to strike another out of fear that it could be decisively disadvantaged if it does *not* strike first.

Formalizing mutual strategic stability among the major powers would be a difficult undertaking today, given the current climate of relations, but it can be pursued through an informal strategic compact made up of a combination of tacit restraint and active reassurance buttressed with international agreements in certain areas.[11] More specifically,

- Each power would show restraint in developing and refining weapons capabilities—either primarily offensive or defensive in nature—that have the practical effect of undermining confidence in the operational effectiveness of another power's national deterrent systems or that could plausibly increase either side's incentives to use nuclear weapons first in a serious crisis or conflict. In cases where strategic intentions were unclear or ambiguous, each power would be obliged to take steps to actively reassure the other power. For example, China is evidently worried about the U.S. deployment of national missile defenses, which in combination with precision strike capabilities—nuclear and conventional—could put in doubt its capacity to retaliate effectively if attacked. Various measures can be taken by the United States to reassure China of the operational purpose of its missile defense systems—namely, to protect the homeland against possible attack from North Korea or Iran. Likewise, China can take steps to reassure the United States about its nuclear force modernization plans and pledge to not increase their overall size significantly.[12]
- Each power would be responsible for ensuring the safety and security of its strategic deterrent forces, including associated delivery systems, and actively reassuring the other power of the measures it had taken to prevent accidental or unauthorized use. If needed, technical expertise and support would be shared for this purpose. Advance warning of missile

and space launches, which already occurs between some of the powers, would be routinized for all. Strategic forces currently in high states of operational readiness—principally U.S. and Russian forces—would be "de-alerted" to reduce the grounds for misunderstanding in a severe crisis.[13]

- Each power would refrain from peacetime activities deemed to be either provocative or threatening to the functioning of another's nuclear deterrent forces. This would include deliberate interference with or simulated attacks on missile early warning systems and associated command and control networks, inflammatory or ambiguous military exercises in the vicinity of national borders, and aggressive or dangerous military maneuvers in close proximity to the strategic forces operated by other powers.[14] Current efforts to develop and test antisatellite capabilities, whether designed with that specific intent in mind or as a by-product of other military systems, would cease as part of a tacit if not formalized moratorium. Current bilateral agreements to prevent and manage dangerous or ambiguous incidents at sea could be expanded and, moreover, extended to outer space.[15] A code of conduct for cyberspace that specified undesirable as well as desirable behavior would also be helpful.[16]

- Each power would agree to manage and resolve accidents and incidents involving its strategic forces in an expeditious and peaceful manner. Extant bilateral measures to assist communication and cooperation in a crisis would be regularly reviewed and improved where needed. The United States and China would establish a dedicated high-level communication link or hotline between senior military and political leaders.[17]

These initiatives would not constitute a radical departure from the intent of current U.S. policy. Indeed, the 2010 U.S. *Nuclear Posture Review* report stated that "maintaining strategic stability in the U.S. China relationship is as important to the Administration as maintaining strategic stability with other major powers."[18] Similar pronouncements underpin U.S.-Russia agreements on the reduction of strategic nuclear forces.

Besides efforts to sustain mutual deterrence, strategic stability can be fostered in other ways. Desisting from activities that can be perceived as politically threatening or provocative is arguably just as important. Thus, efforts that openly or clandestinely challenge the political legitimacy or weaken the authority of major state leaders should also be eschewed. Likewise, activities designed to undermine in a fundamental sense the economic well-being of another state fall into the same category. These all constitute existential threats that go beyond what can be considered normal competitive behavior among major powers jockeying for power and influence in the world.

Perceptions of threat among the major powers will also be influenced by other behavior. The deployment of foreign forces close to one's territorial borders, especially in sizable numbers and configured in an ambiguous if not openly provocative manner is an obvious one;[19] the establishment of new military bases or access arrangements in sensitive areas is another. Military exercises that simulate and thus improve the capacity for offensive action, or deployments that actively probe for weaknesses in a country's defenses, can be additional grounds for concern. Espionage and, increasingly, cyberinterference fall into the same category. Refraining from any of these actions, either through formal constraint or tacit restraint, can further enhance strategic stability among the major powers.

STRENGTHEN THE NORMS AND INSTITUTIONS THAT BOLSTER WORLD ORDER

International order, as discussed in chapter 3, relies on the collective observance of basic rules and norms of behavior, especially as they relate to state sovereignty and the use of force. These rules and the institutions that support them are under increasing stress, however, and have become a source of considerable friction not only among the major powers but in general. The United States should work in concert with like-minded states to bolster these rules and norms so that they remain relevant in the twenty-first century.

With regard to the established norms and rules proscribing the use of force—essentially anything other than national self-defense and UN-authorized collective security missions (so called Chapter VI and Chapter VII missions)—international friction has been steadily growing since the end of the Cold War from two directions. The first derives from the growing pressure to strike either preventively or preemptively before a serious—and conceivably even an existential—national security threat materializes. While there have always been tensions over the right of states to carry out "anticipatory self-defense," these have grown in recent years as more nations—including the United States—have conducted cross-border military strikes (both overtly and covertly) to counter an emerging nuclear proliferation or terrorist threat. As the global diffusion of deadly technologies continues, particularly to nonstate actors, the imperatives to act rapidly and preemptively can only be expected to grow. It is also not hard to imagine how the principle of anticipatory self-defense can be stretched to legitimize the use of force to counter other perceived threats that stem, for example, from the potential spillover effects of political instability, deadly pandemics, or irresponsible environmental behavior in neighboring states—or, for that matter, distant ones, given that geographical proximity is increasingly irrelevant in a globalized and interdependent world.

The second source of pressure on long-standing international norms derives from the growing and widely held conviction that states are responsible for the safety and well-being of their citizens and that if they abuse or fail for whatever reason to uphold this obligation, they forfeit their right to noninterference from the international community to remedy matters and protect endangered civilians. This belief has been translated into an assortment of international conventions and, increasingly, standing institutions—notably, the International Criminal Court—used to prosecute and punish those responsible for the mass killing of civilians or other serious human rights violations, as well as through various UN-sanctioned actions in support of what is formally called the Responsibility to Protect (R2P) principle, most notably in Libya and Cote d'Ivoire.[20] Yet many states, including several powerful ones, are clearly uncomfortable with the invocation of the R2P principle, which may later become the justification for coercive humanitarian intervention and regime change—as indeed happened in Libya in 2011. Such concerns cannot simply be dismissed as the self-interested sentiments of repressive regimes; there are legitimate—and, moreover, fundamental—concerns to be reconciled. As Mark Mazower argues, "The way leaders treat their people is not the only problem that counts in international affairs. A world in which violations of human rights trump the sanctity of borders may turn out to produce more wars, more massacres, and more instability. It may also be less law-abiding. If the history of the past century shows anything, it is that clear legal norms, the empowering of states, and the securing of international stability more generally also serve the cause of human welfare."[21] The pressure to use force in both circumstances can be lessened through earlier nonmilitary preventive measures, including coercive ones, but obviously not completely avoided. Thus, through example and active advocacy, the United States should promote broad support for a practical new set of rules and standards regarding the use of force in cases that involve the breaching of national sovereignty. A potentially useful approach toward pursuing this goal is to advocate where possible the same basic principles that undergird the legitimate use of force for domestic law enforcement that all states more or less adhere to—or at least profess to—as follows.

The most legitimate use of force in the domestic sphere is for self-defense and public security, so the same can apply to fostering international order. Though special circumstances may dictate private resort to force, ordinarily this is the preserve of properly authorized—and, moreover, organized—agents of the state. Likewise, states must restrict the latitude of nonstate actors to wield coercive power, just as they strive to monopolize force within their national boundaries. Acts of anticipatory self-defense and preemptive uses of force to safeguard the public are mostly considered exceptional but not a priori illegitimate. So the same applies to extraterritorial threats to national security that can be legitimately judged to pose a clear and present danger. Mass-casualty terrorism is an obvious case but, as indicated earlier, other threats conceivably meet the threshold criteria.

Similarly, just as generally approved legal mechanisms have evolved to permit the forceful breaching of private property in the interests of public security when it is deemed necessary—notably, with the use of court-approved search warrants and special police protocols—so can the broad practice of seeking the approval of the UN or the relevant regional organization serve the same purpose when it comes to sanctioning comparable international humanitarian missions. And just as exigent circumstances might justify rapid preventive action by law enforcement before formal authorization can be sought and secured, so can the same exceptions be permitted at the international level—again on the understanding that such exceptions are rare and should be followed by subsequent efforts to secure international endorsement. Finally, monitoring how force is ultimately employed—particularly ensuring that it is used in a proportionate and discriminate fashion to minimize civilian casualties and damage, and in accordance with the international laws of war—is necessary in all instances but is especially important in instances where the legitimacy of military action is controversial.

Besides promoting consensus around a new set of norms for the use of force, the United States must ensure that the United Nations remains a viable global institution. Although many Americans remain skeptical of the importance of the UN to U.S. foreign and security policy, no other international institution comes remotely close to its importance for advancing the U.S. preventive engagement agenda. From the normative value of its founding charter and the critical role of the Security Council in providing a venue for major power deliberations and wider global dispute resolution to the myriad conflict management activities and ancillary efforts on the part of its affiliated multilateral agencies to improve the human condition in virtually every corner of the globe, the United Nations is an indispensable institution for promoting a liberal international order. As a permanent member of the Security Council and principal underwriter of the UN system, including being the largest donor to its peacekeeping operations, the United States has considerable influence on what it does on a daily basis as well as in setting its future agenda. The United States should, therefore, not only make the most of what the UN system has to offer but also work hard to make it better at what it does best.

The principal strength of the UN—its universal membership and the legitimacy that this confers—is also, as many have pointed out, its greatest encumbrance. As a vehicle for setting new global norms and regulatory regimes, with their necessary monitoring and compliance mechanisms, it is without equal. The same is true for setting new goals for human development and mobilizing the international community to meet them, whether it is controlling dangerous greenhouse gases or ending extreme poverty in the world. Yet, as a body made up of sovereign nation-states and, moreover, largely dependent on agreement among the permanent members of its Security Council, the UN as an institution can effectively only do what it is allowed to do. For preventive engagement, this translates into being valuable for the "upstream" work of long-term risk reduction and the "downstream" work of crisis prevention, conflict mitigation and, if needed, peacekeeping that has made a demonstrable impact on reducing the risk of countries sliding back into war.[22]

How effective a partner the UN will be in the future will depend in large part on whether it is viewed as a broadly legitimate institution by its members. The legitimacy of an organization can derive from several sources, including whether it continues to perform its intended function effectively. Legitimacy also relates to whether the organization is perceived to represent its members' interests in a manner considered broadly equitable. As many have pointed out, the UN's basic structure was set in the aftermath of World War II, when the global distribution of power was very different from what it is today. The last time the composition of the Security Council was changed was in 1965, when it was agreed that the number of elected temporary members would increase from eleven to fifteen. The lack of broad regional representation is a clear deficiency that will only grow as leading states in the Global South become more prominent members of the international community. That India is not a permanent member given its growing attributes of a major power will become increasingly egregious, which helps explain why the United States rightly endorsed its candidacy for a permanent seat on the Security Council in 2010. The likelihood that India or any other aspirant will gain a seat anytime soon is remote, however, given the institutional hurdles that have to be overcome and the prevailing political interests that will likely continue to block any compromise.[23] This reality should not deter the United States from continuing to publicly endorse Security Council reform and laying out basic principles for its revitalization.

In place of "big bang" restructuring plans, an evolutionary criteria-based approach offers a sensible way forward.[24] In essence, aspirant countries would be encouraged to demonstrate both the capacity and the willingness to make a *sustained* contribution to the work of the UN, particularly with respect to fulfilling its core peace and security responsibilities. This can be assessed in various ways, including financial contributions, involvement in peacebuilding and peacekeeping efforts, and the capacity to employ coercive instruments to uphold global norms and regimes if necessary. Over time, opposition to states' candidacies will become harder to rebuff, especially when their support for other major global initiatives is required, a case that will almost certainly arise in the years ahead. The same logic also applies to those that currently enjoy permanent membership; they, too, have to demonstrate a similar commitment to remain members of the club.

Expanding the size of the Security Council will, however, inevitably make it more difficult for it to reach consensus on controversial issues, though conceivably over the long term this could be offset somewhat should the political complexion of its membership grow more similar. In the meantime, however, the United States should support efforts to lessen the likelihood of council deadlock on issues that do not threaten the core national security concerns of the Permanent Five (China, France, Great Britain, Russia, and the United States). More specifically, the French proposal for permanent members to voluntarily withhold use of their veto power in cases of "mass crimes"—essentially those covered by the R2P principle—deserves support.[25] This suggestion would not require a formal amendment of the UN Charter, nor would it rely on the judgment of any Security Council member or the body as a whole to determine what constituted the relevant circumstances. France has proposed that at least fifty member states would have to request that the UN secretary-general reach such a determination—a threshold that could conceivably be raised to a two-thirds majority of the UN General Assembly to lend such actions greater legitimacy. Alternatively, the International Court of Justice could be asked to make an expedited ruling. In addition, the United States can also work to improve the working practices of the Security Council to make them more transparent to other UN member states.[26]

Besides bolstering the UN for the long haul, it is also critically important that the United States promote the continued viability of the global institutions and regimes associated with the control of dangerous technologies, including not only various weapons of mass destruction—nuclear, chemical, and biological—but also emerging concerns having to do with synthetic biology, robotics, and genetic engineering. Both cyberwarfare and the growing use of armed drones also constitute potentially destabilizing developments. Although some states doubtless do not feel especially threatened by the development of these technologies, either because they are geographically distant from those possessing such capabilities or they have no reason to fear that they might become a target for their use, there are many others that will be acutely concerned. Even when the prospect of invasion and conquest remains exceedingly remote, such technologies could conceivably be used as instruments of political intimidation or be transferred to others, particularly nonstate actors, who may feel little or no inhibitions about using them. Such concerns will likely prompt countermeasures that could raise new insecurities and, as suggested above, encourage states to take preemptive military action.

Ensuring that the current family of global arms control regimes remains relevant and effective for the foreseeable future should therefore continue to be a leading policy priority for the United States. This includes ensuring that the international organizations that support implementation of the principal regimes—the International Atomic Energy Agency as regards the Treaty on the Non-Proliferation of Nuclear Weapons, the Organization for the Prohibition of Chemical Weapons as regards the Chemical Weapons Convention, and the Implementation Support Unit as regards the Biological Weapons Convention—receive adequate international funding as well as political support when challenges arise, as they surely will in the future. It is long overdue, moreover, that the United States finally ratify the Comprehensive Test Ban Treaty; doing so would strengthen the global norm against nuclear testing. The overall running costs of maintaining these arms control regimes are trivial compared to the critical role they play. At the same time, the United States should also push for a set of international legal constraints and behavioral norms surrounding the use of cyberweapons. Regulating cyberwarfare in a technical or numerical way clearly presents a much harder challenge than for weapons of mass destruction and conventional systems, but this should not deter progress in those areas where meaningful constraints can be applied. Similar approaches should also be explored for potentially dangerous dual-use technologies.

Finally, it is vital that the current international regulatory regimes for the use of the "global commons" stay abreast of their increasing exploitation for commercial and military advantage. Besides the atmosphere, the open sea, and outer space, commercial exploitation of the ocean floor and greater use of the polar regions as they become more accessible a result of global warming will in all likelihood make them more "congested, contested, and competitive." This will require strengthening existing regimes—and here again, it is long overdue that the United States has not ratified the UN Convention on the Law of the Sea—while developing new international rules for new areas.

MAINTAIN U.S. REGIONAL SECURITY GUARANTEES

Although America's worldwide system of alliances evolved during the Cold War for different reasons, maintaining them for the indefinite future should be part of the long-term preventive agenda of the United States. Despite the concern that several if not all of America's military alliances have become too costly to maintain and, moreover, risk ensnaring the United States in local disputes of no real strategic importance, their larger import to regional stability should not be overlooked. On balance, America's alliances continue to play a vital stabilizing role at a time of growing geopolitical uncertainty. More specifically, they reassure many countries about their vulnerability to external coercion and aggression and in doing so dampen their incentive to seek other solutions—notably, the development of nuclear weapons, which would undermine regional stability and the larger global nonproliferation regime. The military bases and access arrangements that allies provide the United States also permit it to project its power in defense of other interests while facilitating multinational cooperation on a range of humanitarian operations. These benefits can be illustrated for each of the main regions of concern.

In Europe, NATO's value for regional stability is, if anything, increasing as a consequence of developments on its eastern and southern flanks. Since the 2014 Ukraine crisis, deterring potential Russian revanchism in general and reassuring NATO's eastern members in particular has clearly become a major alliance concern. Similarly, the continuing turmoil in the Middle East and North Africa has made NATO's southern members increasingly nervous about spillover effects on their security. At the same time, growing uncertainty over the long-term future of the European Union brought on by the recent fiscal and migrant crises is also likely to elevate the enduring importance of NATO.

In East Asia, the strategic value of America's "hub and spoke" network of Pacific alliances—especially with Japan, South Korea, the Philippines, and Australia—is also growing rather than declining. The principal reason for this is clearly uncertainty over China's rise, and this has not been helped by China's assertive behavior in managing various territorial disputes in the South China Sea. Should China undergo a fundamental political transformation, it is conceivable that America's Pacific allies may no longer feel the need for U.S. security guarantees, but until that day arrives they will continue to play an important regional stabilizing role. In addition to its defensive functions, the U.S.-Japan alliance will continue to provide basic reassurance to both China and South Korea about Japan's future strategic orientation. As South Korea has grown stronger, and with aspirations to play a more active international role, the same is increasingly true for Japan, and to a lesser extent China, regarding the U.S.–South Korea alliance. For as long as North Korea remains a threat, both alliances clearly remain important to deterring aggression and coercion. Moreover, should North Korea collapse or both Koreas reach a negotiated agreement to reunite, both alliances will likely play a critical role in ensuring regional stability, just as NATO did with assuaging Germany's neighbors when it reunified.

In the Middle East the situation is different given that the United States has no treaty-based alliances other than with Turkey through its NATO commitment. Successive presidents, however, have declared Israel and, to a lesser extent, Saudi Arabia to be allies of the United States and on several occasions have come to their assistance. The long-standing U.S. military presence in the region, including regular air and naval patrols in the Persian Gulf, has clearly also provided an important stabilizing influence both politically and economically given the global importance of unfettered energy supplies from the region. With so many political uncertainties affecting the future of many countries in the region as well as the growing Shia-Sunni rivalry, the value of America's present military role is not likely to diminish in the foreseeable future.

For each of America's alliances, the challenge is to ensure that they remain not only credible military organizations for deterrence purposes but also that they do not inadvertently exacerbate regional tensions and in particular run counter to the strategic reassurance efforts with regard to Russia and China discussed earlier in this chapter. The former requires dedicated alliance management to ensure that members fulfill their security obligations and remain committed partners, while the latter will require careful signaling and special reassurance measures to nonmember states to demonstrate the inherently defensive nature and peaceful intent of each alliance. These can include how military exercises are conducted; where forces are stationed and deployed, even if only temporarily; which weapon systems enter service; and other types of confidence-building measures.

EXPAND GLOBAL TRADE AND ECONOMIC INTERDEPENDENCE

Promoting international trade agreements is another recommendation unlikely to sit well with those who seek a more inward-looking and protectionist posture for the United States. Largely absent in recent public debates over the merits of such agreements, however, is their strategic value and in particular their apparent benefits for lowering the risk of interstate and internal conflict. For this reason the United States should continue to promote free trade as a core element of a long-term preventive engagement strategy.

Since the end of the Second World War, the United States has done more than any other country to support the growth in global trade and investment.[27] Much of this has come about through successive efforts to lower international barriers to trade through global and regional multilateral agreements as well as through bilateral investment treaties. As figure 4.3 indicates, world trade tariffs have progressively declined, and the number of countries that are party to various multilateral and bilateral agreements has increased. Over this period the volume of trade has steadily increased, with the benefits being those of global growth, as noted in this chapter's earlier baseline scenario.

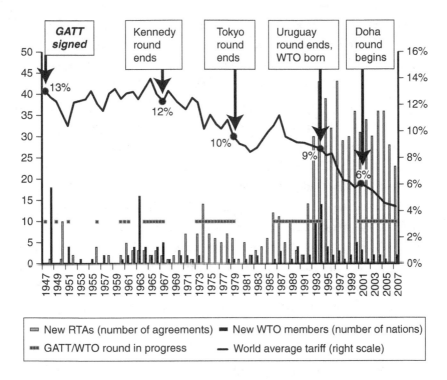

FIGURE 4.3

Tariff Liberalization Since 1947: Regional Trade Agreements and Multilateral Trade Negotiations

Source: Richard Baldwin, "21st Century Regionalism: Filling the Gap Between 21st Century Trade and 20th Century Trade Rules," Staff Working Paper ERSD-2011-08, World Trade Organization, 2011, https://www.wto.org/english/res_e/reser_e/ersd201108_e.pdf.

Further progress at the global level to promote international trade has effectively stalled, however. The latest round of negotiations under the auspices of the World Trade Organization (WTO)—the Doha Development Agenda—has failed to reach a major new agreement after more than twenty years, and most observers believe the prospects are slim that they ever will.[28] This is a reflection of the changing nature of trade and negotiations over trade.[29] The focus of trade has now largely moved beyond the relatively straightforward task of lowering "at-the-border" impediments—essentially, tariffs and quotas—that inhibit the free movement of goods and services to the much more complex challenge of negotiating "behind-the-border" regulatory issues that affect, for example, intellectual property rights, services and investment, safety and labor rights and now, increasingly, the environment. This is in large part due to the changing nature of cross-border economic interactions and in particular the development of complex transnational supply chains that are increasingly used for manufacturing and transporting products. The comparative difficulty of reaching agreement on behind-the-border domestic regulatory issues has in turn been compounded by the growth in the number of countries and interest groups that are now part of any major trade negotiation.

As a consequence, the leading trading nations have increasingly favored negotiating new "super" regional free trade agreements (FTAs). For the United States, the two most important initiatives were until relatively recently the Trans-Pacific Partnership (TPP) agreement and the Transatlantic Trade and Investment Partnership (TTIP). The TPP was launched in 2011 and involved Australia, Brunei, Canada, Chile, Japan, Malaysia, Mexico, New Zealand, Peru, Singapore, and Vietnam, in addition to the United States and potentially South Korea. Collectively these countries are responsible for 40 percent of the world's GDP and one-third of all global trade that is worth approximately US$1.5 trillion in goods and US$242 billion in services. The TTIP, which involves the United States and all twenty-eight members of the European Union (though Britain's future involvement is now doubtful given Brexit), represents a comparable slice of global GDP and trade. Both potential trade deals have been assessed to yield major economic benefits for their members—adding hundreds of billions of dollars and hundreds of thousands of new jobs overall, though the effects are not expected to be uniformly shared.[30]

Both of these prospective agreements, however, are facing growing opposition—albeit for different reasons. Some believe they effectively marginalize and may ultimately weaken the authority of the global WTO arrangements because of their inherently preferential nature.[31] Others, particularly emerging powers like China, see them as essentially designed to counter or contain their rise. Neither view is baseless. Some U.S. scholars openly argue the geopolitical benefits of the TPP and the need to exclude China, if only temporarily, while the TTP is established.[32] Senior U.S.

officials have also explicitly argued the "strategic logic" of both agreements, and the TPP in particular was couched from the outset as an essential element of the Obama administration's policy of rebalancing toward Asia.[33] Although China was not formally excluded from the TPP, no one energetically pursued that nation's membership. Not surprisingly, China has countered with its own set of proposals for trade and investment pacts in the Asia-Pacific region. Similar regionally focused trade blocs are being pursued in other areas; an example is the Eurasian Economic Union advocated by Russia. The possibility of further regionalization of trade into competitive blocs, which is reinforced by underlying geopolitical calculations, is becoming an increasing concern to some.[34]

For these reasons the United States should be sensitive to how its trade policy could inadvertently contribute to various emerging regional tensions and also undermine the intent of the larger "strategic compact" discussed earlier. The TPP and TTIP offer valuable economic benefits and, moreover, an important avenue for reassuring U.S. allies and partners that Washington remains committed to safeguarding their well-being. But these gains should not be realized at the cost of alienating the major powers. For these reasons, the Trump administration should rethink its opposition to the TTP and TTIP from primarily economic reasons while also indicating that it remains open to an expanded membership.

Nor should these massive regional trade pacts come to undermine the vitality of the WTO system. Thus, while the Doha Round can now be considered a failure, the United States should continue to push for less ambitious but still useful trade agreements under the auspices of the WTO. A good example is the Trade Facilitation Agreement negotiated in December 2013, in which all WTO members agreed to improve their customs departments, border crossings, and ports. Less developed countries would also receive aid and technical expertise to help them fulfill the terms of the agreement. Another worthy effort, albeit for a subset of WTO members, is the initiative launched in 2014 to eliminate tariffs on environmental goods like solar panels and wind turbines.[35] Given the challenge of reaching consensus among all of its members, relaxing the WTO's rules to allow for partial agreements, some have argued, is probably a pragmatic course to take in the future.[36] This should not come at the expense of weakening compliance and the credibility of the WTO's vital dispute resolution mechanism after agreements have been reached. An effective WTO will provide an invaluable counterweight to potential recidivism toward more mercantilist tendencies.

At the same time, the United States should continue to encourage—and, where possible, stimulate—intraregional trade in the regions that arguably most need it for its long-term conflict prevention benefits. The Middle East and North Africa (MENA) region, in particular, needs this more than any other; the region accounts for roughly 5–6 percent of the world's population and just less than 4 percent of global GDP, but its share of world trade not based on oil is only 1.8 percent. The MENA level of intraregional trade, moreover, lags well behind other regions—around 8 percent, compared to 25 percent for the Association of Southeast Asian Nations and 66 percent for the European Union.[37] As a World Bank report states, "the MENA region has performed far below its economic potential over the last three decades."[38] This has implications not just for the level of regional integration but also for internal stability. Again, according to the World Bank, over the last decade the number of jobs created—estimated to be around 3.2 million—has been less than half of what is needed to keep up with new entrants into the workforce. To address this employment deficit given anticipated population growth over the next few decades, it is further estimated that the average annual per capita growth would have to nearly double over its current rate (to about 4 percent).[39]

The United States has launched several initiatives to improve the economic performance of the MENA region in general and trade in particular. In 2003, the administration of President George W. Bush proposed creating a Middle East Free Trade Area through essentially a bottom-up process whereby multiple bilateral trade agreements between the United States and countries in the region would eventually merge to create a regional trade bloc based on common standards.[40] While the United States has reached FTAs with five MENA countries (Bahrain, Israel, Jordan, Morocco, and Oman), the goal of a regional agreement has remained elusive. The Obama administration followed up in 2011 with its own program, the MENA Trade and Investment Partnership Initiative, which had broadly similar if somewhat less ambitious goals. The level of U.S. trade to the region has, however, remained low (only 5 percent of total trade and 1 percent of foreign direct investment).[41]

Encouraging greater intraregional trade and economic integration in the MENA region is clearly going to take time given the comparatively high levels of tariffs and nontariff barriers that exist, not to mention the current levels of tension and instability. This will require effort on several fronts: bilateral encouragement to promote unilateral reforms; multilateral efforts through the WTO to lower tariffs; efforts on the part of the World Bank and other donors (notably, China) to improve the regional infrastructure for trade (transportation, ports, and backbone services such as power and financial services); and coordination with the European Union for all of the above. As the current sanctions on Iran are progressively relaxed as it comes into compliance with various international controls on its nuclear program, trade between the Arab world and Iran will hopefully also increase.

The United States can also promote similar changes in South Asia, the other main region of concern. As Daniel Markey has extensively argued, there are a variety of initiatives through which the United States can promote regional trade between Pakistan, India, and Afghanistan that would not only improve their economies but also, over time, alleviate much of the mistrust that currently divides them. These initiatives include negotiating a preferential U.S. trade access deal for the three nations that is conditioned on reduced barriers to intraregional trade, encouraging them to develop a common plan to improve infrastructure for trade that can be funded by the Asian Development Bank and other donors, and promoting the Turkmenistan-Afghanistan-Pakistan-India pipeline project, among other potential programs.[42]

FOSTER GLOBAL DEVELOPMENT

Promoting trade and investment will help with the fourth component of the long game: fostering the political and economic development of fragile states so that they do not pose a variety of risks to the United States in the future. As was discussed in chapter 3, states below a certain threshold of development are far more likely to suffer from political instability and civil violence than are those above that threshold. Helping the most vulnerable states attain sustainable economic growth represents, therefore, a sound investment for not just humanitarian reasons but also strategic ones. Unfortunately, despite the clear evidence in this regard, the United States spends much less on foreign aid as a percentage of its GDP than comparably developed countries even though it remains the largest donor in net terms.[43] Many Americans, moreover, evidently think the United States spends too much on foreign assistance and favors cutting it back.

The reasons for such sentiments are not hard to fathom. The huge amounts of taxpayer funds dispensed on apparently futile nation-building programs in Afghanistan and Iraq have left the American public profoundly disenchanted about the practicality of such efforts, especially at a time when so many feel that various domestic priorities have gone unattended. Also, despite real progress in many countries (particularly in Africa), the prevailing sense is that foreign aid has done little to improve matters and may even have made things worse in certain places. Despite closer attention given to monitoring and evaluating the impact of foreign aid, development experts still do not seem to have a clear idea of what works and what does not, which has probably also contributed to the public's skepticism of the overall value of foreign aid.

Such views are evidently shared by the Trump administration as it has declared its intent to cut U.S. development assistance funding.[44] Doing so, however, would not only gain comparatively little in terms of savings—since less than 1 percent of the federal budget is devoted to foreign aid—but would also jeopardize some potentially important benefits. At the same time, business as usual is also not desirable. Instead, the Trump administration should aim to rationalize and consolidate the many different U.S. development assistance programs into a more focused and integrated effort capable of attracting bipartisan support over the long term.

Currently, U.S. overseas assistance is administered by many different agencies and spread across many countries.[45] These programs need to be reviewed in their entirety because some are legacies of earlier diplomatic initiatives or concerns that no longer pertain. Priorities need to be set, moreover, that conform to assessments of risk. Something like this approach is now used to inform the United Kingdom's decision making regarding the disbursement of its overseas development assistance funds. After first determining which states are most at risk of serious instability or conflict, the UK government then judges those that pose the greatest threat to British interests (using agreed-upon criteria such as the number of UK nationals at risk, the level of UK trade and investment, and other security, economic, and political concerns).[46] These countries are then prioritized accordingly for development assistance.

The United Kingdom also increasingly employs foreign assistance in an integrated whole-of-government way; it has even developed a common pool of funds for relatively short-term conflict prevention efforts, something the United States should adopt.[47] Although the U.S. State Department and U.S. Agency for International Development now produce a joint strategic plan to focus and coordinate their efforts, the much larger Defense Department–led security assistance programs remain for the most part a separate activity even though they are clearly important to the overall objective. These programs also have to be reviewed in their totality and treated as part of a larger whole-of-government endeavor. It is more often than not left to U.S. embassy officials in the recipient country to coordinate these efforts and minimize any contradictions. When the United States has set out to develop an integrated assistance strategy for specific areas—for example, with Plan Colombia and the Trans-Sahara Counterterrorism Partnership—the results have generally been more successful. Recipient countries must also be held more accountable for what they do with this aid and thus become incentivized to receive more through clear performance standards. The approach used by the Millennium Challenge Corporation—a separate government assistance agency created by the George W. Bush administration—is generally seen as a useful model to emulate in this regard.[48]

SUPPORT DEMOCRATIC VALUES AND GOOD GOVERNANCE

The sixth component of a long-term risk reduction strategy is to continue to support the progressive extension of democratic values and good governance around the world. The relationship between democracy and the risk of violent conflict both between and within states is simply too strong for this to not be part of the long game.[49] As noted earlier in this chapter, however, the advance of democratic rule around the world has, by most accounts, stalled in recent years and even regressed in some countries.[50] Although some observers have voiced concern that democracy could experience a more fundamental setback—something that happened once before in the 1920s and 1930s, with calamitous consequences—such fears seem at present to be exaggerated. There have certainly been reversals in Egypt, Russia, Hungary, Uganda, and Thailand, to name some of the more prominent countries to have regressed back into more authoritarian ways, but promising advances have at the same time been made in Kenya, Pakistan, Indonesia, Tunisia, Sri Lanka, and Nigeria. More generally, the number of full or established democracies has not changed, while the number of outright dictatorships continues to decline.

While the prospects for a great leap forward in democratic governance around the world do not look promising in the short term, the United States must continue to remain active in pursuit of this goal. It must put the demoralizing experience of building democratic institutions in Afghanistan and Iraq behind it and revitalize its commitment to democracy promotion despite the headwinds it now faces. To do otherwise would send a profoundly negative message to the many laboring around the world toward this end.

Ensuring that the United States remains an inspiration if not an exact example to replicate is clearly the sine qua non of future democracy promotion. Acknowledging that mistakes were made in the past while being humble and not professing to have all the answers is likewise important. There is clearly no singular prescription or fixed schedule for doing certain things associated with democracy promotion. In some cases, more of a top-down strategy that encourages and supports efforts to build the essential institutions and processes common to all democratic states—constitutions and bills of rights; regular, free and fair elections; and effective party systems—will be appropriate. In others, a bottom-up approach that emphasizes the need to nurture a vibrant civil society, including a free media; encourages the rights of women; and stimulates the involvement of business interests that understand and appreciate the economic advantages of democracies may appear more fruitful. Logically, the two strategies should not be seen as mutually exclusive but as complementary.

Placing more emphasis on one rather than the other approach should clearly derive from an assessment of local conditions and overall "ripeness." As argued in chapter 3, the opportunity to nurture democratic governance will be greater in some countries than in others. The strategy has to be tailored and modified accordingly. When advances are made via either a top-down or bottom-up approach, the United States must be prepared to nurture them to not only lock in the gains but also validate the broader benefits of reform to others who have yet to embrace such change. Transitions to democracy are rarely, if ever, trouble-free; they require sustained support to ensure that they become embedded and resilient to challenge. By the same logic, the United States and other like-minded nations need to be prepared for reversals, whether they be a more active response to turn back what has happened or a more passive containment to reduce the potential for unwelcome spillover effects. In either case, the United States must tread carefully to ensure that what it does is not counterproductive to the larger goal.

Finally, advancing democracy and good governance around the world is clearly not something that the United States should be alone in pursuing or, for that matter, should lead—certainly not all the time and in every context. This has to be a collective effort, not simply as a practical means to share the associated burdens but also to lend the effort the broad legitimacy that is so vital to its success. Encouraging the efforts of emerging democratic powers to advance the cause—particularly in their immediate regions, but also in international forums—is important to underline the message that this is a universal good rather than a narrow American objective.[51]

MITIGATE THE EFFECTS OF CLIMATE CHANGE

The last—but by no means least important—component of long-term risk reduction is slowing the pace of climate change and environmental degradation while preparing to mitigate its potentially destabilizing consequences. The planet's surface temperature has increased by an average of 1.5 degrees

Celsius over the last century as the amount of greenhouse gases in the earth's atmosphere—mainly carbon dioxide and chlorofluorocarbons—has grown. If global warming proceeds unabated and has the projected environmental impact on some regions of the world that many believe it will, the risk of conflict will almost certainly increase as a consequence of the societal and international stresses that will likely be created or exacerbated.

Lowering that risk clearly begins through national and international efforts to reduce greenhouse gas emissions. The initial bilateral U.S.-China accord that paved the way for the historic 2015 Paris Agreement within the United Nations Framework Convention on Climate Change represents a major breakthrough in that signatories have collectively committed to lower their greenhouse emissions to keep global warming below 2.0 degrees Celsius.[52] Some experts, however, remain skeptical that this will be sufficient, especially since the agreement is based on voluntary pledges rather than enforceable constraints.[53] The national commitments, therefore, should be seen as the beginning of more ambitious targets for later years.

As the world's largest emitter of greenhouse gases, the United States must not appear to be vacillating or backsliding on its commitment to manage global warming, as early signs from the Trump administration seem to suggest it will. This would likely undermine the commitments of others, particularly China, to meet their national targets and lead to the unraveling of the overall Framework Convention.[54] In addition, the United States should continue to press for further international efforts to limit greenhouse gases through investment in green technologies and by sharing best practices that incentivize businesses and citizens to conserve energy and use earth-friendly products in daily life. Given that such efforts may still not be enough, the United States must also begin to prepare for international crises triggered in whole or part by environmental change. This includes being able to assess likely stress points and respond with humanitarian aid and other measures when crises arise.

* * *

These seven long-term risk reduction initiatives collectively represent an ambitious agenda that will require diligent attention and persistent upkeep from U.S. policy makers. Progress may seem slow and on occasion even be set back while at other times surprising advances will be possible. This is normal and to be expected. The trick is to not become too discouraged by the former or overly confident from the latter. The American public, moreover, has to be kept informed of the larger imperatives of pursuing these initiatives; otherwise, support will inevitably falter perhaps irrevocably with calamitous consequences. This is something that should not be assumed will happen spontaneously, but rather it requires careful and deliberate education efforts.

5

CRISIS PREVENTION

The Midterm Game

No war is inevitable until it breaks out.

—A. J. P. TAYLOR

Effective engagement at flashpoints is essential, but crisis response is never as good as crisis prevention.

—LAWRENCE SUMMERS

MANAGING EMERGING SOURCES of conflict and instability to reduce the likelihood that they could grow more acute and eventually erupt in dangerous ways arguably represents the most critical element of a U.S. preventive engagement strategy. New crises can not only undermine patient efforts to shape America's strategic environment over the long term to its advantage but also become an unwelcome distraction and added burden to policy makers grappling with more immediate challenges. Crises may indeed provide opportunities to do things that were not possible beforehand, but this is hardly a compelling reason to tempt fate and risk the possibility that events get out of hand and lead to costly new military commitments.

Looking ahead over the next three to five years, it is possible to discern many plausible crisis contingencies that would pose a variety of risks to the United States. The first part of this chapter, therefore, will examine these contingencies more closely using the preventive foresight methods outlined in chapter 2. The principal goal here is to ascertain which are deserving of greater attention than others. The second part of the chapter will discuss how the United States can manage these risks and potentially avert the most dangerous crises using the range of preventive strategies outlined in chapter 3.

MIDTERM RISKS AND PRIORITIES

Drawing on both official estimates (particularly the Annual Worldwide Threat Assessment delivered to Congress by the director of national intelligence[1]) and numerous nongovernment assessments, it is possible to draw up a list of plausible crisis contingencies of concern to the United States. To briefly recap the preventive foresight assessment criteria, some of these potential crises can be classified as High Consequence Contingencies (Category 1) in that they could be very harmful to America in their own right and potentially lead to war with a major power. Others fall into Medium and Low Consequence Contingencies (Categories 2 and 3) and thus pose lesser but still significant risks to the United States. Their relative priority for preventive action can then be determined by plotting their relative likelihood and impact on a standard risk matrix. The contingencies discussed here will not include those that could evolve from ongoing conflicts. These will be addressed in chapter 6. Moreover, the discussion of potential midterm crises below should not be considered to be exhaustive; rather they represent the most prominent risks at the time the assessment was conducted. Since the world is a dynamic place, the assessment of medium-term risks and the ordering of preventive priorities should be regularly reviewed and adjusted accordingly.

CATEGORY 1 CONTINGENCIES

Although the likelihood of a general war breaking out between the United States and either China or Russia remains very low in the medium term, the risk of a serious military confrontation involving either major power is undoubtedly growing.[2] More specifically, as a result of various treaty commitments, the United States is directly or indirectly implicated in several territorial disputes that involve either China or Russia. These disputes are not new, but they have grown more acrimonious in recent years to the extent that under quite plausible circumstances they could escalate in ways that bring the armed forces of the United States in direct confrontation with those of China or Russia. Besides the inherent risk of further escalation, such confrontations could have a profoundly harmful impact on subsequent relations between the major powers involved with potentially far-reaching consequences for cooperation on a range of pressing global concerns.

Looking first at potential contingencies involving China, the most worrisome revolve around several maritime disputes in the East and South China Seas as well as long-standing differences about the status of Taiwan and the potential demise of North Korea. These disputes have gained greater strategic significance in recent years as the relationship between the United States and China has evolved and in many respects grown more mistrustful. Each of the disputes, moreover, is highly charged with strong nationalist emotions that increase the likelihood of escalation and decrease the prospects for compromise in a crisis.[3]

East China Sea Confrontation

Until relatively recently, the dispute between China and Japan over their respective sovereignty claims to what are referred to as the Diaoyu Islands by the Chinese and the Senkaku Islands by the Japanese had been largely dormant. This group of small uninhabited islands that lay approximately 205 miles from China's coast, 105 from Taiwan, and about the same distance from Okinawa, the nearest Japanese island, have been under the administrative control of Japan since 1895 when they were annexed following the first Sino-Japanese war. It was not until 1971, however, that China lodged a formal diplomatic note avowing its claim, followed soon after by Taiwan. The timing was no doubt driven by several factors: the impending transfer of U.S. administrative control of Okinawa (which it had occupied since the end of World War II) to Japan; the release of the results of a 1969 United Nations survey indicating the presence of sizable energy resources under the seabed close to the islands; and the beginning of commercial

134

discussions between Japan and Taiwan to exploit them. Having lodged their claims, the parties more or less agreed to disagree and not let the dispute interfere with their burgeoning economic relationship.

This state of affairs prevailed until 2010, when a Chinese fishing trawler rammed two Japanese Coast Guard vessels patrolling close to the islands, resulting in the detention of its captain and a serious diplomatic spat with China. The crisis subsided with the release of the captain, but was reignited two years later when the Japanese government decided to purchase three out of the five islands from their private owner to preempt a mounting public campaign by the nationalist mayor of Tokyo to do the same.[4] Rather than calm matters, as was the intention of the Japanese government, the purchase inflamed Chinese public opinion—doubtless fanned by the authorities—which led to widespread anti-Japanese demonstrations and extensive vandalism to Japanese companies based in China. The Chinese government soon after issued new legal claims to the islands, including declaring to the UN that China's continental shelf extended to include the Senkaku Islands, which it now indicated should be considered part of its exclusive economic zone under the terms of the UN Convention on the Law of the Sea (UNCLOS).

Since then Chinese marine surveillance vessels and Fisheries Enforcement Command ships have regularly sailed within Japan's twelve-nautical-mile territorial zone around the islands in a clear attempt to assert China's sovereignty and undermine Japanese administrative control. On November 23, 2013, China also announced the creation of an Air Defense Identification Zone (ADIZ) in the East China Sea that extends over the Senkakus and overlaps Japan's own territorial ADIZ, thus increasing the risk of dangerous military interactions between the two countries in the contested airspace. Chinese surveillance aircraft and drones have since passed close to the islands on numerous occasions, provoking the dispatch of Japanese air defense interceptors and angry complaints from Japanese authorities.

Should a serious incident occur that involves Japanese and Chinese aircraft or ships, it is not hard to imagine how the crisis could escalate: decision makers in both capitals would likely feel intense pressure to respond in a vigorous fashion to demonstrate national resolve, including bolstering their military presence in the disputed area. The possibility that Japan or China could decide to press their respective positions by force majeure also cannot be dismissed. Japan, for example, could choose to permanently occupy and fortify the islands in an effort to consolidate its administrative control, while China could decide to assert its sovereign claim by impeding Japan's air and maritime access, thereby undermining Japan's claim to administrative control. Given the political challenge such action would represent to either country, neither would be inclined to back down, and the crisis would almost certainly intensify further.

In such circumstances, the United States would find it extremely difficult to stay detached from the crisis. Although the official U.S. stance regarding the Senkaku Islands is that it does not take a formal position on who has ultimate sovereignty, senior U.S. officials, including most recently President Trump in February 2017, have unequivocally stated that the United States considers the Senkakus to be under the administrative control of Japan and thereby covered by article 5 of the U.S.-Japan Treaty of Mutual Cooperation and Security.[5] The United States, as a result, is obligated to come to Japan's assistance if the Senkakus are attacked or occupied by China.[6] Although the U.S. declarations are clearly intended to deter Chinese actions, Beijing might calculate in a crisis that the United States would not intervene given its lesser stake in the dispute or alternatively that it could be dissuaded to do so by the threat of further escalation in the form of an even larger display of force. The basic elements for a dangerous U.S.-Chinese military confrontation are thus present.

South China Sea Confrontation

The comparable territorial disagreements in the South China Sea are no less serious. These mostly concern two sets of island groups—the Paracels and the Spratlys. In both cases there are multiple claimants besides China. Although tensions have periodically flared up over both island groups since at least the 1970s, when oil and gas exploration began in earnest, the intensity of the various disputes has grown significantly since 2009, when the deadline for submission of claims under the terms of UNCLOS took effect. In particular, China's assertion of sovereignty over virtually the entire

South China Sea with the formal release of a map demarcating its claim with the Nine-Dash Line has been the most provocative. Since then China has been involved in many heated incidents with other claimants, but principally the Philippines and Vietnam, to physically control those areas it considers to be under its sovereign jurisdiction. This has resulted in several serious diplomatic spats and overt displays of force. In 2015 China also began an intensive effort to consolidate control of several of the disputed islands by physically enlarging them by dredging up nearby sand and coral. Though it is not the first country to have resorted to this tactic, China has become the most active in doing so. In addition, China rejected the UN Permanent Court of Arbitration's ruling on a case brought forth by the Philippines beginning in 2013. In July 2016 the court sided with the Philippines and found China's claim of historic rights, as well as its construction of artificial islands and other aggressive actions, to be invalid and unlawful.

As with the Senkaku dispute, the United States has avoided taking sides, insisting instead that claimants settle their differences peacefully and in accordance with international law. For similar reasons, however, the United States could still find itself in a direct military confrontation with China. The most obvious scenario is that the Philippines requests military assistance from the United States (under the terms of the 1951 U.S.-Philippines Mutual Defense Treaty) should China aggressively assert physical control over disputed territory, especially if it results in an armed clash and the loss of Filipino life.[7] Such an appeal would undoubtedly put the United States under considerable pressure to come to the aid of its ally or risk the repercussions of appearing weak and unreliable.

Similar incidents could arise in other parts of the South China Sea, and while the United States would not be treaty bound to respond, the need to take sides or at least be resolute in the face of what might be characterized as Chinese aggression would be considerable. Potential scenarios of this kind include a serious military clash between China and Vietnam over commercial exploitation rights in disputed areas (the likelihood of which has grown in recent years) and similar incidents involving Indian commercial interests in the region.[8] The United States would likely feel compelled to intervene, if only to ensure that a dispute of this kind did not undermine freedom of navigation or interfere with international trade. Each year, trade worth an estimated US$5.3 trillion passes through the South China Sea, with the United States accounting for US$1.2 trillion of that total.[9] A major disruption of the principal trade routes could be very harmful to regional economies and also resonate globally. In short, the United States would find it difficult if not impossible to stay detached from a serious crisis in the South China Sea.[10]

Renewed China-Taiwan Confrontation

Since the end of the Chinese Civil War in 1949, when defeated nationalist forces fled to the island of Taiwan and established their own government, mainland China has viewed Taiwan as a renegade province and vowed that it will prevent it from ever becoming an independent sovereign state—if necessary, by force. Although the United States adheres to a formal "one China" policy in which the government of the People's Republic of China is recognized as the sole legal government of China and that "there is but one China and Taiwan is part of China," the U.S. government has on numerous occasions intervened to support Taiwan in response to threatening actions from the mainland, including sending air and naval forces into the Taiwan Strait to deter Chinese military action while also supplying it with defensive weapons under the terms of the 1979 Taiwan Relations Act (TRA). The United States does not support or oppose Taiwan's independence, but believes that its contested status with mainland China should be resolved in a purely peaceful and consensual manner. In the language of the TRA, any attempt to determine Taiwan's future by force would be treated as "a threat" to the peace and security of the Western Pacific and "a grave concern" to the United States.[11]

The risk of a dangerous U.S.-China clash over Taiwan has receded greatly since the last serious crisis in 1995–1996, when the United States diverted two carrier battle groups through the Taiwan Strait to counter China's increasingly belligerent military actions (which included "test-firing" ballistic missiles into the vicinity of the island and even issuing thinly veiled warnings that it was prepared to entertain a nuclear exchange with the United States) to prevent what it considered a growing independence movement by the first democratically elected president of Taiwan, Lee Teng-hui.[12] The 2008 election of President Ma Ying-jeou from the Kuomintang Party, which espouses a "three no's" policy (no unification, no independence, and no use of force), led to a significant improvement in cross-strait relations, including deeper economic ties and more regular official contacts.[13] Although the presidency since reverted back to the opposing Democratic Progressive Party with the election of Tsai Ing-wen in 2016, China-Taiwan relations are not expected to change suddenly.

The passions that lay below the surface of this dispute remain no less charged, however, and the potential for them to be unleashed suddenly with unpredictable consequences remains very real. As security expert Richard Betts reminds us, the importance of Taiwan as a "core national interest" for China has not diminished, and reunification remains "a question of when, not whether."[14] China, moreover, has never renounced the use of force against Taiwan; indeed, its climb down following the dispatch of American carriers during the 1996 crisis evidently spurred it to embark on a formidable buildup of ballistic and cruise missiles along with other military capabilities directly across from Taiwan so as to give it an expanded range of coercive options should circumstances demand it. The presence of these forces has in the process raised the costs of intervention for the United States in any future crisis.[15] The elements of a serious crisis, while currently dormant, have not disappeared. As Betts notes,

> The possibility of war over Taiwan could be the biggest danger that American security policy faces. No other flashpoint is more likely to bring the United States into combat with a major power, and no other contingency compels Washington to respond with such ambiguous commitment. Americans and Chinese see the issues at stake in the dispute over Taiwan in different terms; U.S. policy on the defense of Taiwan is uncertain, and thus so is the understanding in Beijing, Taipei, and Washington over how far the United States might go under different circumstances; and because Taiwan is more independent than either Washington or Beijing might prefer, neither great power can fully control developments that might ignite a crisis. This is a classic recipe for surprise, miscalculation, and uncontrolled escalation.[16]

It is not difficult—certainly in general terms—to imagine how another Taiwan crisis might erupt and bring tensions between the United States and China to a head.[17] Leaders in Taipei could for a variety of reasons embark on a course to change the status quo in cross-strait relations, if only incrementally.[18] China would immediately and vigorously oppose such actions, and that would likely trigger a rerun of the 1996 crisis. Having substantially built up its military forces across from Taiwan over the last two decades, Beijing may feel more confident that it can intimidate Taipei and deter a potential U.S. intervention. An alternative scenario is one in which Chinese leaders decide for a variety of domestic reasons that the time is propitious to settle the Taiwan question once and for all. A serious crisis somewhere else in the region or the world that consumes the attention of the United States could also help to push China in that direction.

Regardless of what triggers another China-Taiwan crisis, it could escalate in a variety of ways. Inflammatory rhetoric, diplomatic threats, and displays of force could quickly propel a crisis toward a dangerous tipping point. Leaders in Beijing and Washington would come under intense pressure to demonstrate national resolve given their prior commitments regarding Taiwan and the perceived stakes of the confrontation in the larger context of the changing U.S.-China balance of power. Self-restraint and compromise in such circumstances would likely be especially difficult to project for fear of losing face and communicating weakness. Crisis management could also be complicated by the actions of Taiwanese leaders who might calculate that they could pursue maximalist objectives or resist China's demands in the conviction that the United States would ultimately protect them.[19]

Collapse of North Korea

In the aftermath of the Cold War, North Korea has defied repeated predictions from outside experts that it would collapse and ultimately cease to exist as a sovereign entity. Yet for all the many extreme shocks and setbacks it has experienced—the loss of Soviet support, the death of its founding father, a catastrophic famine, the imposition of punishing international sanctions, and further leadership changes—North Korea lives on and shows no outward signs that it will fail anytime soon. Authoritarian regimes, however, especially ones as internationally isolated as North Korea, have been known to collapse with little or no warning and thus it is prudent to consider this contingency especially given the larger risks associated with its demise. What might trigger the collapse of North Korea has been the subject of considerable speculation.[20] The emergence of a popular movement in North Korea that agitates for change and eventually topples the current regime seems unlikely given the very limited opportunities for dissent to coalesce and be mobilized effectively. More likely is that the ruling Kim family regime is challenged from within by a faction either seeking fundamental reform or one conceivably resistant to such change because of the threat it poses to its political influence and economic standing. The role of the military and domestic security agencies would clearly be pivotal to the outcome of any such challenge to the regime given their capacity to either quash or support it. That they could orchestrate a coup to oust the regime is, of course, another possibility.

Numerous scenarios could play out as consequence of such instability, though they fit broadly into two categories: "soft landings," those amounting to a relatively peaceful transformation of North Korea, and "hard landings," which cover various contested and extremely violent contingencies. In the latter case, an internal power struggle could be settled relatively quickly, albeit bloodily, or lead to prolonged civil strife that might produce spillover effects on neighboring countries in the form of large-scale refugee flows, high-level defections, border incidents, provocations, and appeals for assistance (to list the more obvious scenarios). Depending on either the amount of spillover or the level of internal strife, South Korea, the United States, and China would all come under considerable pressure from various domestic constituencies, humanitarian nongovernmental organizations, and other international organizations to intervene and restore order. Should the North Korean regime begin to unravel and lose internal control, other considerations are likely to come to the fore.[21]

For South Korea the most vexing question will be whether to view rising unrest or other sources of instability as a historic opportunity to reunify the peninsula after decades of division. Its leaders would understandably not want to squander what could be a fleeting chance to shape and accelerate events toward that end. They would also be acutely concerned about potential Chinese actions to thwart potential reunification either by installing a new regime in Pyongyang that would be sympathetic to Beijing or, conceivably, intervening militarily and carving out a buffer zone along the China–North Korea border for ostensibly humanitarian reasons. Such anxieties could exert a powerful motive for Seoul to move quickly and intervene unilaterally. Although the U.S. and South Korean militaries work closely with one another under common command arrangements, the latitude for independent action clearly exists. Given that it is generally known that South Korea has developed its own plan for unifying the peninsula—details of which have only been shared in very sketchy terms with the United States—it would be very surprising if it had not also developed options for unilateral military intervention.

Likewise, China would also be worried about the possible course of events—and particularly what the end of North Korea might presage. Besides securing its own borders from potentially large outflows of refugees, China would be likely to use whatever influence it had to ensure that North Korea survives in one form or another, right up to point that it becomes completely untenable—and certainly if Beijing had not been convincingly reassured about the nature of what could follow. Just as South Korea might believe it better to move sooner rather than later in a crisis, China might conclude the same. As a formal ally of North Korea, moreover, it is quite conceivable that it could be asked for assistance, especially if South Korea and the United States intervene. In short, we cannot assume that China would watch passively on the sidelines, much like the Soviet Union did as its eastern European satellites broke away.

The United States would find itself in a very difficult position: on the one hand, having to support South Korea's legitimate and understandable aspiration for national unity and, on the other hand, ensuring that America is not dragged into a major regional conflict that leads to a serious confrontation with China. At the same time, the fate of North Korea's nuclear arsenal and long-range missiles would also be a major concern for the United States and it would likely have to decide very quickly whether to destroy or secure them in some way. The relevant nuclear and missile sites are for the most part located close to the border with China, and thus any such action—unless coordinated beforehand with China—carries obvious risks. All of these fears and impulses could come together and lead to a serious confrontation with China should North Korea begin to unravel.

* * *

Turning now to U.S.-Russian contingencies of concern, the risk of a military confrontation has grown in recent years as relations have steadily deteriorated over a range of issues. NATO's 2011 intervention in Libya for ostensibly humanitarian reasons but which eventually became the pretext for regime change was viewed as a major affront to Russia and probably represented the beginning of this decline. Although there has been cooperation in some areas—strategic arms reduction and, more crucially, with regard to curbing Iran's nuclear program—mutual mistrust has intensified with Russia's meddling in Ukraine and annexation of Crimea in 2014, followed by its intervention in Syria to support its beleaguered president, Bashar al-Assad, in 2015. Furthermore, expectations that relations would improve after the election of Donald Trump have now been set back with allegations that Russia interfered with its outcome. Officials in both Russia and the United States now view each other in openly adversarial terms.

Numerous scenarios can now be imagined in which U.S. and Russian forces are involved in a dangerous military incident. As regrettable as such events would be, they are unlikely to precipitate a serious rupture in relations or escalate further. More worrisome, however, is the possibility of a major crisis stemming from miscalculations or misperceptions of hostile intent in areas that Russia considers especially sensitive to its security and status as a regional power. More specifically, several points of contention along Russia's western periphery could conceivably become the source of a serious confrontation. Of these, a potential crisis in the Baltic region represents the most plausible Category 1 contingency.

NATO-Russia Confrontation in the Baltic Region

Since the outbreak of the Ukraine crisis, apprehension has steadily grown in the Baltic states of Estonia, Latvia, and Lithuania that Russia might employ similar tactics to exert influence and undermine their close ties with the West—principally NATO, which they joined in 2004, the same year they also became members of the European Union. As former republics of the Soviet Union, their membership of NATO was especially resented by Russia, which engaged in thinly veiled threats and aggressive military exercises in the region soon thereafter. In fact, well before the Ukraine crisis, Russia's actions had convinced NATO of the necessity of developing contingency plans to come to the Baltic states' defense if they were threatened.[22]

An unprovoked Russian military invasion of the Baltic states—even with the relatively limited objective of occupying and eventually annexing those areas where ethnic Russians predominate—seems improbable given that such actions would be tantamount to declaring war on NATO, but a serious crisis could still occur for other reasons. Russia could, for example, foment unrest within the Russian-speaking communities or carry out ambiguous military exercises close to the Baltic states as a diversionary tactic for actions elsewhere or to generally keep NATO off balance. In doing so Russia might calculate that it could create divisive schisms within NATO over how to respond to such provocations; this in turn would undermine the credibility of the regional organization's mutual security guarantees enshrined in article 5 of the North Atlantic Treaty. For example, a crisis that exposed the unwillingness of some NATO members to assist one or more of the Baltic countries with precautionary defensive actions would likely be seen as a highly desirable outcome for Moscow.

Alternatively, a crisis might also arise less as a consequence of Russia's desire to exert control over the Baltic states and more out of its sense of insecurity over NATO's intentions and Russia's relative decline in the world.[23] Comparatively small incidents—for example, a pro-Russian demonstration or parade, or the temporary disruption of rail or maritime links to Kaliningrad, the Russian oblast surrounded by Poland and Lithuania—could gather momentum as a result of the overreaction of local officials, thus enflaming Russian sensitivities and putting Moscow in the position of either having to escalate more forcefully or back down in humiliation. NATO's defensive actions could also be perceived as yet another flaunting of Western power or, more ominously, the precursor of a more serious challenge, much as the November 2013 crisis in Kiev was viewed by Moscow as a West-instigated regime change, thus causing it to react aggressively. And should Russian and NATO military forces begin to move to a higher state of readiness they would inevitably start to operate in closer proximity to one another, increasing the risk of accidents and unintended escalation that could ratchet up tensions in a dangerous way.

CATEGORY 2 CONTINGENCIES

Category 2 contingencies are harder to identify in the medium term because of the unpredictability of U.S. actions in circumstances where treaty allies are neither threatened nor attacked. Despite this uncertainty, several contingencies warrant being classified in this category either because of their likely impact on U.S. interests and/or the risk of significant military engagement.

Military Confrontation with Iran

For much of the early 2000s the prospect of a U.S. and/or Israeli military strike on Iran to prevent it from developing nuclear weapons was very real—such was the seriousness of the threat. Iranian retaliation and the risk of a wider regional conflict breaking out as a consequence was also a genuine fear. However, following the successful conclusion of negotiations leading up to the July 2015 agreement between Iran and the five permanent members of the UN Security Council plus Germany (the so-called P5+1), known as the Joint Comprehensive Plan of Action (JCPOA) that has placed strict and verifiable limits on Iran's capacity to produce weapons-grade nuclear materials for fifteen years, the risk of a U.S.-Iranian conflict has significantly diminished.[24] While the JCPOA is evidently being observed by all parties, it has not led to a significant improvement in relations. Indeed, other sources of tension have emerged that have increased the risk of armed conflict with Iran.

First, Iranian special forces as well as militia groups trained and armed by Iran have been operating inside Syria and Iraq in ways that are generally viewed as inimical to U.S. objectives in both countries. Iran also continues to lend support to Hezbollah, the militant Islamist group, in Lebanon and more recently the Houthi insurgency in Yemen, both of which separately threaten America's main allies in the region—Israel and Saudi Arabia, respectively. Second, Iran continues to develop long-range ballistic missiles capable of delivering nuclear weapons—in violation of the spirit, if not the explicit word, of the 2015 nuclear agreement.[25] A missile test carried out in early 2017 elicited the imposition of new sanctions on Iran by the Trump administration as well as a sharp rebuke that it was now "on notice."[26] Third, U.S. and Iranian maritime forces in the Persian Gulf continue to operate in close proximity to one another, and this has led on more than one occasion to dangerous incidents that have prompted similar warnings by U.S. officials, including President Trump, of potential retaliatory action.

From these developments it is possible to imagine a variety of plausible scenarios that could lead to a military confrontation with Iran. At some point, for example, the United States could decide to take punitive action against Iran for any of the activities just mentioned. This could range from relatively discreet cyberattacks and "surgical" military strikes against Iranian-backed militia groups to ultimately attacking specific targets inside Iran. Though carried out with the limited goal of deterring further provocations, such actions could nevertheless prompt Iran to retaliate either overtly or covertly against U.S. (and possibly Israeli and Saudi) targets in the Middle East. Maritime traffic through the vital Strait of Hormuz might also be disrupted by Iran. All this could clearly trigger additional military actions against Iran by the United States, either alone or in concert with its partners in the region.

Iran could also conceivably determine in the future that its security environment is deteriorating in ways that warrant either revoking the nuclear agreement and openly "racing for the bomb" or restarting its covert weapons program with the goal of eventually presenting the world with a fait accompli. Either way, in the ensuing international crisis the United States could conclude that it had no choice but to strike Iran and prevent it from developing an operational nuclear arsenal because of the threat it would pose to allies in the region, the U.S. homeland in the future, and the integrity of the global nonproliferation regime. It might also calculate that this could be accomplished in a discrete enough way to dissuade Iran from retaliating—much like Israel was able to do when it carried out preventive military strikes against nuclear facilities inside Iraq in 1981 and Syria in 2007.[27] Such an outcome cannot be assumed, however, and Iran could respond in the ways outlined above; this in turn could drive both parties toward a much larger conflict.

Alternatively, Washington might demur from taking military action because of the risk of escalation. Israel and potentially Saudi Arabia, on the other hand, might decide that a nuclear-armed Iran posed an existential and thus unacceptable threat, leading them to take matters into their own hands.[28] Depending on how their actions played out, the United States could eventually be drawn into the ensuing conflict, either to assist its allies or to protect its interests in the Middle East, including keeping the Strait of Hormuz open for commerce. Even though America's dependence on Middle Eastern oil has been dramatically reduced as a result of increased domestic supply, it still maintains an interest in ensuring that this vital artery of the global economy not be cut for a significant length of time.[29]

The United States could also find itself in conflict with Iran for reasons other than preventing its acquisition of nuclear weapons. Judging from the numerous violent contests for influence in the Middle East (notably, in Lebanon, Iraq, Syria, and Yemen), the political and religious rivalry between the Sunni states of Saudi Arabia and the Persian Gulf on the one hand and Shia Iran and various affiliated nonstate actors on the other is clearly intensifying. This is also manifested in a major increase in weapons purchases by many states in the region, which in some cases provide them with formidable offensive power projection capabilities. Although there are few obvious points of contention that could become immediate flash points and thus potential triggers for military escalation, the rivalry could nevertheless grow more dangerous and unstable in a number of ways. For example, the current conflict is conducted largely by proxy forces in contested areas, but it could escalate to include the targeting of high-value political and commercial interests beyond these areas that could prompt tit-for-tat retaliation. This shadow war, moreover, could conceivably also begin to play out in the territories of the leading protagonists, which up to now have been largely untouched. This could take the form of cyberattacks or various kinds of violent political warfare that might grow in scope and intensity. It is also conceivable that armed groups could emerge to prosecute this war independent of state control and beyond the ground rules and confines of the current conflict, thereby taking it in an unpredictable direction. If this were to happen, the potential for unintentional escalation from misattributed acts would certainly grow. And just as al-Qaeda chose to attack the United States—the "far enemy"—to help its campaign to unseat what it viewed as corrupt and apostate states in the Middle East, so warring groups in the Shia-Sunni rivalry might do the same. In short, for all these reasons, the United States could find itself drawn into the Shia-Sunni contest for supremacy regardless of how much it may desire to stay out of it.

Nuclear-Related Contingencies in Pakistan

For a variety of reasons the United States may feel compelled in the future to take military action to secure or otherwise neutralize Pakistan's nuclear arsenal and associated delivery systems. Although Pakistani officials have repeatedly insisted that their nuclear weapons facilities are secure from theft, diversion, or unauthorized use, such fears have persisted, albeit waxing and waning in relation to the general level of instability and violence in the country.[30] Militant groups have in the past targeted bases believed to be part of Pakistan's nuclear infrastructure and could likely do so again. Potential sympathizers and supporters of various militant causes within Pakistan's military establishment could conceivably divert sensitive materials and devices to a terrorist organization. Should the country fracture as a result of civil war—a scenario that remains a possibility—the security of sensitive sites could also be compromised. And finally, the possibility of state-sanctioned diversion of nuclear weapons to another state cannot be dismissed.

Depending on the specific scenario, the United States could take various measures ranging from relatively small and surgical "render-safe" military missions to large-scale "nuclear disablement" operations.[31] It is possible that Pakistan would invite such actions or not actively resist them under certain circumstances. On the other hand, it could treat them as a hostile act, and the United States could find itself in an adversarial if not openly war-like relationship with Pakistan, potentially for a prolonged period.

Russian Intervention in Georgia

Besides a crisis in the Baltic region, the other plausible flash point along Russia's periphery in the medium term is a renewed military confrontation in Georgia.[32] This could arise in several ways: as a consequence of Russian efforts to reassert its influence over Georgia or to prevent Georgia from moving closer to the West (and especially seeking membership in NATO), or as a result of actions—inadvertent or not—on the part of local players in the breakaway republics of South Ossetia and Abkhazia seeking to cement closer ties to Moscow.[33] Although the risk of a full-blown war between Georgia and Russia is low, a renewed confrontation could still lead to the mobilization and deployment of armed forces by each side against the other; these would be potentially violent clashes that could result in the loss of life and the displacement of a large number of civilians as well as other dangerous interactions short of sustained combat operations. Since Georgia is not a NATO member and thus not covered by the article 5 defense guarantees, the United States would not be obligated to come to its aid. Depending on the circumstances, however, the United States could still come under considerable pressure both domestically and internationally to respond to Russia's actions. Much will hinge on contextual factors—the state of U.S.-Russia relations at the time and what events preceded the crisis—as well as whether Russian motives are viewed as essentially defensive or aggressive in purpose.

CATEGORY 3 CONTINGENCIES

There are many more conceivable Category 3 contingencies in the medium term that could lead to limited regional military engagements by the United States. As discussed in chapter 2, the ensuing military missions are likely to be launched for one or more reasons: counterterrorism efforts, political stabilization and humanitarian assistance (including atrocity prevention and noncombatant evacuation operations), and peacekeeping support.

In the Middle East, potential political instability in Saudi Arabia as a result of a combination of declining oil revenues, internal frictions within the ruling royal family, and public disaffection with the cost of the military campaign in Yemen is a growing concern. Although Saudi Arabia is not a formal ally of the United States, it is clearly an important partner in many endeavors in the Middle East, not to mention a major supplier of oil to the world market. Instability in Saudi Arabia could also resonate in Bahrain, headquarters of the U.S. Fifth Fleet in the Persian Gulf. The United States also has a strong interest in preventing the destabilization of Jordan and Lebanon as a consequence of the stressful spillover effects of the civil war in neighboring Syria. Aside from not wishing to see the violence and disorder already prevalent in much of the Levant grow even larger, there is also the risk of renewed conflict between Israel and Hezbollah in southern Lebanon. Given the latter's ties to Iran and the changing nature of the Middle East more generally, renewed fighting between Israel and Hezbollah could have larger ramifications than did earlier clashes.

The political stability of Turkey in the medium term is also a growing concern following the attempted coup in 2016 and the increasingly authoritarian tendencies of the Erdogan government. As an important NATO ally and host to several large U.S. military bases as well as being a major partner in the fight against ISIS, the United States has important interests at stake in Turkey remaining politically stable. Finally, the future trajectory of Egypt has to be of concern; its economy remains very weak, and the undercurrents of popular disaffection with the current authoritarian regime are not very far below the surface. A reoccurrence of the political instability witnessed in the aftermath of the Arab Spring cannot be discounted.

Compared to the Middle East, the risk of U.S. military intervention in Africa has historically been much lower. With militant Islamist groups affiliated with either al-Qaeda or ISIS becoming more active in the Sahel region, however, the likelihood of U.S. counterterrorism operations will grow. Arguably of much greater concern to the United States, however, is the political trajectory of Africa's larger states—notably, Kenya, Nigeria, the Democratic Republic of the Congo, and even South Africa. Though preventing violent instability in these countries represents a desirable U.S. goal, the likelihood of significant military intervention beyond evacuation missions remains remote to say the least. The exception would be a potential mass atrocity contingency. Much would hinge on the scale and intensity of the killing and in particular whether it reflected a clear genocidal motive rather than the by-product of a civil war, as well as instrumental calculations as to whether military intervention could make a significant difference. Closer to home, drug-related violence and instability in Mexico and other parts of Central America have been long-standing U.S. concerns given the spillover effects of migration and organized crime into the United States. U.S. military and development agencies are already providing assistance, which could conceivably increase if the situation deteriorates. Here again, the likelihood of direct U.S. military intervention appears very remote given the obvious political sensitivities surrounding such action. In South America, the only plausible contingency on the horizon concerns the possible breakdown of the peace agreement between the Colombian government and the Revolutionary Armed Forces of Colombia insurgent group that was reached in 2016. The United States has provided substantial support to Colombia to defeat this insurgency and also to counter drug trafficking in the country. Should the agreement unravel and violence surge again, the United States will likely feel compelled to further support the Colombian government given America's already considerable investment, but once more, the level of military involvement is unlikely to rise above what it has been in the past.

Using the approach to prioritizing contingencies proposed in chapter 2, the leading medium-term preventive priorities for the United States can be plotted on a risk matrix as illustrated in table 5.1. Specific contingencies have been placed on the matrix according to both their assessed category as well as a rough estimate of their likelihood over the next three to five years using the three levels of probability discussed earlier—High (probable to almost certain), Medium (even chance of occurring), and Low (improbable to highly unlikely).

TABLE 5.1 U.S. CRISIS PREVENTION RISK MATRIX (CA. 2017)

CONTINGENCY/ LIKELIHOOD	HIGH	MODERATE	LOW
Category 1	• South China Sea confrontation	• East China Sea confrontation • NATO-Russia confrontation in the Baltic region	• Renewed China-Taiwan confrontation • Collapse of North Korea
Category 2	• Military confrontation with Iran	• Nuclear-related contingencies in Pakistan	• Russian intervention in Georgia
Category 3		Instability in: • Egypt • Lebanon • Turkey	Instability in: • Jordan • Bahrain • Saudi Arabia

This translates into the following U.S. crisis prevention priorities:

- Tier I: South China Sea confrontation; East China Sea confrontation; NATO-Russia confrontation in the Baltic region; Military confrontation with Iran
- Tier II: Renewed China-Taiwan confrontation; Collapse of North Korea; Nuclear-related contingencies in Pakistan
- Tier III: Russian intervention in Georgia; Instability in Egypt, Lebanon, Turkey, Jordan, Bahrain, and Saudi Arabia

MIDTERM PREVENTIVE ENGAGEMENT

TIER I PRIORITIES

With respect to the South and East China Sea contingencies there seems little prospect in the medium term that the various territorial disputes can be resolved in a mutually satisfactory fashion. Accordingly, the United States should pursue a preventive strategy designed to reduce the likelihood of dangerous incidents and inadvertent escalation arising while also improving the ability of those involved in any future crisis to manage it peacefully. This strategy would have three complementary policy elements that would be carried out simultaneously.

The first element entails being clear and consistent about U.S. interests and intentions regarding the potential flash points. With China, the United States should continue to emphasize that while it takes no position on the sovereignty of the disputed areas, it would oppose any coercive or forceful measures to advance individual claims. U.S. actions must also be seen as genuinely evenhanded and based on recognized international principles that are uniformly applicable.[34] Thus, the United States should support the 2016 ruling of the Permanent Court of Arbitration in The Hague regarding the South China Sea. Other recognized principles for adjudicating and resolving maritime disputes should also be emphasized. This would include continuing to reject the notion that "historic rights" can override commonly accepted legal principles—that is, China's claims in the South China Sea via its contentious Nine-Dash Line.

At the same, the United States should be equally clear and consistent about its treaty obligations to defend Japan and the Philippines without providing either state with the misconception that it can pursue its claims in ways inconsistent with the general principles. Such commitments should be made credible not only via the regular presence of U.S. forces in the region but also by maintaining the operational viability of both alliances consistent with their defensive purposes. This includes regular military exercises to enhance readiness and coordination, as well as any needed material assistance. To the extent possible, such activities should be carried out in a transparent fashion to reassure others of their defensive intent. Conversely, as some have argued, the United States should avoid making declarations and promises that it is ultimately unwilling to back up if called upon to do so.[35]

The second element to the U.S. preventive strategy should be to support a variety of tension reduction measures.[36] The United States should in the first instance encourage the disputants to freeze or desist from activities

likely to incite tensions—that is, China's construction of military facilities on disputed territories in the South China Sea or unnecessary asser-
tions by Japan of its administrative control of the Senkaku Islands. China
and Japan should also be encouraged to contain these disputes within their
overall bilateral relationship and not let them affect how they approach
other issues, including other territorial disputes. If circumstances permit,
the United States can also actively support various cooperative ventures
between the disputants, such as jointly managed projects to regulate fishing and exploit energy reserves.[37] Several precedents already exist that can
be the model for such projects.

The third element consists of efforts to manage the risk of military escalation. This covers informal and formal efforts to reduce the likelihood of
deadly accidents and dangerous incidents along with measures to help facilitate the management of potential crises that may arise for whatever reason.
The United States should continue to support regional efforts by the Association of Southeast Asian Nations to develop a code of conduct among its
member states and China. These discussions have been ongoing since 2002,
and like many multilateral negotiations they have become hostage to numerous competing interests. Rather than waiting for a comprehensive agreement to emerge, there is merit to encouraging disputants to pursue interim
arrangements. Developing emergency communication arrangements and
related crisis management protocols, for example, can be instituted separately. The United States should likewise support nascent efforts by Japan
and China to develop bilateral crisis management procedures.

Aside from actively supporting these multilateral and bilateral efforts,
the United States can also provide technical assistance to nations in the region to improve their own understanding and management of potentially
dangerous incidents through improved surveillance and command and control systems. And since the United States has been involved in several such
incidents, it should continue to pursue its own bilateral crisis prevention and
management arrangements with China.

With regard to a potential armed confrontation with Russia over the Baltic states, there is no territorial dispute to be resolved, so crisis prevention
rests primarily on deterring potential Russian provocations and avoiding
unintended escalation caused by accidents and misunderstandings. The for-

mer requires enhancing the credibility of NATO's defensive commitments in a way that does not goad Moscow. The NATO defense support initiatives announced in 2015 do this by increasing the temporary presence of alliance forces in the Baltic region without committing to permanent deployments. The scope for much larger and more prolonged NATO military deployments in the Baltic states clearly exists as the next step if circumstances require it. Contingency planning and military exercising have also been upgraded significantly to improve the ability of the alliance to respond rapidly in a crisis.

As for the risk of unintended escalation, the United States and its NATO allies should seek to reduce it through a combination of unilateral and cooperative measures with Russia. Besides emphasizing the need for local authorities to be especially cautious around historically delicate anniversaries and in response to incidents in culturally sensitive areas and along the border with Russia, NATO should operate with maximum transparency to the extent that that is feasible. This entails being clear in advance about its deployments, exercises, and patrolling plans. The decision by the NATO secretary-general in 2015 to share with Russia a list of planned NATO exercises is to be commended for this reason; hopefully the courtesy will be reciprocated.[38] At the same time, more formalized arrangements should be proposed to avoid dangerous accidents and help manage them if and when they occur. This includes reliable military-to-military communications and other relevant protocols for crisis management. Although the United States and some NATO members have worked out bilateral arrangements for avoiding dangerous military incidents with Russia, no alliance-wide arrangement apparently exists, and that is something that would be desirable.[39]

Over time it may also be possible to modernize and upgrade the related set of confidence-building measures that were originally conceived between NATO and the Warsaw Pact states in the dying days of the Cold War. The observance of the Organization for Security and Co-operation in Europe's confidence and security building measures, often known as the Vienna measures, as well as those negotiated in the context of the Conventional Forces in Europe (CFE) Treaty, have largely lapsed in recent years—and certainly since Russia declared in 2015 that it was no longer observing the CFE Treaty.

These measures were all designed to increase the level of predictability and transparency in major military operations across the European continent. While the current political climate may not be propitious to conclude a new pan-European arms control treaty and overarching security pact, as some have advocated, initiating discussions would still be valuable to improve the general level of mutual understanding between Russia and the West.[40]

Reducing the risk of armed conflict between Iran and United States will require a careful balance of diplomatic and military measures designed to deter and counter destabilizing Iranian behavior in the region while simultaneously encouraging a longer-term normalization of relations. Ensuring that the JCPOA nuclear agreement remains in force should be the top policy priority. While extensive surveillance and inspection provisions are part of the agreement, these will need to be fully supported financially and with appropriately trained personnel over the life cycle of the agreement. This includes ensuring that the International Atomic Energy Agency is appropriately funded and prepared for the task, since the primary monitoring burden will rest on its staff.[41] Iran will also need to be convinced that the parties to the agreement will not waver in restoring sanctions should serious violations be detected. The JCPOA includes provision for so-called snapback sanctions, but this process must remain credible if it is to deter Iranian cheating.[42] At the same time, care must be taken to avoid unnecessary friction or misunderstandings over how to interpret and resolve apparent violations. This, after all, was a major factor in the eventual undoing of the inspection regime created to prevent Iraq from acquiring weapons of mass destruction in the wake of the First Gulf War.

Iran's willingness to comply with the nuclear agreement will clearly be influenced by its own national security calculations. Indications that other countries in the region are moving ahead in developing military capabilities threatening to Iran or that the international community is less than evenhanded in how it addresses other proliferation concerns could weaken Iran's commitment to the JCPOA. For this reason, the United States must calibrate its military activities and security assistance to regional actors in ways that deter and neutralize Iranian assertiveness while reassuring Iran's leadership that U.S. policy is not to seek regime change or otherwise undermine Iran's national security. This requires supporting U.S. partners in the region to counter the activities of Iranian-backed militias in a variety of ways, including military intelligence sharing, cybersecurity measures, counterterrorism training, arms interdictions, and the implementation of financial sanctions. At the same time, U.S. military exercises (beyond current war zones), arms sales, and technology transfers to allies should be perceived as primarily defensive in character. Ideally the United States should also initiate a dialogue with Iran on preventing dangerous incidents on or over maritime areas, especially in the Persian Gulf, so as to avoid accidents, misunderstandings, and potential escalation.[43] Range restrictions and confidence-building measures relating to ballistic missile testing may also be realizable.[44] If such talks are not possible, then the United States should convey in the clearest possible terms to Iranian officials the potential consequences of various types of provocative behavior, thus hoping to reduce the scope for misunderstanding and overreaction in the event of a deadly incident. Establishing emergency consultation channels between senior political or military officials is likewise desirable to resolve potential disputes in a timely and peaceful manner. Beyond these measures—and certainly not before situations stabilize in Iraq, Syria, and Yemen—it is hard to imagine that a more formalized effort to reduce tensions and prevent conflict with Iran can be initiated. Even then, the best that may be attained is a reciprocated process of mutual restraint that produces a stable modus vivendi of sorts.

TIER II PRIORITIES

To manage the risk of renewed cross-strait tensions for the United States, two broad policy preventive options can be considered to replace the approach taken by successive U.S. administrations since the normalization of relations with China. Both essentially entail recalibrating the level of America's commitment to the defense of Taiwan though in diametrically opposite ways. The first would require the United States to substantially increase the defensive capabilities of Taiwan's armed forces while demonstrably upgrading U.S. preparedness to defend the island to deter China from using force to change the status quo. The second would be to renounce America's current security commitment to Taiwan in order to encourage its peaceful absorption by China—in much the same way Hong Kong and Macau were "unified" with the mainland—and in so doing, dramatically reduce if not entirely remove U.S. exposure to becoming embroiled in any future war over the status of the island.[45]

Both options carry substantive risks to the United States. The former would immediately change the tenor of U.S.-China relations to one that was overtly adversarial and thus affect cooperation on a wide range of issues of interest to America, including the peaceful resolution of other disputes in the Asia-Pacific region. The latter option—almost certainly characterized as America appeasing China and abandoning Taiwan—would immediately affect how U.S. allies in the region perceive their security, potentially causing them to either move closer to China or pursue other solutions including developing their own nuclear deterrent. On balance, therefore, the current U.S. policy toward Taiwan—for all its deficiencies for *resolving* the dispute—still represents the most prudent way to deter Chinese coercion and opportunism while also reassuring America's regional allies that the United States remains committed to their well-being and security. As before, America's posture toward Taiwan will require constant attention and careful adjustment to ensure that the commitment to provide weapons "of a defensive nature" match the level of threat posed by mainland China and that U.S. policy pronouncements and security-related activities on or around Taiwan cannot be construed as violating the cardinal principles upon which the current status quo rests.

More practically, the United States should continue to support cross-strait trade and investment that will dissuade the use of force while also encouraging Taiwan and mainland China to explore a range of potentially useful military confidence-building measures that lessen the risk of dangerous accidents and unintended military interactions. In the short term these include enhanced information sharing, advance notification of military exercises, and modifications to current deployments; in the long term they include the establishment of crisis hotlines and inter-military exchanges.[46] At the same time, the United States must regularly review its own crisis management preparedness for a cross-strait contingency.

As for the risks associated with the collapse of North Korea stemming from the onset of a serious economic or political crisis, U.S. policy makers face an acute dilemma. On the one hand, events that raise the prospect of a swift end to the odious regime in Pyongyang and the eventual reunification of Korea would be considered attractive. Certainly the United States would not want to take actions that diminish that prospect especially if it also ran counter to policies being pursued by its South Korean ally to achieve that goal. Yet, U.S. policy makers would just as fervently not want to see North Korea collapse in a way that ignites another Korean war and potentially puts the United States on a collision course with China.

In theory, this predicament can be avoided through negotiations and a political process that brings about a fundamental reconciliation between the two Koreas. There is no reason to expect, however, that this will happen anytime soon. Various schemes to bring about peaceful reunification of the peninsula have been proposed for over sixty years but have never gained serious traction. Less ambitious confederative "one nation, two systems" arrangements that more or less codify peaceful coexistence have also been discussed but have fared no better.

Deliberately hastening the collapse of North Korea through a variety of subversive and coercive measures to bring about regime change and, ultimately, reunification—as some advocate—represents another way to address the problem.[47] Besides removing a major threat to regional stability and emancipating the long suffering North Korean people from a horrendously repressive regime, accelerating North Korea's demise could also be accompanied by preparations to manage the transition and aftermath rather than risk the messy improvisation that follows being caught by surprise. Though this approach is superficially appealing, there is every reason to believe that China would actively undermine such efforts by helping North Korea resist external economic coercion and political subversion because of its own concerns about the potential spillover effects and, moreover, what might follow regime change, particularly a unified Korea allied to the United States with military forces deployed on its northeastern border. In short, China is highly unlikely to cooperate unless regime change was considered imperative for its own interests and it had some input, moreover, in what political and security arrangements would pertain in a united Korean Peninsula thereafter. From a practical standpoint, it is also questionable whether a "controlled collapse" of North Korea could even be engineered and managed in a way that would not unleash the very perils that everyone wishes to avoid. For this reason, risk-averse policy makers are unlikely to support such measures unless the threat posed by North Korea reaches truly intolerable levels.

These arguments do not obviate the need, however, for the United States to be better prepared to manage the downside risks of acute instability and regime collapse in North Korea should events for whatever reason suddenly move in that direction. This requires in the first instance a great deal of precrisis consultation and planning between South Korea and the United States to manage the potential spillover effects and "spill-in" pressures. Although much progress has been achieved in recent years to improve the level of U.S.–South Korea preparedness and planning, it is evidently still very rudimentary. Sharing sensitive national plans is obviously difficult, but through regular exercises and consultations, potential surprises and misunderstandings in a crisis can be avoided.

Japan also needs to be included in such contingency planning—certainly more than it has been to date. Although there are obvious political sensitivities to be navigated, and this is not helped by continuing friction over how the historical facts of imperial Japan's role in World War II are remembered and taught in schools, there are important reasons for trilateral discussions to take place. Resurrecting or re-creating something similar to the previously established but currently moribund U.S.–Japan–South Korea Trilateral Coordinating and Oversight Group for this purpose makes a great deal of sense.

Where feasible, consultations with Chinese officials and officers should also be pursued, even though such efforts have to date not been fruitful. If the Chinese continue to be reluctant to discuss the potential demise of North Korea, which would not be surprising, there is still benefit in raising specific concerns and discussing potential responses so as to reduce misunderstandings in a real crisis. Establishing reliable communication channels and proper protocols for crisis consultation should at the very least be a priority.

Beyond the immediate challenges of managing political instability and possible state collapse in North Korea, consultation and planning between South Korea and the United States should also extend to the so-called day-after issues. Many very delicate issues will quickly come to the fore once the demise of North Korea appears certain and—if

Germany's experience with reunification is any guide—they will need to be resolved in a very compressed time frame. Many of the issues are in fact quite similar: besides the fundamental questions concerning how North Korea would be absorbed politically and economically, a unified Korea would have to reassure neighbors and allies about its borders, nuclear weapons status, alliance relationships, and the future presence of foreign forces on its soil (among other security-related issues), just as Germany had to as part of a final settlement during reunification.[48] Until comparatively recently, raising such questions—at least publicly—was more or less taboo. However, the U.S.–South Korea Joint Vision Statement of 2009, which declared that a reunified Korea would be based on "principles of free democracy and a market economy," has provided the essential platform for more detailed discussions.[49] Such discussions may seem academic and unimportant while North Korea remains so defiantly full of life, yet having a clearer understanding of the desired end state in Korea is helpful to managing the likely endgame. This is particularly true for assuaging plausible Chinese concerns, and it may influence how China behaves in a serious crisis. Reassuring Japan about the status of a unified Korea is second only in importance to China. And as a country with a shared border, albeit a very short one, Russia also has a legitimate interest in what might emerge from Korean reunification.

The third Tier II priority—preventing various nuclear weapons-related contingencies in Pakistan—will require the United States to maintain utmost vigilance of both political developments inside the country, particularly signs of serious instability, as well as the security of its nuclear weapons-related facilities and arsenal. Despite the "double game" that Pakistan has played in Afghanistan by covertly supporting the Taliban and thus undermining U.S. counterinsurgency goals, it is still in America's interest to help Pakistan confront internal security threats to its own stability. Continuing with economic and other forms of development assistance to put the country on a stable and sustainable path remains a desirable policy objective. Various locally focused programs with this goal in mind have evidently proven effective and provide a useful model for the future.[50] Encouraging other actors, including China, to help in this respect should likewise be energetically pursued.

The United States should also continue its quiet efforts to pressure Pakistan's government and relevant military authorities to minimize the risk of a security breach to its various nuclear-related facilities. By most accounts such efforts have been successful; both U.S. officials and some nongovernmental watchdogs have recently acknowledged improvements in several areas of nuclear safety and security.[51] Going forward, important progress can be made to improve the level of confidence about the security of Pakistan's nuclear arsenal. Specialized advice and equipment to enhance the security of Pakistan's nuclear facilities and the reliability of the related personnel should be shared where possible though there are limits to how much assistance the United States can provide and Pakistan will accept.[52] At the same time, pressure must be maintained on Pakistan to change the current trajectory of its nuclear posture, which is increasing, not diminishing, the risk of a potentially dangerous crisis. Its insistence on developing a "full spectrum" nuclear capability, including the deployment of a growing number of tactical nuclear weapons able to launch with little warning; its continuing production of weapons-grade fissile material beyond levels sufficient for a strategic deterrent; and the collocation of civilian and military nuclear facilities are all risks that Pakistan should take steps to minimize.[53]

TIER III PRIORITIES

Averting a renewed confrontation between Georgia and Russia requires at a minimum that the United States privately indicate to Russia that it would not recognize the annexation of South Ossetia and/or Abkhazia, and that any attempt to do so would invite further sanctions on Russia.[54] At the same time, the United States and its NATO allies should also insist that Russia live up to its commitment to implement the 2008 six-point cease-fire agreement, which it has failed to do. With the support of monitors from the Organization for Security and Co-operation in Europe, any effort to redraw the associated demarcation lines should also be resisted. Having already raised the possibility of Georgia (and Ukraine) one day being able to join NATO, it would be wrong and potentially dangerous of the West to suggest that this is permanently off the table. Likewise, the

United States and its partners should not desist from providing Georgia with defensive arms in the belief that this would antagonize Russia. The West's support for Georgia should not be unconditional, however. Georgia must remain on the democratic path and avoid actions that antagonize Russia needlessly.

The remaining Tier III priorities are all Middle East contingencies and mostly concern the risk of internal political instability. America's ability to foster their political and economic development to ultimately lessen this risk will always be limited, but other forms of preventive engagement are available. For Jordan and Lebanon, where the principal source of internal stress is the adjacent civil war in Syria and in particular the huge number of refugees that they have had to absorb, the United States can continue to provide humanitarian assistance—both directly and indirectly through multilateral agencies. Providing resettlement opportunities and encouraging host governments—again directly and indirectly—to improve the educational and employment prospects for refugees should also be pursued.[55] The European Union countries are natural partners in such efforts. Furthermore, in Jordan at least, where the United States already provides considerable intelligence and internal security assistance, additional support in such areas as border surveillance can be increased. In Lebanon, enlisting the help of regional actors—notably the Arab Persian Gulf states as well as Iran—to dampen rising sectarian tensions and in particular overreach by Hezbollah either internally or against Israel, should also be pursued. However, bringing the Syrian civil war to an end so that most if not all of the refugees can return represents the most significant contribution the United States can make to easing the pressure on both countries.

For Saudi Arabia, much will hinge on the success of the ambitious national plan to transform and diversify the economy.[56] Huge challenges confront these initiatives and besides providing technical assistance in some areas, there is not much the United States can do to assist Saudi Arabia directly beyond encouraging further progress. Indirectly, however, America can help Saudi Arabia disentangle itself from its costly intervention in Yemen by actively supporting a viable peace process (to be discussed in chapter 6) that would lessen the risk of rising public disaffection with the social and economic costs of the war. The United States can also encourage Saudi Arabia to be more open to political and social reforms in Bahrain over which it has considerable leverage, thereby reducing the threat of internal unrest to U.S. interests there.

Egypt, by contrast, represents the toughest preventive engagement challenge for U.S. policy makers. Its sheer size, entrenched interests, and widespread corruption all make it very difficult to enact the necessary economic reforms to raise the standard of living for most Egyptians. Working through third parties, whether it be multilateral agencies or the Gulf Arab states, to nudge Egypt in the right direction is probably the best that can be accomplished in the medium term. The United States does retain some leverage with its long-standing security assistance programs and military-to-military contacts—though not as much as sometimes asserted—and this can also be used in some cases to promote progress and manage emerging risks.

As for less specific Tier III humanitarian contingencies, particularly where the threat of widespread mass atrocities is very real, the United States should continue to lessen the overall risk by developing tailored crisis prevention plans for the most vulnerable countries as originally proposed by the Genocide Prevention Task Force.[57] More specifically this would include

- A detailed target country assessment by the intelligence community that identifies potential points of leverage and policy intervention. This assessment would provide basic political, military, economic, and demographic information; details about the senior leadership, its sources of support (domestic and foreign), internal opposition, and potential motivations to authorize or permit mass atrocities; details about the potential perpetrators, their motivations, command and control arrangements, and potential methods of mass killing; and details on the identity, number, location, and vulnerability of the potential victims.
- An atrocities estimate and impact assessment. This would assess, among other things, the potential scale of violence, the risk to U.S. citizens and property, the impact on the political stability of the country, the probable effect in terms of internal or external migration, the risk of intervention

from neighboring states, and the likely political and economic consequences both regionally and globally if action is not taken.

- A policy options assessment that draws on the target country analysis to lay out a range of potential U.S. responses matched to rising levels of crisis escalation. This assessment should be generated by a standard planning framework to speed the process but also ensure that a comprehensive review of all the options takes place. More specifically, this would tailor specific responses to the relevant target groups in latent or emerging genocidal situations: those planning, authorizing, and fomenting genocide/mass atrocities (to affect their decision calculus); those likely to carry out the genocide/mass atrocities (to reduce their operational effectiveness); the potential victims (to improve their chances of survival); and other relevant domestic and foreign actors (to persuade and mobilize them to play a positive role).

On the basis of this analysis, different policy packages or playbooks would be developed that could be mixed and matched to respond to a variety of contingencies for different phases of a crisis. The crisis response plan would draw on these assessments to create a detailed interagency operations plan that would define (among other things) U.S. interests, objectives, a desired end state, lead agency responsibilities and tasks, potential international partners, lines of authority and coordination, sequencing, and necessary preparatory measures. Preparatory measures would cover a host of requirements: appointing a congressional liaison, diplomatic coordination, consultation with necessary legal authorities, funding, and media coordination. Provision should be made to rehearse the crisis response plan and subject it to "red team" review—that is, gaming in which a group is designated to play the role of the adversary—so long as this would not delay timely response.

* * *

The detailed policy planning necessary to develop and implement the various crisis prevention initiatives proposed here require dedicated and suitably empowered structures within the U.S. bureaucracy. Staff has to be properly trained to carry out contingency planning based on prior experience of what has and has not worked in comparable cases. Moreover, this effort has to be "mainstreamed" in the sense that senior officials are engaged and supportive. Finally, flexible funds to implement the identified preventive engagement initiatives also have to be available; otherwise, this planning effort will be worthless. In other words, business as usual will not suffice. Chapter 8 will discuss what this should entail in further detail.

6

CONFLICT MITIGATION

The Short Game

To see what is in front of one's nose needs a constant struggle.

—GEORGE ORWELL

You never want a serious crisis to go to waste. And what I mean by that it's an opportunity to do things you think you could not do before.

—RAHM EMANUEL

T HE THIRD AND FINAL component to a preventive engagement strategy is the "short game"—managing existing conflicts so that they do not deteriorate in ways that threaten U.S. interests and potentially lead to new or more costly military commitments. Evaluating such risks would appear to be straightforward compared to either long- or medium-term assessments in that real rather than hypothetical developments are being appraised. Making sense of the present can still be hard, however, while the urgent can easily become confused with the important. Having a clear sense of priorities is thus just as necessary with the short game as it is with addressing long- and medium-term risks.

Resolving the underlying drivers of an ongoing conflict clearly represents the most satisfactory way to reduce the risk it poses. In many cases, however, preventing a dangerous situation from getting worse will seem the best that can be accomplished given what appear to be insurmountable obstacles to do anything more. Careful judgment is needed at all times, however, to ensure that temporary expediencies do not preclude more sustainable solutions. De-escalating tensions to buy time for a more propitious moment to resolve a conflict can certainly be justified in some instances, but conflicts have a habit of hardening over time, turning them into permanent features of the international landscape. At the same time, crises can provide a fleeting window of opportunity to focus attention and mobilize political capital to overcome long-standing logjams that have potential benefits for the medium and long term. Being prepared for those moments is an essential element of the short game.

SHORT-TERM RISKS AND PRIORITIES

A survey of ongoing conflicts of interest to the United States can be organized according to the same set of categories used to evaluate medium- and long-term priorities.

CATEGORY 1 CONTINGENCIES

Several contingencies qualify as Category 1 concerns in terms of their immediate impact on critical U.S. interests or their propensity to involve the United States in a major armed conflict.

Major Terrorist Attack on U.S. Homeland

It is reasonable to conclude that the United States will remain at risk of a serious terrorist attack for the foreseeable future. How much of a risk is difficult to gauge given the inherent uncertainties of evaluating threats from nonstate actors. Judging by the increase in the number of terrorist groups now considered hostile to the United States, the threat has grown since 9/11.[1]

The original perpetrators of the 9/11 attack, now often labeled core or central al-Qaeda, have evidently been severely degraded from a relentless campaign to kill or capture the group's leaders in Afghanistan and Pakistan—including, of course, the killing of its founder, Osama bin Laden, in 2011. Al-Qaeda, however, has since spawned many regional offshoots or affiliated groups, some of whom—notably al-Qaeda in the Arabian Peninsula—have attempted to attack the U.S. homeland.[2] The leaders of other terrorist organizations have also from time to time expressed their hostility toward the United States. This includes two Pakistani groups—the Tehrik-e-Taliban Pakistan, which trained and deployed Faizal Shahzad to explode a car bomb in New York City's Times Square in 2010, and Lashkar-e-Taiba, which carried out a sophisticated attack on the Indian port city of Mumbai in 2008.[3] To these groups must now also be added the self-proclaimed Islamic State of Iraq and Syria (ISIS, also known as ISIL or Daesh), which the United States is actively involved in military operations to destroy.

Having the motivation to attack the United States is one thing, but having the capacity to do so is quite another. The opportunity to plan and prepare for a major operation on U.S. soil has undoubtedly been rendered more difficult by what is now a worldwide counterterrorism surveillance effort conducted by the United States and its network of intelligence-sharing partners. The ability to dispatch operatives and materials into the United States or support an operation financially has likewise become much harder due to enhanced screening procedures. Such barriers are especially pertinent to assessing the more extreme risk: an attack involving the use of improvised weapons of mass destruction, which al-Qaeda is at least known to have actively pursued.[4] Clandestinely acquiring and certainly importing nuclear, biological, or chemical materials into the United States, and then assembling a usable device from them clearly represents a formidable challenge that should not be trivialized.

Other considerations, however, have to be weighed before discounting the risk of a major terrorist attack further. In particular, there is growing concern with what are classified as homegrown violent extremists— essentially, individuals and groups living within the United States who become radicalized and motivated to carry out terrorist acts. This has already occurred on a small scale with the attack on a military facility in Chattanooga, Tennessee, in July 2015; at a regional center serving the developmentally disabled in San Bernardino, California, in December 2015; and the attack on a nightclub in Orlando, Florida, in June 2016; all of these were carried out by individuals inspired by ISIS. In 2015, the FBI made approximately five dozen arrests of U.S.-based ISIS supporters, up from a dozen the year before.[5] The capacity of lone wolves, as they are sometimes called, to organize and carry out a mass casualty attack is clearly significantly less than an organized group, but it cannot be entirely dismissed given the progressive diffusion of technical knowledge and the potential use of publicly available materials that can be put to harmful uses.

Should there be another major terrorist attack or even a string of coordinated smaller attacks, the public pressure to retaliate against the perpetrators and especially any country known to be implicated in the attack would surely be intense. Whatever reservations many Americans would have about responding militarily in such circumstances given what has happened since 9/11 could easily become overcome by the raw emotions of the moment. They would be hard to resist.

Renewed Korean War

Although there have been no major and sustained breaches of the armistice that ended the Korean War in 1953, tensions have waxed and waned but never completely subsided. A resumption of hostilities would immediately involve the more than 28,000 U.S. military personnel deployed in South Korea and would almost certainly entail many more being sent from Japan and elsewhere as reinforcements. Estimates of the potential cost of a new Korean conflict depend, as always, on its character and how long it would last. The 1950–1953 Korean War is now estimated to have cost the lives of well over a million people. Over 36,000 Americans died while more than 100,000 were wounded. The financial cost for the United States was also high, ranging from around $300 billion to over $600 billion in inflation-adjusted dollars depending on whether indirect costs are included. By 1994, at the height of the first nuclear crisis with North Korea, the U.S. military estimated that if war broke out there would be 52,000 Americans killed or wounded and nearly half a million South Korean military casualties.[6] Many more Americans now reside or work in South Korea—approximately 120,000, with around 30,000 living in the capital, Seoul. More than 50,000 American citizens, moreover, live and work in Japan.

Until relatively recently, the renewal of open hostilities on the Korean Peninsula would have been classified as a clear Category 2 contingency. This can no longer be considered the case, for three important reasons. The first is the potential involvement of China (and conceivably even Russia) in a way that would present a very different risk to U.S. interests from what was the case during the Korean War. The second is the growing effort by North Korea to threaten the U.S. homeland with long-range ballistic missiles armed with nuclear warheads (among other capabilities). Finally, as South Korea's economy and trading links to the world have grown, the economic consequences of renewed conflict would affect the global economy on a much greater level today.[7]

There are several ways a new Korean war could break out. The least likely scenario is the one that most preoccupied U.S. war planners during the Cold War—a premeditated North Korean invasion of South Korea to forcibly reunify the peninsula. What confidence North Korea's army may have once had about executing such an operation has steadily eroded as its military capabilities have grown more antiquated from the lack of modernization, while the quality of U.S. and South Korean forces have over the same period steadily improved. Even a limited North Korean military incursion into South Korea—for example, a quick grab for the capital Seoul from across the demilitarized zone (DMZ)—as a desperate gambit to relieve pressure from sanctions or suing for peace on terms that preserve its long-term future also seems far-fetched given the near certainty of massive retaliation. To paraphrase Otto von Bismarck's famous line about preventive war, such action would be akin to committing suicide out of fear of death.

The more plausible contingency in the short term is the inadvertent escalation of a deliberate North Korea provocation. These occur regularly and range from bellicose threats of massive devastation that are often timed to coincide with a nuclear weapons or missile test to aggressive if limited military skirmishes with South Korean forces. The latter has in recent years included the torpedoing of the naval corvette *Cheonan* in March 2010 and the shelling of Yeonpyeong Island in the Yellow Sea in November 2010, both of which resulted in the loss of South Korean lives.

Such provocative behavior is clearly reckless and irresponsible, but from the perspective of North Korea's leaders it is likely viewed as serving a useful purpose. On the one hand, it projects fearlessness and resolve to the outside world and potentially intimidates South Korea and the United States into making concessions such as sanctions relief. On the other hand, any negative reaction can be used internally by the North Korean regime to justify actions that further consolidate its hold on power and convince the general public that outside powers harbor hostile intentions. The risk, of course, is that North Korea's leadership may miscalculate the long-standing reluctance of South Korea and the United States to retaliate militarily to such provocations for fear that that may lead to another war. Since the *Cheonan* and Yeonpyeong incidents, the allies have worked together to develop the joint Counter-Provocation Plan in 2013 to deter and respond to similar actions by North Korea in the future.[8] South Korea has also declared its intention to adhere to a policy of "proactive deterrence"—namely, that it reserves the right to take self-defense measures against the source of the provocation as well as any supporting facilities and command posts associated with that source. Although this is a wholly understandable posture to adopt to deter North Korean provocations, it nevertheless increases the risk that a dangerous chain reaction of strikes and counterstrikes could occur in a crisis that progressively undermines self-restraint and propels the peninsula toward outright war.[9]

Besides the inter-Korean dynamics of any serious crisis, there is now the additional and growing possibility that the United States might decide to take preventive or preemptive military action—either alone or with South Korean support—against North Korea's nuclear weapons and ballistic missile programs that place not only South Korea and Japan at risk but also, increasingly, U.S territory.[10] Declarations of intent, combined with credible evidence of preparations during a crisis to ready such capabilities for operational use, would rightly be viewed with the utmost concern by U.S. officials and potentially precipitate preemptive action. The United States would likely be similarly predisposed to use force against North Korea it if transferred nuclear weapons or other weapons of mass destruction to a terrorist organization or some other dangerous nonstate entity. There is no evidence of any intent or inclination by North Korea to do this, but it has nevertheless demonstrated a highly disturbing disregard for international nonproliferation controls with its evident transfer of nuclear technology to Syria and perhaps other states—not to mention its ballistic missile exports. Despite having limited military and political objectives, a preemptive or punitive U.S. strike could nevertheless spur retaliation by North Korea and trigger a larger conflict.

More generally, management of a serious crisis on or around the Korean Peninsula could also be complicated by other factors. Pyongyang's grasp of potentially fast-moving events could be quite limited and slow, given North Korea's relatively unsophisticated intelligence and communication systems. Furthermore, the limited options for communicating with the North Korean leadership could hinder attempts to bring a rapidly deteriorating situation under control. Since the *Cheonan* incident, North Korea has shut down the intermilitary hotline established in 2004 for maritime emergencies in the Yellow Sea; it also regularly turns off the UN fax machine communications link at Panmunjom in the DMZ to demonstrate its displeasure. (The United States from time to time has had to use a bullhorn to announce planned military exercises.) Likewise, the Seoul-Pyongyang telephone "hotline" maintained by the Red Cross is regularly disconnected for the same reason while various ad hoc military and intelligence links between the two Koreas cannot be considered timely and reliable conduits for crisis management. The same is also true for official U.S.-North Korea diplomatic connections, including the so-called New York channel through North Korea's UN representative. This is maintained by its foreign ministry and thus does not represent a direct link to the leadership.[11]

Renewed Indo-Pakistani War

Another major war between India and Pakistan—there have been three since they gained independence from Britain in 1947—also warrants being considered as a short-term Category 1 contingency for at least three reasons. First, the risk of renewed fighting remains very real, and various scenarios for how India and Pakistan could once again go to war are not hard to imagine. The most plausible is another successful terrorist attack by a Pakistani militant group, acting with or without the support of government officials, that targets, for example, India's leadership or a particularly sensitive political or religious site and, regardless of the target, results in mass casualties.[12] In December 2001, terrorists from two Pakistani militant groups with ties to Pakistan's intelligence service attacked the Indian Parliament building in New Delhi, which prompted India to mobilize over 500,000 troops and send them to the border where a tense standoff ensued for nearly two years. In 2008, Pakistani militants attacked the port city of Mumbai, killing 164 and wounding more than three hundred others in various locations. Only after considerable U.S. pressure and Indian self-restraint was another war averted.[13] Much, of course, would depend on the nature and scale of a terrorist attack, but if it were particularly egregious, military retaliation from India certainly cannot be ruled out. This would thus raise the prospect of Pakistan responding in similar fashion and further escalation ensuing.

A less likely but still plausible scenario involves the escalation of relatively localized violence in the disputed region of Kashmir—the focal point of Indo-Pakistani antagonism since the two nations' partition and independence from British rule. Skirmishes continue to take place regularly along the Line of Control that marks the de facto division of Kashmir. As recently as September 2016, Pakistani militants attacked an Indian army outpost in Uri, killing seventeen soldiers, which led in turn to cross-border retaliatory strikes against Pakistan.[14] Separatist related violence in the Indian controlled part of Kashmir also flares up from time to time, prompting angry condemnation from Pakistan. Although both sides have developed various formal and informal mechanisms for managing conflict in Kashmir, it remains a serious flashpoint and potential trigger for a larger war.[15]

The second reason why preventing an Indo-Pakistani war constitutes a Category 1 priority is the manifest risk that it could lead to the use of nuclear weapons by one or both sides.[16] Since May 1998, when India and Pakistan each tested nuclear devices and openly declared themselves to be nuclear powers, both countries have steadily built up their arsenals.[17] It cannot be assumed, however, that a stable nuclear deterrent relationship based on a mutual understanding of the risks will be maintained indefinitely. As two seasoned experts on Indian and Pakistani nuclear relationship have argued,

> Government officials tend to believe that the signals they send are received and interpreted correctly. Yet, most scholarship on this subject finds precisely the opposite: the recipient of signals interprets them very differently than the sender expects. Pakistani officials and politicians have regularly "played the nuclear card" that the signaling value of such statements has diminished in India. And India's hype around its "proactive strategy" is both discounted as bluster and used to justify the development of tactical nuclear weapons in Pakistan. Deterrence requires communication of a credible willingness to use force but when both sides discount the signals as well as the credibility of the threats, there is plenty of room for error.[18]

A relatively "localized" nuclear war between the two countries might be considered by some Americans to be a distant threat with negligible lasting consequences for the United States, but the harmful effects would in all likelihood be far-reaching and prolonged.[19] One rigorous assessment of two plausible nuclear exchange scenarios—ten Hiroshima-size bombs (of a fifteen-kiloton airburst) on ten Indian and Pakistani cities, or twenty-four nuclear warheads (of a twenty-five-kiloton ground burst) on fifteen cities—estimates that the casualties would be approximately 2.8 million killed (with 1.5 million severely wounded) and 22.1 million killed (with 8 million severely wounded), respectively.[20] Aside from the massive and immediate humanitarian catastrophe, the use of nuclear weapons would almost certainly produce a huge disruptive shock to the international financial and trading system. India and Pakistan are not a major part of the most important global supply chains but widespread devastation of their cities would almost certainly have very adverse regional economic consequences. Moreover, depending on the magnitude of a nuclear exchange, the radiological fallout as well as the likely dust and debris that would be thrown into the atmosphere could have very serious global health and environmental consequences.[21]

The third reason to make a potential Indo-Pakistani war a Category 1 preventive priority is the potential involvement of China, which has a long-standing strategic partnership with Pakistan.[22] The conventional wisdom is that Pakistan is not high up on the list of China's foreign policy concerns and it would likely remain on the sidelines in any future Indo-Pakistani crisis—certainly in the foreseeable future. Beijing is not looking to compromise a peaceful and burgeoning trading relationship with New Delhi nor be potentially at odds with Washington on yet another issue.[23] Yet China's calculus is surely changing. The nuclear rivalry between India and Pakistan, with its latent potential for unintended escalation in a crisis, must be of growing concern. On any given day there are roughly ten thousand Chinese engineers working on various projects inside Pakistan and thus potentially at risk.[24] And if the worst were to happen, China would probably suffer the most, economically and environmentally, of all the external affected powers. Whether all of this could translate into a more interventionist posture in a future Indo-Pakistani crisis, and especially one openly supportive of Pakistan, is difficult to determine in the abstract. But it clearly raises the stakes for both Washington and New Delhi.

CATEGORY 2 CONTINGENCIES

Several contingencies can also be identified as Category 2 conflict mitigation priorities for the United States in the short term.

Escalation of Civil War in Syria

Since antigovernment protests began in Syria in 2011, the ensuing civil war has steadily escalated into a much larger conflict that has cost over half a million lives and caused one the largest humanitarian disasters in this century. Approximately 6.5 million Syrians have been internally displaced, and another 2.8 million have fled as refugees to neighboring countries—in particular, Jordan and Lebanon.[25] Hundreds of thousands have also sought asylum in Europe, causing serious political divisions within and among the European Union (EU) member states. Moreover, the Syrian civil war now involves many outside powers, each with differing military and political goals.

This has increased the potential for further escalation and certainly made the war's resolution more difficult. The most relevant external actors are:

- Iran, which has supported the regime of Syrian president Bashar al-Assad with financial and military assistance from the outset to maintain its influence in Syria and also maintain a land bridge to Hezbollah, the Islamist militant group in Lebanon that serves as a strategic asset in its conflict with Israel.

- The United States, which along with Saudi Arabia and its Arab partners in the Persian Gulf has provided training and material assistance to various opposition groups to remove the Assad regime while also engaging in a multinational military campaign to degrade and destroy ISIS. In 2017, the United States also struck a Syrian airbase with cruise missiles in retaliation for the use of chemical weapons.

- Turkey, which has intervened militarily to counter the growing influence of Kurdish groups in northern Syria, some of whom, to complicate matters, are battling both the Assad regime and ISIS as well as the Turkish state.

- Russia, which since 2015 has provided airpower and some special forces to prevent the Assad regime from falling.

Because of the complexity of the war, creating a sustainable cease-fire, much less an acceptable political resolution, has proved elusive. The UN has tried and failed several times, while it remains to be seen whether a Russian-Iranian-Turkish–led effort following the recapture of Aleppo from opposition forces in December 2016 will succeed. The track record of peacemaking in civil wars of this nature is not encouraging; they typically last over a decade before being resolved one way or another.[26] Until this happens, the risk of deeper U.S. military engagement will remain very real. This could come about in several ways.

First, the fight against ISIS may require more U.S. military involvement than originally anticipated, including forces to maintain order in places liberated from its control. Attacks organized or inspired by ISIS against targets in Europe and especially the United States could lead to an intensification of the military campaign to remove the threat once and for all.[27] Second, preventing Turkish-Kurdish tensions from escalating further may require U.S. forces to be deployed increasingly in an interpositional role to keep the peace in northern Syria and northern Iraq. Third, systematic mass killings by government forces of remaining opposition groups and their perceived civilian sympathizers would likely provoke outrage in Europe and the United States especially if it involved the further use of chemical weapons. Pressure to punish the Syrian regime and deter additional mass killings would inevitably grow along with calls that the United States impose safe havens or no-fly zones inside Syria. Once initiated, such limited responses could turn into a much larger intervention to satisfy new operational demands and political objectives. And, finally, there is the ever present risk of military incidents involving U.S. and Russian as well as Iranian forces operating inside Syria, leading to a further deterioration of relations between them.

Violent Disintegration of Iraq

After the withdrawal of U.S. forces in 2011, the political and sectarian divisions within Iraq have steadily worsened. Although the country has not descended into an open civil war on a scale comparable to that of neighboring Syria, large parts of Iraq have fallen under the control of ISIS, and government forces and Kurdish Peshmerga militia supported by the U.S. Air Force and special operations units have since sought to reclaim these territories through military action. Iran is also providing material support to Iraq and using its special forces to combat ISIS.

To date the United States has calibrated its military operations against ISIS to avoid being dragged back into another costly counterinsurgency campaign in Iraq. As with Syria, however, the United States could become more involved militarily to ensure not just the defeat of ISIS but also to keep the peace thereafter. More specifically, the United States could end up deploying considerably more forces to Iraq to help stabilize areas liberated from ISIS, potentially as part of a major multinational force. Unless a major effort is undertaken to reincorporate the predominantly Sunni areas liberated from ISIS control and convince them they have a future within Iraq, then they are likely to remain restive and resistant to Baghdad's authority.

The United States could also feel pressured to take a more active role in managing the various manifestations of the growing Kurdish problem whether it be deterring Turkish military intervention or protecting Iraqi Kurds from forces loyal to Baghdad in the event that they declare their intention to create an independent sovereign state. The latter in particular could prompt a bloody military campaign to prevent not just Kurdistan breaking loose from Baghdad's nominal control but also other parts of Iraq that may feel emboldened to do the same.[28] The United States is likely to feel torn between feeling obligated to support the aspirations of Iraqi Kurds, especially given their support in fighting ISIS, and preventing the disintegration of Iraq with all the dangerous consequences this could have on the stability of the region.

Strategic Reversal in Afghanistan

The reimposition of Taliban control in many rural areas of Afghanistan, combined with chronic governance problems at the national level, is jeopardizing the U.S. and NATO goal of eventually leaving Afghanistan in a reasonably stable and secure condition. In 2015 the Taliban made steady advances in several rural provinces and briefly took control of Kunduz, a large provincial capital. According to U.S. estimates, areas under uncontested government control have declined from 72 percent in November 2015 to 59 percent in November 2016.[29] Other urban areas are vulnerable to attack, and the possibility of a simultaneous coordinated offensive against several of them that overwhelms the already overstretched and underequipped Afghan National Security Forces is conceivable.[30] Although the capture of Kabul still appears beyond the capacity of the Taliban, the chronic weakness of the Afghan national government as a result of infighting and endemic corruption will undermine its capacity to conduct an effective counterinsurgency campaign.

A serious deterioration of the situation in Afghanistan would present the United States and its NATO allies with an immensely difficult decision as to whether to recommit sizable forces to bolster the national government and counter the advances made by the Taliban. After more than fifteen years of fighting in Afghanistan, the sentiment that the United States should cut its losses and withdraw completely will likely be strong. The competing argument—that the United States must stay and fight, if only to prevent Afghanistan from once again becoming a safe haven for al-Qaeda and possibly even ISIS—will also be compelling. A complete U.S. withdrawal could also lead to dangerous meddling and even proxy conflicts inside Afghanistan by neighboring states, which undermines regional stability.

Escalation of Conflict in Ukraine

Although the United States is not directly involved in the conflict in Ukraine, the risk of a serious confrontation with Russia and potential military engagement in the ongoing crisis clearly exists. Since popular protests in the capital Kiev forced Prime Minister Viktor Yanukovych to flee in November 2014, Russia has annexed Crimea through covert military action and provided support to armed separatists in eastern Ukraine. While the February 2015 Minsk II accords brokered a cease-fire in eastern Ukraine, sporadic violence continues to erupt on a regular basis.[31] The situation remains very volatile and the underlying conflict could easily escalate. Government forces, for example, could decide to roll back the gains made by the separatists, thus leading to Russia intervening militarily to protect them. Russia might also decide to intervene for other reasons, such as to create a land bridge to Crimea or in response to developments elsewhere on its periphery. Whatever the scenario, should Russia be seen to be taking an aggressive role in Ukraine, the United States and other European powers would almost certainly come under intense pressure to provide more than nonlethal assistance to the Ukrainian government, especially if it appealed formally to the UN for help. The United States, if not the whole of NATO, would essentially be involved in a proxy conflict against Russia.

CATEGORY 3 CONTINGENCIES

Several ongoing conflicts qualify as Category 3 contingencies in that they either already involve limited U.S. military engagement that could conceivably expand in the near term or they could evolve in ways that lead to completely new involvement from the United States. Among the former contingencies, Yemen, Libya, and Somalia stand out, while South Sudan constitutes a potential new case of U.S. military engagement in the short term.

Intensification of the War in Yemen

Following the attack by al-Qaeda on the USS *Cole* in the Yemeni port of Aden in 2000, the United States has provided substantial security assistance to the government of Yemen to prevent it from becoming a safe haven for terrorists. Since 9/11 the United States has also used armed drones and Special Forces to attack al-Qaeda in the Arabian Peninsula (AQAP), which is operating mainly in Yemen. These efforts have in recent years been affected by a civil war that has wracked Yemen since the departure of long-standing president Ali Abdullah Saleh in 2012. His vice president, Abd-Rabbu Mansour Hadi, assumed office as interim president in a transition mediated by the Gulf Cooperation Council and backed by the United States. As part of this transition, the UN sponsored the National Dialogue Conference to come up with a new constitution for Yemen, but this effort ultimately failed. Popular unrest caused by the removal of fuel subsidies in 2014 eventually led to an overthrow of the Hadi government by forces made up predominantly of Houthis, a Shia group with ties to Iran. The fear that Iran would increase its influence in Yemen, along with Houthi cross-border attacks, prompted Saudi Arabia—with support from other Arab states—to invade Yemen in 2015. While the United States has lent military support to the Saudi-led campaign in Yemen, there is growing concern that it will radicalize many Yemenis and drive them into the hands of al-Qaeda and ISIS. By January 2017, the United Nations estimated that more than ten thousand civilians had been killed and more than three million Yemenis had been displaced by the fighting. Around 80 percent of Yemenis are considered to be reliant on some form of humanitarian assistance.[32] The risk of the United States becoming increasingly involved in Yemen could grow if AQAP takes advantage of the conflict to mount new attacks on U.S. targets.

Further Fracturing of Libya

In the aftermath of the 2011 NATO intervention in Libya, which ultimately led to the removal and death of its longtime leader Muammar al-Gaddhafi, the country has effectively fractured into two government entities vying for control, each with its own militia. As a result, more than 435,000 people have been internally displaced. Given its proximity to Europe, Libya has also been used as a passageway for Libyan refugees and refugees from other North African and sub-Saharan African countries. As of May 2017, more than 50,000 refugees and migrants have made the journey by sea to Italy, almost all of them departing from Libya.[33] Amid the general chaos both Ansar al-Sharia (the Libyan terrorist group allegedly responsible for the attack on the U.S. consulate in Benghazi in 2012) and ISIS also increased their presence inside Libya. In November 2015, the United States bombed ISIS targets in Sirte, Libya, to prevent them from gaining a larger foothold, which seems to have been effective. Should the situation deteriorate in a way that prompts or facilitates major new outflows of refugees toward Europe or if Libya becomes a significant springboard for militants to attack targets in Europe and North Africa, then the pressure to intervene militarily, including the use of ground forces, will once again grow.

Strategic Reversal in Somalia

The United States has been engaged in counterterrorism operations against the militant Islamist group al-Shabab in Somalia since at least 2006, when it emerged and formally affiliated itself with al-Qaeda. Al-Shabab's control of large parts of Somalia probably peaked in 2011; since then it has contracted significantly, in large part due to an international coalition of forces, including the United States, organized under the auspices of the African Union (AU) to establish a viable government in Mogadishu. In that year, troops from Kenya operating as part of the African Union Mission in Somalia (AMISOM) entered Somalia and successfully pushed al-Shabab out of most of its strongholds. U.S. drones and the Special Forces have also been used on a regular basis to degrade al-Shabab's leadership. Moreover, attacks on commercial shipping off the coast of Somalia by pirates, many with ties to al-Shabab, elicited a major international response that has further reduced its means of support.

Al-Shabab has not been defeated, however, and continues to launch deadly attacks within Somalia and also in Kenya. In April 2015 it attacked a Kenyan college campus, killing 148 people, and an attack in 2013 on a mall in Nairobi killed at least 67. Al-Shabab could conceivably make a comeback and imperil the gains that have been made to create some semblance of order inside Somalia. If this happens, the United States will almost certainly feel pressured to commit more military resources to fighting al-Shabab. While the United States has deployed dozens of soldiers to Mogadishu to help train and equip African Union and Somali government forces, no major deployments of U.S. combat forces to Somalia have taken place since 1994.[34] This could change if recent gains are imperiled and especially if al-Shabab succeeds in mounting a major terrorist attack against the United States that causes significant casualties.

Genocide in South Sudan

Tens of thousands of people have been killed and almost two million have been internally displaced since civil war broke out in South Sudan in December 2013. What began as a political struggle between President Salva Kiir and Vice President Riek Machar has descended into a civil war, pitting armed fighters from the two largest ethnic groups—the Dinka, which is aligned with President Kiir, and the Nuer, which supports Riek Machar— against each other. Since the outbreak of violence, additional armed groups have emerged that have targeted civilians and looted villages, committed rape and sexual violence, and recruited children into their ranks.

After several rounds of negotiations and the threat of sanctions from the United States, the Intergovernmental Authority on Development (IGAD)— the principal regional security organization for East Africa—brokered a peace agreement in August 2015 among the parties to the conflict that also included a new political road map for South Sudan. Despite cease-fire violations and little progress toward implementing the agreement, Machar returned to Juba in April 2016 as part of the peace deal.[35] Less than three months later, major clashes broke out between Kiir and Machar's factions, killing three hundred people and two UN peacekeepers.[36] The violence in July 2016 caused massive displacement, with approximately 600,000 South Sudanese fleeing to northern Uganda in less than nine months. Uganda hosts almost 900,000 South Sudanese refugees and averaged around 2,800 new arrivals per day in March 2017.

The peace agreement, which faced huge political challenges due to the proposed power-sharing agreement that essentially spurred the start of the civil war, has failed and the humanitarian situation is dire. The UN declared famine in parts of the country in February 2017, warning that 4.9 million people (more than 40 percent of the country's population) were in need of urgent food.[37] The risk of a much larger ethnic war that could include genocidal violence is now considered to be very high by UN officials. Besides the immediate humanitarian consequences, such a war could also be hugely destabilizing for the region.[38] After great objection and stalling from South Sudan's government, the first of four thousand regional peacekeepers authorized by the UN to use force deployed to Juba in May 2017, but there is no functioning peace process or progress toward a political settlement. Pressure for the United States to intervene, especially given its role in supporting South Sudan's independence from Sudan, is likely to grow should the situation continue to deteriorate.

* * *

The priority afforded each of these short-term contingencies will, of course, vary as circumstances change. At the time of this writing, however, they can be ranked into three tiers of priority using the methodology for ranking contingencies discussed in chapter 2, as illustrated in table 6.1.

SHORT-TERM PREVENTIVE ENGAGEMENT

Using the range of conflict mitigation techniques discussed in chapter 3, the United States can lessen the risk posed by various conflicts identified above.

TABLE 6.1 SHORT-TERM U.S. CONFLICT MITIGATION PRIORITIES (CA. 2017)

CONTINGENCY/ LIKELIHOOD	HIGH	MODERATE	LOW
Category 1	• Renewed Korean war	• Major terrorist attack on U.S. homeland	• Renewed Indo-Pakistani war
Category 2	• Escalation of civil war in Syria • Strategic reversal in Afghanistan	• Escalation of conflict in Ukraine • Violent disintegration of Iraq	
Category 3	• Intensification of the war in Yemen • Genocide in South Sudan	• Further fracturing of Libya • Strategic reversal in Somalia	

Following the ranking schema used in chapter 5, the short-term conflict mitigation priorities are as follows:

- Tier I: Renewed Korean war; Major terrorist attack on U.S. homeland; Escalation of civil war in Syria; Strategic reversal in Afghanistan
- Tier II: Renewed Indo-Pakistani war; Escalation of conflict in Ukraine; Violent disintegration of Iraq; Intensification of the war in Yemen; Genocide in South Sudan
- Tier III: Further fracturing of Libya; Strategic reversal in Somalia

TIER I PRIORITIES

The highest preventive priorities in terms of relative likelihood and impact are the following contingencies.

Renewed Korean War

Preventing a renewed outbreak of hostilities on the Korean Peninsula will, for the foreseeable future, rest on doing three things: maintaining a robust and credible military deterrent, defusing or at least containing the principal sources of tension, and minimizing the risk of inadvertent escalation. The first is relatively straightforward in that it requires U.S. and ROK forces to regularly demonstrate their capacity and readiness to counter potential North Korean intimidation and aggression across the full spectrum of possible threats. The main prerequisite here is that this be done in a way that is perceived to be defensive in purpose and does not undermine the two other requirements.

The second area of conflict mitigation entails essentially diplomatic efforts to lessen tensions on the peninsula. The primary focus of such efforts has, to date, been on preventing North Korea from developing nuclear weapons and long-range missiles. This effort, as discussed earlier, has failed on both accounts and it appears highly unlikely that North Korea's weapons programs can be rolled back in a total and fully verifiable manner. Constraining North Korea's production of additional fissile material, capping its operationally ready nuclear arsenal, and limiting its development of long-range missile systems through arms control negotiations should now be the overriding goal. This will require coordinated efforts by the United States and China to both pressure and incentivize North Korea economically to freeze further testing and development using the threat of further punitive sanctions and the promise of development assistance.[39] The immediate goal of this effort would be to buy time and lower the risk of additional provocative developments that increase the likelihood of war. While it would suspend—for the time being, at least—the goal of a denuclearized Korean Peninsula, it would not permanently abandon it. Indeed, a parallel diplomatic process also involving South Korea and Russia should also be pursued to reach a formal end to the Korean War and to bring about a more stable political relationship that will hopefully include formal constraints on nuclear weapons development.

The third area of effort is to encourage the two Koreas to lessen the potential for dangerous incidents to occur and escalate along their common border. The most contentious section in recent years has been the maritime

portion in the Yellow Sea known as the Northern Limit Line.[40] Supporting a formal international adjudication over where this maritime boundary
should be would be consistent with U.S. policy on other territorial disputes,
but this would almost certainly not be welcomed by South Korea or even
North Korea. Instead, a more promising avenue for tension reduction would
appear to be various confidence-building initiatives that facilitate commercial access and exploitation of the area for fishing and possibly joint energy
exploration.[41] Some productive inter-Korean discussions have been made
to reach such agreements, but these have fallen victim to the latest freeze
in inter-Korea relations. Should North-South dialogue resume in the near
future, these kinds of joint economic initiatives should be explored. Establishing a reliable means for emergency communication in a crisis is another
initiative worth pursuing. As discussed previously, the current channels are
unsatisfactory for various reasons. Enlisting the support of China and potentially Russia to maintain a high-level link to North Korea's leadership
probably represents the best option given their shared interest in preventing renewed conflict.

Major Terrorist Attack on U.S. Homeland

Efforts to prevent a major terrorist attack on the United States—especially
one that involves the use of a modified weapon of mass destruction—will
continue to depend on the various homeland security and counterterrorism measures that have been put in place since 9/11 to deter and disrupt
terrorist threats. Continuing these programs without a thorough review,
however, would be unwise. The number of radicalized individuals and organized groups with motive to attack the United States has, as discussed
earlier in this chapter, grown and not diminished. Moreover, their ingenu-
ity in devising new ways to accomplish an attack has not remained static.
Thus it is important to assess whether current homeland security and
counterterrorism measures are evolving to meet the changing threat. Some
programs instituted since 9/11 may now serve little or no purpose, while
others may be deficient or underfunded. Similarly, some efforts may actually be counterproductive to lessening the risk of attack. More specifically,
much criticism has been leveled at what is sometimes characterized as
overly kinetic or militarized counterterrorist measures—essentially, the

use of drones and special forces; some consider these methods to be blunt instruments that create more terrorists than they take off the battlefield.

Such a comprehensive review is beyond the scope of this book, but some basic principles should guide U.S. efforts to prevent mass casualty terrorist attacks against the United States:

- First, denying the means and opportunity for groups and individuals to carry out a *truly catastrophic* attack against the United States should remain the overriding priority. In particular, ongoing bilateral and multilateral efforts to secure nuclear materials and prevent them from being acquired by terrorist groups, smuggled into the United States, and assembled along with other critical materials must be maintained with the same level of urgency.[42] The continued attention given to nuclear terrorism should not obscure, however, other emerging mass casualty threats that could become a greater concern in the future. The weaponization of biological agents (and, in particular, the emerging field of synthetic biology) deserves special attention, even though the scope for preventive action appears distressingly limited given that the barriers to entry are apparently very low.[43]

- Second, the United States should place the overwhelming emphasis of its overseas counterterrorism efforts on groups and individuals with the avowed intent of attacking the homeland and major U.S. allies. This seems an obvious invocation, but it is clear that the United States has over the last decade progressively expanded the scope of its counterterrorism operations to include militant groups with essentially local or regional political agendas, albeit ones antithetical to U.S interests. U.S counterterrorism programs and operations are now routinely carried out in dozens of countries around the world where the putative benefit to lowering the threat to the U.S. homeland is questionable. To the contrary, it might be adding to the risk that leaders and adherents of essentially localized militant groups will target the United States in the future.[44]

- Third, the use of lethal force, including armed drones and special operators, will continue to be necessary against implacable foes that cannot be deterred or dissuaded. There is no easy formula when it comes to such operations other than being constantly mindful of the strategic rather than merely tactical effects of using force. Nonkinetic activities designed to sow doubt and dissension within the leadership of known groups to create schisms and generally destabilize them organizationally should receive just as much effort even if the metrics of success are not as clear.

For the foreseeable future, lethal counterterrorism operations would appear to be necessary in Afghanistan, Pakistan, Syria, Iraq, Yemen, and Somalia where the United States faces groups that have declared their intent—both in words and deeds—to attack the homeland. Given that anti-American sentiment is already high in these places, special care must be taken not to enflame it unnecessarily through actions that appear unilateral and indiscriminate.[45] In particular, the governments of these and other countries bearing the brunt of U.S. counterterrorism operations have to be seen as leading the fight for the common good rather than acquiescing under sufferance to U.S. operational diktats. This requires a delicate balancing act. On the one hand, the United States must make it in these nations' interest to cooperate in counterterrorism operations; on the other hand, it must also be abundantly clear that there would be severe repercussions were an attack on America to emanate from their territories.[46]

Finally, preventing the radicalization and recruitment of *new* adherents to the cause of militant groups wishing to do harm to the United States and its major allies should receive as much attention as killing or capturing *existing* ones. Preventive efforts cannot just be about regularly culling the number of recruits—"mowing the lawn," as Israeli counterterrorism officials often describe this approach; it has to limit the number of "susceptibles."[47] This principle harks back to the question posed by former secretary of defense Donald Rumsfeld in his famous "snowflake" (internal Pentagon memo) on the topic in 2003: "Are we capturing, killing, or deterring and dissuading more terrorists every day than the madrassas and radical clerics are recruiting, training, and deploying against us?"[48] What drives radicalization and recruitment—and thus what might in turn counter it—remains a contested issue. There is compelling evidence, however, that many if not all recruits to terrorist groups are motivated more by personal than political goals—at least in the initial stages. More specifically, it is the attraction of becoming part of a social group, particularly one comprising like-minded individuals, and the sense of kinship or belonging that goes with it rather than the organization's political agenda that motivates many to join.[49] This especially appears to be truer for groups like ISIS than it was for al-Qaeda.[50]

The policy implication of this is that these primary preventive efforts should focus on particular at-risk countries that have historically provided fertile sources of recruitment—more specifically, "diaspora communities in western countries that host large unassimilated, dislocated populations such as the Maghrebis in France; single, unemployed, Islamist men residing in comparatively secular Muslim countries such as Pakistan; restive, youthful populations that feel estranged from the state such as in Saudi Arabia; and prison populations, which, by definition, are home to the socially isolated and dislocated."[51] Ultimately, lessening the sense of marginalization and alienation among this vast pool of potential recruits will require improving their economic prospects, fostering more impartial law enforcement, and building up civil society groups and places of worship that offer support networks, social ties, and mentoring without radical proselytizing—all in all, a huge and long-term undertaking. In the short term, however, these efforts should be complemented by deliberate measures to undermine the social appeal of radical groups by discrediting the motives of their leaders and deromanticizing the notion of life as a recruit. Various programs have been established with this goal in mind under the U.S. Department of Homeland Security's Countering Violent Extremism program. This includes an active effort to counter the use of the Internet for recruitment by delegitimizing the arguments commonly used and also exposing the reality of life as a militant. Reducing the opportunity to recruit individuals in prisons, religious centers, and sports clubs is another common tactic.

The challenge for the United States is that the success of these efforts will rest largely on the commitment and dexterity of others. Its ability to influence and shape related initiatives will be limited, and even trying to support them may be counterproductive. For these reasons, the United States must tread very carefully, at times working indirectly through others and forsaking whatever short-term benefits may accrue from advertising its role.

Escalation of Civil War in Syria

Bringing an end to the Syrian civil war represents a daunting challenge given its multiple dimensions, the deep antipathy among the core protagonists, and the competing interests of their external supporters—notably, Saudi Arabia, Iran, Russia, and the United States.[52] For the foreseeable future, therefore, U.S. conflict mitigation efforts should follow three parallel tracks: humanitarian relief to those displaced from Syria in neighboring countries and, where possible, to those within Syria; military operations to degrade ISIS and contract the area it controls spanning the Syrian-Iraqi border; and diplomatic efforts that aim to bring the fighting to a halt and lay the basis for a durable political settlement, preferably with Syria remaining as a unitary state.

The diplomatic track is clearly the most difficult of the three, but a negotiated solution is not out of the question. Indeed in many respects the interests of the principal protagonists are becoming more aligned. The Assad regime has now regained control over large parts of Syria, including major urban centers, and its continued survival no longer seems in doubt. The war aims of its principal supporters—Iran and Russia—have thus been accomplished, and they are likely keen to want to decrease the economic burden their support has imposed on them; the financial transfers are substantial, especially at a time of depressed energy prices and thus reduced state revenues for both nations. The United States and Saudi Arabia both recognize that whatever opportunity existed to bring about regime change in Damascus has now passed and are also keen to bring the fighting to an end, even if it means accepting that Assad remains in power for the time being. The primary U.S. goal is to defeat ISIS, while for Saudi Arabia the situation in Yemen is now a more pressing concern.[53] The European Union, China, and India can likewise add their weight behind a diplomatic solution given their interests and influence with some of the main actors.

Several cease-fire arrangements have been proposed that all more or less accept the need to maintain Syria as a unitary state with Assad—for the time being, at least—the nominal if not de facto ruler in every part of the country.[54] Discussion of a final political settlement of the war would be deferred in order to establish a robust cease-fire and thus create the conditions for such negotiations to take place. A decentralized power-sharing arrangement would appear to be the most stable outcome over the long term. In the meantime, the principal external powers would use their influence over local actors and combatants to observe the cease-fire, allow humanitarian access, and maintain order in their respective zones of control. In certain areas, such as those hitherto under the control of ISIS, a special UN stabilization force may also be necessary.

Strategic Reversal in Afghanistan

After more than fifteen years of costly military engagement in Afghanistan, U.S. policy makers and the American public in general can be forgiven for wanting to finally end the mission and leave for good. While al-Qaeda has not been definitively vanquished, its use of Afghanistan as a base to mount attacks on the United States—the precipitant for American military intervention in 2001—has effectively been eliminated. The threat posed by the Taliban to the legitimate government of Afghanistan, however, remains and, as discussed earlier in the chapter, is evidently growing. Withdrawing U.S. forces entirely now would almost certainly undermine Afghanistan's unity government led by Ashraf Ghani as it simultaneously endeavors to pursue much-needed economic and anti-corruption reforms while beating back the advances of the Taliban. For the United States to leave in the short term would embolden the Taliban, demoralize the Afghan government, and undermine the will of its army to continue the fight. It would likely also encourage neighboring countries to engage in meddlesome behavior in anticipation of the American departure.[55]

The United States, therefore, should continue to help train and equip the Afghan national security forces while using its air assets and special forces to prevent any easy or significant victory by the Taliban. At the same time, however, the United States should use whatever diplomatic leverage it has to reinvigorate the Afghan reconciliation process. Although this is ultimately an internal matter between the Afghan government and representatives of the Taliban, the United States must encourage other interested parties to play a positive role.[56] These include China, Russia, India, Iran, and other Persian Gulf states, and especially Pakistan, which continues to harbor the Taliban leadership. These states have a significant stake in ensuring that Afghanistan does not collapse altogether given the likely spill-in and spillover consequences for regional security. The challenges to achieving a stable and sustainable peace agreement with the Taliban are formidable but if the main external actors can cajole and incentivize the principal protagonists into making what will unavoidably be painful compromises, a peace agreement remains possible. The engagement of external actors in an Afghan peace process, however, should not stop with its conclusion. Success will ultimately depend on them collectively overseeing and investing in its implementation for many years thereafter.

TIER II PRIORITIES

Several of the contingencies ranked here as Tier II priorities will likely strike some readers as deserving of a higher designation given the potential consequences were they to materialize. To reiterate, however, the relative ranking of contingencies is an aggregated assessment of both their likelihood and their impact.

Renewed Indo-Pakistani War

Historically, America's role in averting war between India and Pakistan has primarily involved being willing and able to manage a serious crisis at the first sign of danger. This remains an important task but the United States should do more to lessen the risk *before* the onset of a crisis and, furthermore, enlist the help of other powers to help constrain the principal protagonists from going to war.

The risk of a serious escalation of tensions between India and Pakistan will clearly be higher when relations between them remain contentious and mistrustful—and vice versa. The ability of the United States to shape this relationship is limited but it can press both India and Pakistan—preferably with the direct support of other countries and organizations that they depend upon like China, Saudi Arabia, the EU, and the World Bank—to normalize their diplomatic and economic interactions. In particular, improving bilateral trade and investment—for example, easing cross-border restrictions, developing special economic zones, and joint infrastructure projects—clearly represents the best way to lessen the underlying risk that any crisis would escalate.[57]

More tailored conflict mitigation efforts should focus on the specific crisis scenarios discussed earlier in this chapter. Again, the options are limited but not nonexistent. The United States should continue to pressure Pakistan to curb the activities of various militant groups like Lashkar-e-Taiba and Jaish-e-Muhammad from attacking Indian targets. Further U.S. and other foreign aid can be conditioned on evidence that progress is being made to this end. Pakistani authorities, particularly the ISI, should also be privately warned that they will be held accountable for any attacks where compelling evidence exists of their complicity. The United States, moreover, can help India thwart militant attacks by sharing intelligence information it may acquire and offering tactical counterterrorism advice that reduces its vulnerability to major attacks likely to prompt military retaliation against Pakistan.[58] As for lessening the risk of a crisis emanating in Kashmir, a final political settlement represents the ultimate solution but it is no closer to being realized. The best the United States can hope to do is to encourage both sides—again with Chinese help—to reduce the likelihood of dangerous incidents along the Line of Control escalating into something more serious. Several confidence-building and crisis communication measures already exist to manage dangerous military interactions but there is scope for more. The same is also true for managing dangerous incidents that occur elsewhere between the two militaries, including reducing the risk of misperceptions arising from the alerting and deployment of their nuclear forces in a crisis.[59]

These conflict mitigation initiatives will only lessen the risk of war, not eliminate it, and thus the United States must be prepared through regularly updated contingency planning to act swiftly in a serious crisis. Options or specific playbooks that match likely scenarios need to be developed in advance so that they can be quickly executed. Besides being prepared to mediate a crisis as before, American Intelligence, Surveillance and Reconnaissance (ISR) assets could also prove helpful to help pierce the fog of crisis and lower the risk of misunderstandings arising from a poor or erroneous appreciation of events. And, just as China needs to be brought into discussions of various North Korean contingencies, so it should also be solicited about managing a potential Indo-Pakistani military crisis.

Escalation of Conflict in Ukraine

U.S. policy options to mitigate the ongoing conflict in Ukraine are often characterized as a choice between two polar opposites: either a vigorous pushback of recent and expected Russian moves toward Ukraine or some form of accommodation of them. The former entails ramping up Western political, economic, and security assistance to Ukraine, including the provision of lethal military aid and support for its eventual accession to NATO and EU membership. The latter option involves seeking Ukrainian acquiescence to the loss of Crimea and possibly even agreeing to the partitioning of the eastern Donbas region. Ukraine would also become a neutral buffer state, much like Finland during the Cold War, aligned with neither Russia nor the West. Both options, however, carry major risks. The former might provoke Russia into taking a more aggressive stance toward Ukraine, which would in turn require the West to either take additional offsetting measures that ultimately lead to a dangerous confrontation with Moscow or, alternatively, lead to a humiliating climb down that damages the credibility of America's political and military commitments in Europe and beyond. The other option, however, could convince Russia that the West is weak and unwilling to stand behind the hitherto bedrock principles of national self-determination and the inviolability of sovereign borders; this could embolden Russia (and conceivably others) into more assertive and destabilizing policies.

For these reasons, therefore, U.S. policy should steer a middle course. It should continue to be supportive of the government of Ukraine and its freedom of action as an independent state while also sending a resolute message to Russia that any intimidation or activities that undermine the Minsk II accords will be countered in a way that harms Russian interests. This would include further political and financial sanctions and conceivably the provision of lethal military aid to Kiev. The United States should also continue to deny the legitimacy of the annexation of Crimea—at least until an internationally sanctioned and supervised plebiscite approves its transfer to Russia. The same is true of the Donbas. At the same time, the West should not rule out the possibility of Ukraine one day joining NATO and the EU should it so choose. As with previous accession processes, this must be conditional on basic internal reforms and other factors. America must also be clear to the Ukrainian government that U.S. support cannot be construed as license to take measures that actively contest Russian annexation of Crimea, undermine the terms of the Minsk II accords, or otherwise provoke Russia.

This middle course remains sensible for as long as Russia abides by the terms of the latest cease-fire and does not seek to enlarge the territory held by the separatists in eastern Ukraine. This should be monitored through the robust presence of the OSCE. Although this arrangement would essentially mean accepting that Russia had succeeded in achieving its short-term objectives, it would not amount to ceding the lost territories in perpetuity. Russia would continue to incur financial and economic costs for its actions and may decide under different leadership in the future to change its current policy. Meanwhile, with European Union and International Monetary Fund assistance Ukraine can steadily improve its standard of living in ways that make reintegration for the citizens of Crimea and the Donbas an attractive option. If, however, Russia chooses to subvert the current cease-fire or carry out other destabilizing actions against Ukraine, then it will be a clear signal to adopt a more active and broad-based strategy to counter Russian aggression. Such a strategy, however, cannot be solely a U.S. response; it must represent a collective international campaign in support of Ukraine.

Violent Disintegration of Iraq

Preventing the violent disintegration of Iraq will depend to a large extent on the success of efforts to defeat ISIS and bring effective governance to the areas it has occupied. If this goes badly, then the challenges confronting Iraq will progressively multiply and likely become insurmountable. Several interlocking issues will have to be managed almost simultaneously to avoid this outcome. Thus, ensuring that Kurdish militia forces are employed in the fight against ISIS in both Syria and Iraq in ways that mollify Turkish concerns and forestall major military intervention is one immediate concern. Addressing the status of the predominantly Kurdish areas of northern Syria in any future peace negotiations must be sensitive to the same concern as well as its implications for fomenting secessionist sentiments in Iraqi Kurdistan. Similarly, the restoration of government control and basic services by Iraqi forces in areas liberated from ISIS must be handled in a way that neither incites local resistance nor inflames anti-Baghdad sentiments in other restive parts of Iraq.

These are all, to say the least, complex challenges that will require great skill to navigate much less resolve. America's capacity to influence the calculations and behavior of the numerous players involved in both the campaign against ISIS and in the Syrian civil war is limited but some leverage exists. The United States has assembled a major multinational coalition for the former, which it can also use to help address post-ISIS concerns. Relations with officials in Iraqi Kurdistan have also been strengthened through various assistance programs. And as a result of its efforts to train and equip Iraqi forces to defeat ISIS, the United States has regained some influence in Baghdad. Although the United States cannot ultimately prevent any of the main parties from doing things that undermine the integrity of Iraq, it can at least try to dissuade them by laying out the likely consequences of such actions. If Iraq's recent past doesn't serve as a warning of what could transpire, then what has happened in neighboring Syria should. Ultimately, fundamental reform of Iraq's 2005 constitution that established the current federal system may be required. A confederal arrangement that gives even greater autonomy to specific regions within the framework of a unified Iraqi state may ultimately be the only viable solution.

Intensification of the War in Yemen

The decision by the Trump administration in early 2017 to provide additional military assistance to the Saudi-led coalition fighting the Houthis in Yemen may also help the U.S. effort to counter a resurgence of AQAP, and by extension reduce the threat that this group poses to U.S. national security. Whatever battlefield success is achieved against AQAP is likely to be short-lived, however, if the larger war in Yemen drags on, creating more resentment over the U.S. role and with it more recruits to the group's cause. Besides urging greater care and restraint in how the coalition prosecutes the campaign in Yemen, the United States should help mobilize humanitarian relief efforts and, more importantly, support a reinvigorated international mediation effort to end the conflict. The UN-led process still represents the best hope for this.

Genocide in South Sudan

The South Sudan peace agreement brokered by IGAD in August 2015 provided for the establishment of the power-sharing Transitional Government of National Unity for a thirty-month period to oversee an ambitious plan for political, security, and economic reforms, including the approval of a permanent constitution and elections for a new government. This plan, which was supported by the United States, collapsed in July 2016 after fighting broke out in Juba between the two major factions. The best hope now for South Sudan is an AU-brokered cease-fire supported by the United States, the UN, and other external actors that can provide for the creation of an international transitional administration to restore order and govern the country until a stable and sustainable indigenous arrangement can take over. In the meantime, the United States should pressure South Sudan's government to allow humanitarian access to reach populations in dire need and support any efforts toward cease-fires to calm the fighting and reduce the suffering.[60]

TIER III PRIORITIES

Two contingencies are categorized here as Tier III priorities though, here again, this could change depending on the perceived trajectory of events in each conflict.

Strategic Reversal in Somalia

The United States is pursuing a two-pronged strategy in Somalia: providing financial and logistical support to AMISOM in its counterinsurgency operations against al-Shabab while also conducting its own counterterrorism operations, including drone strikes and special operations forces raids, against suspected militants.[61] Since 2007 the United States has provided more than $500 million to train and equip AU forces battling al-Shabab; it has also been active in countering the Somali piracy threat off the Horn of Africa. Such efforts will likely suffice while AMISOM and its principal contributors stay committed to the fight, but that cannot be assumed. Building up some Somali national capacity to carry out counterinsurgency missions in support of the federal government in Mogadishu must thus take place or al-Shabab will almost certainly stage a major comeback. The United States should also continue to provide intelligence support to Kenya in its effort to counter potential cross-border attacks. Ultimately, however, efforts to build a viable state in Somalia—whether it be a federal system, as currently envisaged, or a confederal one—has to gain real traction. The hope is that progress in some areas of Somalia will act as compelling examples for other parts to emulate.

Further Fracturing of Libya

Efforts by the UN to broker a government of national unity accepted by all the rival authorities in Libya have proven unsuccessful. With little or no prospect that any of the rival authorities will be able to prevail militarily and claim victory in Libya, the long-term solution remains a negotiated political accommodation. The best that the UN, the EU, and the United States can do in the meantime is to encourage political dialogue and incentivize compromise at the negotiating table primarily through the promise of economic assistance and commercial ties. Egypt, however, may ultimately offer the best hope of brokering a deal since it has the most to gain and arguably the most to lose from the further fracturing of Libya.[62] The UAE, Turkey, and Qatar also have to play a positive role in supporting this process even though their interests do not align perfectly.

* * *

This discussion of short-term conflict mitigation efforts concludes the detailed description of what the three principal elements of a U.S. preventive engagement strategy would mean in practice. As should be clear by now, implementing this strategy requires the United States to partner with others—states, international organizations, civil society groups, and business interests—to achieve its desired objectives. This is unavoidable; the magnitude and complexity of the task is simply too big for America to go it alone. Nor should it. Though preventive engagement is conceived herein primarily for America's benefit, others stand to gain from U.S. efforts to lower the long-term risk of conflict, prevent new crises from arising, and manage ongoing sources of violence. What the United States can do to nurture the support of others and in the process enhance their role as preventive partners is the focus of the next chapter.

7

PARTNERS IN PREVENTION

I think the world that we are living in right now is going to call for us to be engaged—not alone, because we can't do this alone—with many of our friends all over the world. And I don't just mean in a fight but in ways that both respond but also hopefully prevent fights from breaking out.

—MICHAEL MULLEN

F OR MANY AMERICANS, the argument that international collaboration can help the United States avoid costly military commitments in the future will seem either counterintuitive or unpersuasive. To them, such cooperation will actually increase the likelihood that America will become either ensnared in problems of no real concern to its national interest or encumbered by the need to work with others when the stakes are indeed real. Many existing partnerships, moreover, are judged to be one directional in their benefits; most of the costs and risks are borne by the United States, which is seen to get little in return. Indeed, a commonly voiced criticism is that American engagement has perversely incentivized others to do less not more for the common good.

Such beliefs, however, ignore or underestimate not only the general value of international collaboration to the United States but also the more specific benefits of partnerships to the many different areas of preventive engagement discussed in previous chapters.[1]

First, American allies and partners routinely provide valuable—sometimes critical—information and analysis about what is happening in the world. Even with its vast intelligence-gathering apparatus and global diplomatic presence, the United States is not omniscient and has only limited information about certain areas and actors in the world. Other states and international organizations, in contrast, often have better physical access or more reliable sources of information that they will share with the United States. In many cases, nongovernmental organizations (NGOs) and corporations are the principal providers of information, especially when official travel to and within certain countries is difficult for, if not denied to, U.S. officials.

Second, partners can bring additional resources and special—even unique—assets to bear in support of U.S. preventive efforts. These can be financial, military, political, economic, and logistical in nature. In cases where coercive strategies are considered necessary, the contribution of partners may derive more from what they can deny to others rather than what they provide to the United States. This may include access to financial capital, advanced technologies, communications, travel opportunities, and economic markets.

Third, having partners, particularly the support of major multilateral institutions like the United Nations, can be an important source of international legitimacy for U.S. initiatives. This is especially useful when the actions being contemplated are for whatever reason considered politically or legally controversial. Securing the imprimatur of a major international organization can thus provide important political "cover" to the United States and allow it to utilize its resources, including the direct help of its members. Such assistance can in turn help generate and sustain the support of the American public for what might be considered unpalatable actions.

These benefits may not be attainable all the time, and in some cases it may be preferable for the United States to go it alone. As a practical matter, however, these instances are likely to be rare. When it does partner with other states and organizations, it is important that the United States acknowledge the benefits that accrue from cooperation as too often it is the costs or associated constraints of collective action that garner public attention with the result that continued U.S. support can suffer. Where it can, the United States should also deliberately enhance the capacity of other actors to be more effective partners, especially in managing risks that are not necessarily top tier U.S. preventive priorities.

The range of actors that the United States can partner with and benefit from as it pursues the three different levels of preventive engagement strategy is very large indeed. Major and emerging powers, allied countries, global and regional institutions, and myriad civil society organizations and private corporations all have a lesser or greater stake in preventing growing disorder and violent conflict. In some cases the partnerships will be loose and informal; at other times they may be more formal and institutionalized. This chapter will examine how each of these prospective partners can help the United States with its preventive agenda and, where relevant, how the United States can also help them with theirs.

MAJOR AND EMERGING POWERS

Growing geopolitical friction with Russia and China clearly complicates U.S. preventive engagement efforts, but it does not preclude progress. All the major powers, after all, have overlapping interests in important areas of the long-term preventive engagement agenda—notably, promoting global trade and economic development, inhibiting climate change, and keeping weapons of mass destruction out of the hands of nonstate actors and rogue states.[2] Gaining broad consensus and backing for new norms of sovereignty, more representative global institutions, and the continued extension of democratic governance around the world are likely to remain contentious issues, however. Progress in these areas will require persistent and patient effort on the part of the United States to maintain the unity of like-minded states to keep up a common front while widening the circle of new adherents and especially new standard bearers willing to take the lead. Emphasizing that such efforts serve a common rather than a U.S. agenda will be critical.

Several existing international forums can be useful in this regard. The annual G-7 summits among United States, Britain, Canada, France, Germany, Italy, and Japan with other European Union (EU) representatives also usually in attendance, continue to serve as an important coordinating mechanism among the leading Western powers and, moreover, a powerful collective voice on issues of concern.[3] The Organisation for Economic Cooperation and Development (OECD) has likewise proven useful for coordinating and guiding foreign assistance to fragile and conflict-afflicted countries.[4] The relatively new coalition of G-20 nations could also play a useful role in the future given its inclusive membership, but its capacity for collective decision making on anything other than macroeconomic measures has yet to be demonstrated. In the meantime, it is important that the United States nurture strong working relationships with the major emerging regional powers such as Brazil, Indonesia, Turkey, and South Africa to build support for the broad goals of preventive engagement.

The collective management of regional threats to peace and stability by the major powers presents similar challenges, but once again common interests provide the basis for cooperation in some areas. The United States, China, and Russia worked closely together in the Middle East to limit Iran's nuclear ambitions. Less encouraging, however, has been the management of the civil war in Syria, with Russia, China and, to a lesser extent, India, repeatedly blocking efforts by the United States and others in the UN Security Council to pressure the Assad regime to step aside. Should the situation deteriorate further in Syria and the larger Shia-Sunni conflict metastasize in highly destabilizing ways, then Russia, China, and India could conceivably be more open to cooperating with the United States in Middle East diplomacy. Although some in Russia and China may welcome America's continued entanglement in the region as a useful distraction to it being involved in areas of more direct importance to them, both powers and India can no longer view what happens in the Middle East with quite the level of detachment they once did. Besides the threat of transnational terrorism and nuclear proliferation, the geopolitical importance of the Middle East to China, India, and to a lesser extent Russia, is unquestionably growing.

Currently, just over half of China's total oil imports come from the Middle East, with the level of dependence expected to rise to 70 percent by 2020 and still higher thereafter according to the International Energy Agency.[5] India's reliance on Middle Eastern oil is already close to that level.[6] Other trade has increased substantially in recent years; total trade volume between China and the Middle East rose 87 percent between 2005 and 2009, and investment has also steadily grown. For example, China is now the largest investor in Iraq and Iran.[7] Although the importance of the Middle East to China's overall trade balance is still minor, this is not the case for India: nearly one-third of its imports come from the region, and nearly one-fourth of its exports go there.[8]

For similar reasons, the logic of major power cooperation in South Asia is arguably growing stronger. In Afghanistan, China is taking a more active role in facilitating reconciliation talks between the Afghan government and representatives of the Taliban.[9] Besides its interest in preventing Afghanistan (with which it shares a border, albeit a small one) from once again becoming a terrorist safe haven, China has also made substantial commercial investments that it does not want to see threatened by prolonged conflict.[10] The United States has also proposed various regional schemes to enhance Afghanistan regional integration through energy pipelines and power grids with its neighbors. In this respect, the interests of China, India, and the United States are growing more aligned in Afghanistan. In contrast, there is still considerable divergence among the major powers over how to deal with the threat posed by Islamist militant groups in Pakistan and reduce tensions in Kashmir, though here again commercial interests may help ameliorate mistrust over the longer term.

In Africa there are encouraging signs that the major powers can work together to manage instability and conflict. The United States, Britain, and France have long cooperated at the UN and in many peacemaking efforts in Africa. India has also been a long-standing contributor to UN peacekeeping operations on the continent in the Democratic Republic of the Congo, South Sudan, and Liberia, among other places. These traditional players have now been joined by China. In recent years it has helped with mediation efforts in South Sudan, sent small contingents of peacekeepers to the Democratic Republic of the Congo, Liberia, Mali, and South Sudan, and begun to contribute to the African Union's operating budget. As China's investments in Africa grow, its active involvement in conflict prevention and management is likely to increase.

Elsewhere, the prospects for major power cooperation appear less promising. In Europe, neither China nor India appears willing to support U.S. and EU efforts to manage the Ukraine crisis. Indeed, if anything China has provided Russia valuable relief from international opprobrium. For the foreseeable future, America's main partners in managing relations with Russia will be Germany (as a result of its substantial commercial ties), along with Britain and France given their role as permanent members of the UN Security Council. In East Asia, the major powers are aligned on only the importance of maintaining peace and stability on the Korean Peninsula and even on that point there are significant tactical differences between China, Russia, Japan, and the United States on how to manage the growing threat posed by North Korea's nuclear arsenal and development of long-range ballistic missiles. In the South China Sea, however, India could become a more valuable partner in the future as its military deployments and commercial interests in the region grow. The United States has also begun to nurture better relations with other emerging regional powers—notably, Indonesia and Vietnam.

GLOBAL INSTITUTIONS

No other global institution is more important for the U.S. preventive engagement agenda than the UN. Over the long term, the UN will be critical for sustaining broad international support for the norms affecting national sovereignty and the use of force, general access to the global commons as well as numerous critical arms control agreements that regulate weapons of mass destruction and the global arms trade. The UN will also continue to be a champion for global economic development; in particular the Sustainable Development Goals established in 2015 will help mobilize international efforts to improve the quality of life and thus reduce the risk of conflict in many of the fragile states of concern to the United States. And while progress toward limiting global warming will depend for the most part on the commitment of the major carbon dioxide emitters, it will be the UN that will be tasked with upholding the eventual global climate control regime.

* * *

In the medium and short term the UN will continue to be critical to various crisis prevention and conflict mitigation efforts around the world. It has demonstrated on numerous occasions its ability to make important contributions in both areas particularly through low-key "quiet diplomacy." In recent years this has included the following:

- Helping to prevent electoral violence and deter improprieties with technical assistance and monitoring. Recent examples include Mauritania and Sierra Leone (2007); Ghana, Kenya, and the Maldives (2008); Lesotho and Madagascar (2009); the Solomon Islands (2010); and Kenya (2013). International endorsement of election results has also helped improve the winner's legitimacy and lay the basis for economic or diplomatic penalties for fraudulent elections.
- Quiet mediation to dissuade civilian or military leaders from taking extraconstitutional political actions. In 2010 the UN Office for West Africa successfully encouraged military leaders in Guinea, Togo, and Niger to fulfill their commitments to transfer power to civilian authorities. The UN has also lent its substantial experience in crafting new constitutions during tense political transitions, as in Kyrgyzstan following the ouster of its president in 2010.
- Arbitrating border disputes and other boundary issues. For example, the UN Assistance Mission for Iraq helped address contested land rights between Arabs and Kurds in the city of Kirkuk. In 2010 the UN International Court of Justice worked with the UN Office for West Africa to adjudicate a tense border dispute—exacerbated by the discovery of oil deposits—involving Cameroon and Nigeria. The UN Regional Center for Preventive Diplomacy for Central Asia has achieved success in resolving water rights issues in the region.
- Conducting special investigations of potentially destabilizing events in countries where the capacity or impartiality of the government is questioned. Examples include an investigation of human rights violations at the end of the Sri Lankan civil war in 2009, an independent panel of inquiry into the Israeli raid on the flotilla of ships carrying aid to Gaza in 2010, a committee of inquiry into war crimes in Syria since 2011, and the outbreak of violence in Juba, South Sudan in 2016.

Aside from these primarily political missions, the UN can in principle also authorize the deployment of military forces for preventive (as distinct from peacekeeping) missions. It has done so only once, however, with the UN Preventive Deployment Force in the Republic of Macedonia from 1992 to 1999 to deter spillover from the conflicts in Bosnia and Kosovo. Though a useful precedent, it was a rare conjunction of circumstances—unanimity among the nations of the Permanent Five (P5) members of the UN Security Council (China, France, Great Britain, Russia, and the United States), the acquiescence of a small host country, and the availability of UN forces nearby—that made this possible. In contrast, the deployment of peacekeepers in the wake of a cease-fire or negotiated settlement has proven easier to orchestrate.

Several recent high-level UN expert study groups have recommended that the UN put more emphasis on crisis prevention and rapid conflict management.[11] Whether such commitments will be translated into practice remains to be seen, however, especially given the basic structural impediments the UN faces in engaging in early preventive action. In particular, no formal apparatus exists for conflict early warning, as member states will not allow anything they consider to be either unduly intrusive or judgmental of their intentions and actions, especially when it relates to internal matters.[12] This is not likely to change in the foreseeable future, and the UN will thus continue to rely on informal information gathering and sharing mechanisms to anticipate potential sources of instability and conflict—a situation that is hardly ideal or efficient.[13] The greater challenge, however, is generating the necessary consensus for collective action even when there is broad appreciation among UN officials of a potentially serious crisis. The common obstacles highlighted in chapter 3 become even bigger at the UN. Member states and, crucially, members of the P5 typically have different interests at stake and differing assessments of the likelihood of violent conflict. As a result, the UN will typically only swing into action once a crisis has erupted or is about to erupt and even then only when it does not involve one of the major powers or impinge significantly on their interests.[14]

With these limitations in mind, the UN will likely be most helpful to the United States in managing Tier II and especially Tier III priorities. Although the United States already provides considerable financial support to UN peacekeeping operations, it should reallocate some of its budget support toward helping the work of the UN Department of Political Affairs (DPA) for its crisis prevention efforts. In recent years, the DPA has grown more operational, with thirteen field missions around the world engaged in a variety of activities, including electoral assistance, facilitating dialogues through their "good offices," and quiet mediation efforts. In 2006 the DPA created its small Mediation Support Unit of experts and augmented this with its Standby Team, which has been deployed at short notice to backstop specific negotiations. Funding these efforts remains a perennial problem, however, and the DPA remains underresourced given its expanding mandate. More specifically, the UN's capacity to support unanticipated missions remains a serious problem and relies principally on ad hoc donations from individual countries. The United States should support the recommendation of the 2015 High-Level Independent Panel on Peace Operations that the DPA's conflict prevention efforts be part of the regular UN budget rather than supported by voluntary donations.[15]

REGIONAL INSTITUTIONS

Regional institutions can likewise play a valuable role in supporting U.S. preventive engagement in the long, medium, and short terms. Over the long term, they can help reinforce global norms of peaceful behavior among their members, foster political cooperation and economic development, and build mutual trust and confidence through greater functional cooperation on a wide range of issues. In the short to medium term, some regional and subregional organizations will also be helpful for crisis prevention and conflict mitigation since they have already developed capacities and competences in specific areas for this purpose. For others, however, such a role still remains largely aspirational. Before turning to how regional organizations can help with the specific preventive priorities of the United States, it is useful to give a general overview of what they do now in the main areas of concern.

In Europe, NATO represents the most important regional organization for the United States given its primus inter pares standing. Since the end of the Cold War, NATO has progressively expanded its traditional collective mission to incorporate a broader conception of its role. Thus, the 2010 Strategic Concept declared crisis management to be one of its three essential core tasks whereby NATO "has a unique and robust set of political and military capabilities to address the full spectrum of crises—before, during and after conflicts. NATO will actively employ an appropriate mix of those political and military tools to help manage developing crises that have the potential to affect Alliance security, before they escalate into conflicts; to stop ongoing conflicts where they affect Alliance security; and to help consolidate stability in post-conflict situations where that contributes to Euro-Atlantic security."[16] In practical terms, however, NATO's contribution to conflict prevention still mostly derives from the deterrent effect of its collective defense capabilities, though it has tried in various ways to also reassure Russia through various initiatives.[17] These include establishing a high-level consultative body and pledging not to station NATO military forces permanently on the territory of new members close to Russia.[18] In comparison to NATO, the EU plays a much broader conflict prevention role through various elements of its Common Foreign and Security Policy (CFSP).[19] After the European Council adopted the Program on the Prevention of Violent Conflict in Göteborg in 2001, the EU established a variety of special initiatives and institutional mechanisms for this purpose; these range from foreign assistance programs intended to reduce the underlying risk of conflict through economic development and institution building in specific countries (particularly in Africa) to the Instrument for Stability, a short-term emergency assistance program for states in crisis. The EU also maintains its own watch list of countries at risk of violent conflict. Following the adoption of the European Security and Defense Policy (ESDP) in 2003, the EU's capacity to deploy political and military missions for crisis management purposes has steadily grown,[20] and to date there have been thirty-four crisis management operations, with sixteen ongoing as of March 2016.[21] These include police missions in Afghanistan, Bosnia and Herzegovina, Kosovo, and the Palestinian territories; rule of law missions in Kosovo and Iraq; and a monitoring mission in Georgia.[22] All have been led by EU special representatives who can be serve double duty to oversee both military and diplomatic missions.

Reforms introduced by the 2009 Lisbon Treaty are designed, in theory, to improve the EU's crisis responsiveness abilities and institutional flexibility.[23] The high representative for foreign and security policy (who also serves as vice president of the European Commission) now directs the European External Action Service. The Lisbon Treaty provides the high representative with considerable latitude to initiate foreign policy proposals; set the agenda of important EU bodies, including the Foreign Affairs Council (which the high representative would chair); and convoke "extraordinary meetings [of the EU council] on emergency matters."[24] The Lisbon Treaty has also established new procedures to provide "rapid access" to the EU budget and create a start-up fund of member state contributions outside the EU budget. Both procedures can finance "urgent initiatives" under the CFSP and, in particular, preparatory activities for ESDP missions. Decisions can be made by qualified majority voting, with the high representative authorized to disperse the funds. Yet as the fragmented responses to the democratic uprisings in North Africa and the Middle East demonstrated, member states still tend to act independently and sometimes at odds with the consensus positions agreed to by the EU in Brussels.

In parallel with the development of a civilian expeditionary capability, the EU has also developed rapidly deployable military forces. Two "battle groups" are theoretically capable of deployment on five to ten days' notice for conflict prevention missions (preventive deployments, embargoes, counterproliferation, and joint disarmament operations).[25] To date, six military ESDP missions have been deployed to Ukraine, Georgia, Kosovo, Libya, Mali, and Somalia.[26] Assuming Britain does eventually withdraw from the EU, many of these initiatives will likely be affected, though by how much is hard to determine. Brexit, however, is unlikely to cause the EU to become less committed to playing an active role in international conflict management or being a valuable partner to the United States. Moreover, it is more than likely that Britain will continue to participate in many EU conflict prevention initiatives without being formally bound by them.

Besides the EU, there is also the Organization for Security and Cooperation in Europe (OSCE), which has a more inclusive membership, with fifty-six states spanning a region "from Vancouver to Vladivostok." In addition to monitoring conventional force levels and activities among member states, the OSCE helps democratic institution building, promotes and safeguards minority rights, monitors elections, helps secure sensitive borders, and assists with security sector reforms. As an instrument for crisis prevention and crisis management, however, the OSCE has significant structural deficiencies that have hindered it from playing a significant role despite its declared intentions and array of diplomatic mechanisms.[27] In particular, the need for unanimity among member states has stymied rapid collective action on sensitive matters, as in the August 2008 crisis in Georgia, where Russia effectively blocked the OSCE from playing an active role, and in the delayed response to deadly ethnic riots in southern Kyrgyzstan in July 2010 and the Russian annexation of Crimea in 2014.[28] Recommendations amending the organization's decision-making rules to allow for greater initiative on the part of senior officials in crisis circumstances have been regularly rejected—most often by Russia.[29]

In Latin America, the Organization of American States (OAS) has made important strides toward playing a more active preventive role, even though its charter does not formally mandate it to do so. Its principal contributions to regional peace and stability relate to the promotion of democratic principles (through the Inter-American Democratic Charter and the Resolution 1080 mechanism that allows for violators to be condemned and isolated) and human rights (primarily through the Inter-American Commission on Human Rights [IACHR], which regularly issues reports of abuses).[30] Both activities exert a powerful normative influence throughout a region long blighted with coups and other extraconstitutional crises. Moreover, after being moribund for most of the Cold War, the OAS's various international dispute settlement mechanisms (principally the secretary-general's "good offices" and use of special missions) have also successfully mediated territorial disputes involving Guatemala and Belize, Honduras and Nicaragua, and Guyana and Suriname.

OAS members, however, remain protective of the principle of nonintervention in internal disputes without host nation consent. Thus, not surprisingly, OAS officials have been ambivalent in their support of norms like the Responsibility to Protect (R2P) principle and, at times, even the concept of *conflict prevention*, preferring instead the more consensual-sounding term *peacebuilding*. The OAS's role in managing various ongoing internal conflicts in Latin America has consequently been relatively modest. Currently the organization has some analytical capabilities to warn of both internal instability and interstate disputes, but unless a member state appeals to the OAS Permanent Council and there is consensus to act, such warnings go unheeded.[31] Even when the will to act exists, the OAS's resources for mediation missions are limited.[32] Should peaceful preventive measures fail, the organization has no deployable military or police forces within the region, though member states contribute to UN peacekeeping and special political missions. How the OAS evolves to fill some of these gaps will also depend on the development of a rival regional organization, the Union of South American Nations, which excludes the United States. Some members see this organization as becoming the premier political mechanism to resolve disputes, as demonstrated during the 2010 Colombian-Venezuelan crisis.

In East Asia, the Association of Southeast Asian Nations (ASEAN) adheres to the same core principles as the OAS with regard to nonintervention and consensus-based decision making. These principles are enshrined in the organization's Treaty of Amity and Cooperation and the 2008 ASEAN Charter, which commits signatories to settle their disputes peacefully, including refraining from threats to use force;[33] in 2009 the United States became a signatory. Unlike the OAS, however, ASEAN has done little to promote or uphold other normative principles conducive to stable peace—notably, democratic governance and human rights. It has no electoral assistance or monitoring capabilities and few dispute resolution mechanisms or dedicated resources to facilitate mediation. The ASEAN Charter allows disputants to request the chair or secretary-general to act "in an ex officio capacity, to provide good offices, conciliation or mediation," but on the rare occasions when this mechanism has been invoked, for example to resolve the Thai-Cambodian border dispute, it has not fared well.[34] Similarly, plans to develop a rudimentary conflict early warning system as part of an expanded operational role for the secretary-general and the ASEAN Secretariat have also not been implemented.[35] In contrast, ASEAN's efforts to develop a code of conduct to manage maritime disputes are beginning to bear fruit.[36]

Elsewhere in Asia the situation is even less developed. The South Asia Association for Regional Cooperation has no pretensions of playing a conflict prevention role other than by providing a regular venue for state leaders on the subcontinent to discuss their differences. The same is true for the Shanghai Cooperation Organization of central Asian states, though it is more security oriented in promoting cooperation on counterterrorism, border security, and even collective military action. As for Northeast Asia, no dedicated subregional organization exists, nor does one look likely to emerge anytime soon.[37]

In Africa, institutional development has improved markedly in recent years, although it still falls short in important areas. In addition to the continent-wide African Union (AU), multiple subregional organizations—notably, the Economic Community of West African States (ECOWAS), the South African Development Community, the Inter-Governmental Authority on Development, and the Economic Community of Central African States (ECCAS)—have all committed themselves to the goal of conflict prevention and have initiated related programs. The AU has increasingly emphasized norms that actively promote peace and stability in Africa and also developed a set of institutional arrangements known as the African Peace and Security Architecture (APSA). Whereas the AU's predecessor, the Organization of African Unity, was founded on principles of mutual noninterference among African states that had just become independent from colonial rule, the AU has from its inception emphasized that it would not be indifferent to the consequences of humanitarian disasters and violent conflict within the sovereign territory of its member states.[38] Indeed, it is the only regional organization to explicitly adopt such a formal position. Thus, while the Constitutive Act of the African Union still expresses respect for national borders and the sovereign right of noninterference by any member state in the internal affairs of another, it also affirms "the right of the Union to intervene in a Member State pursuant to a decision of the Assembly in respect of grave circumstances, namely war crimes, genocide and crimes against humanity" as well as "the right of Member States to request intervention from the Union in order to restore peace and security."[39]

The AU has also strongly endorsed the norm against unconstitutional political change in Africa, even permitting its Peace and Security Council the right to call on members to impose sanctions.[40] To date, the AU has called for sanctions three times: in May 2009 it sanctioned Eritrea for its assistance to Islamic militants fighting to overthrow the Transitional Federal Government in Somalia, thus causing Eritrea to withdraw from the AU; in October 2009 it sanctioned the military junta that took power in a coup in Guinea; and it barred the Ivory Coast from participating in the organization from December 2010 until April 2011, during an internal power struggle when then president Laurent Gbagbo refused to step down after losing an election. Acting independently, or in conjunction with the AU, several African subregional organizations can also impose sanctions, with ECOWAS consistently being the most assertive at doing so.

To buttress the AU's overall conflict prevention goals, various institutional capacities are being developed. The Continental Early Warning System was created in 2002 to report potential threats to the chairperson of the Commission of the African Union and, in turn, the organization's Peace and Security Council so that it can recommend timely action.[41] The leading subregional organizations have also begun developing conflict early warning systems of varying degrees of effectiveness.[42] The AU has two primary dispute resolution mechanisms for conflict risk reduction and crisis mitigation. The first is the Panel of the Wise, consisting of five respected African leaders—one from each subregional organization—with a broad mandate to advise and support the Peace and Security Council and the chairperson of the commission.[43] The panel has undertaken five fact-finding and mediations missions and played an active role in the successful mission in Kenya in 2008. The second mechanism comprises ad hoc high-level groups that have a poor track record, with failed missions in Darfur in 2009 and Libya in 2011.

Finally, in 2003 the AU endorsed the concept of the African Standby Force to conduct a range of military missions, including "observation and monitoring . . . peace support . . . [and] intervention in a Member State in respect of grave circumstances [and] preventive deployment" when mandated by the Peace and Security Council within the framework of the UN Charter.[44] The Standby Force aspires to include five multidisciplinary brigades—one provided by each African subregional organization—and to be able to deploy anywhere on the continent within thirty days for peacekeeping missions, ninety days for complex peacekeeping operations, and fourteen days for interventions "in genocide situations where the international community does not act promptly."[45]

Although these considerable strides toward operationalizing preventive action in Africa should be lauded, their practical effect has been minimal. Even with the principle of nonindifference to political instability and violent conflict within member states enshrined in the AU's constitutive act, member states have not embraced the R2P principle, and this is a stance that will likely harden in light of the controversial 2011 Libya intervention. Moreover, the AU's ability to implement its peace and security norms is hampered by the dynamics of the organization, which operates by consensus. Some African leaders pay lip service to AU principles while actively blocking the more interventionist inclinations of others. Meanwhile, the new capacity-building initiatives are struggling to gain traction. The under-resourced Panel of the Wise is often ignored by the Commission of the African Union or the Peace and Security Council. In light of its low profile and competing bodies—such as the AU high-level groups and the Elders, an organization formed by Nelson Mandela—there is deep concern within the AU that the panel will become irrelevant.[46]

Similarly, the AU's Military Staff Committee, which was established to manage and implement the goals set for the Standby Force, has made some initial steps in developing a common doctrine and guidelines for training and evaluation, but it has limited institutional capacity to do strategic planning, deploy soldiers, or conduct peacekeeping operations. Most important, because the Standby Force cannot yet deploy as a unit, AU member states continue to provide the vast majority of the twenty-three thousand peacekeepers and police officers supporting the joint AU/UN hybrid operation in Darfur and the ten thousand African soldiers and police deployed in support of the AU mission in Somalia.

Compared to the other regions, the Middle East remains the most underdeveloped institutionally. Other than its rhetorical commitment to the peaceful resolution of disputes, some capacity for mediation, and a venue for dialogue among leaders in the Middle East, the Arab League plays virtually no significant role. Indeed, the league's well-known March 2011 resolution on Libya requested that "the UN Security Council fulfill its responsibilities" but made no requirements of its own member states to attempt to resolve the conflict in Libya.[47] The Gulf Cooperation Council (GCC) has historically been used only for functional collaboration that indirectly benefited regional stability.[48] A Saudi proposal in 2011 to transform the GCC into the "Gulf Union" to counterbalance Iran's activism in the region was met with only lukewarm support. Since then, divisions among members of the GCC, particularly over the 2015 Saudi-led military intervention in Yemen and in 2017 over Qatar's support for various Islamist groups, have provided further evidence of a basic lack of unity within the organization.

American capacity to shape the actions of these various regional bodies is obviously limited; the United States is only a full-fledged member of three of them—NATO, the OSCE, and OAS—yet in numerous ways it can indirectly influence their work and profit from their actions. In Europe, the EU and to a lesser extent the OSCE will be important for managing Russia and the uncertain situation in many parts of eastern Europe. The EU is both a major market and source of economic assistance that provides it with considerable leverage in negotiations over Ukraine and elsewhere. The same is just as true for managing instability in the Middle East and North Africa, where it has substantial investments and donor arrangements. The EU will also remain a major player in the implementation of the nuclear agreement with Iran, with which it also has diplomatic relations—unlike the United States. Beyond Europe's immediate periphery, the EU has burgeoning trade and aid relationships with many countries in Africa while also being involved in various diplomatic initiatives of importance to the United States. As a major trading partner with China, India, and other countries in the Asia-Pacific region, the EU cannot be easily ignored when it makes its preferences known regarding various political disputes.

For how long the EU can stay an effective partner of the United States will depend on how long it remains a cohesive and energetic organization. Various crises in recent years—the Greek debt bailout, the massive influx of migrants and refugees in 2015, and the UK Brexit vote in 2016 to leave the union, to name the most prominent—has dented confidence in the EU and raised uncomfortable questions about its long-term vitality. In particular, if Brexit proceeds, other countries could conceivably follow, and this would at the very least be a huge distraction for the EU and possibly even trigger an existential crisis.

In East Asia the primary conduits for exerting U.S influence and partnering with regional powers will continue to be its bilateral security alliances.

The United States, however, has become more engaged in recent years in various ASEAN forums, and it will press ASEAN to play a more active role in helping to defuse tensions in the South China Sea as well as other conflicts in the region. Its capacity to influence the body is limited but growing. In June 2010 the United States became the first non-ASEAN country to open a dedicated mission, placing an ambassador in residence the following year. In 2013 the first high-level US-ASEAN summit was held, and the United States has begun to lead regional discussion on a wide range of issues. Of particular interest are ASEAN's efforts to develop a code of conduct for activities in the South China Sea.

A similar evolution has characterized the United States' relationship with African institutions. In 2006 the United States established a permanent mission to the AU and has since contributed to its work. The United States has assisted the African Standby Force as it works to become fully operational. The U.S. government has also contributed resources and expertise to the ongoing development of a regional maritime strategy and to improving the medical planning capability of the AU's Peace Support Operations Division. The United States has also provided much-needed communication equipment and training to support the AU's goal of developing a continental communication architecture that includes regional standby brigades and ongoing peace support operations. Training is a significant component of U.S. support to the AU's peace and security initiatives—notably, in the areas of strategic communications, conflict monitoring and analysis, and military planning. Since 2007 the United States has provided support valued at $258 million to the African Union Mission in Somalia, making it the largest individual financial contributor to AU peacekeeping operations in Somalia.

The United States and the AU share a commitment to democratic principles, including free and fair elections, just transitions of power, and sound governance. To support these goals, the U.S. Agency for International Development (USAID) works with the AU's Democracy and Electoral Assistance Unit to improve election processes across Africa. USAID also assists the AU to promote the African Charter on Democracy, Elections, and Governance. More broadly, the U.S. government looks to the AU as a respected voice on the continent that builds consensus on African issues among member states and stakeholders. In this context, the United States and the AU engage in substantive and frank dialogue about how to address such issues as unconstitutional changes in government in Africa and the threat posed by violent extremism.

CIVIL SOCIETY ORGANIZATIONS

Since the end of the Cold War civil society organizations (CSOs) have begun to play an increasingly important role in crisis prevention and peacebuilding. Although there is no generally accepted definition of a CSO, they are typically viewed as entities that are independent of government control and not organized for profit seeking.[49] This covers an extraordinarily diverse set of actors, ranging from community organizations, professional associations, and special interest groups to faith-based entities, advocacy organizations, think tanks, charities, and foundations, among others.[50] Some have relatively narrow goals confined to a specific locale, while others transcend borders with global agendas. Some are partisan and self-interested; others claim to function for the common good, such as religious organizations. And some are policy focused, while others are operationally oriented.

In very broad terms, CSOs are helpful as sources of information, for the resources they can deploy (people, funding, and organization), and for their ability to access far-reaching networks of other like-minded groups. In comparison to state-controlled government entities, CSOs can also be easier to mobilize and more operationally agile. At the same time, however, they clearly do not have the resources of states, their base of support can be quite narrow, and their ability to sustain themselves operationally is often limited. In some contexts, governments or other entities target CSOs because their work may criticize, counter, and drum up support against policies on certain issues. On balance, however, CSOs collectively represent a powerful set of potential partners for both short- and long-term preventive engagement.

In the short term, CSOs can be useful for countering violent extremism—in particular, by making communities especially susceptible to terrorist recruitment more resistant and resilient to radicalization. For example, community organizations and leaders of faith-based groups are now widely viewed as being on the front lines of public messaging campaigns to delegitimize militant narratives and also offer more compelling alternatives. In areas at risk of instability and conflict, these and other kinds of CSOs can provide valuable early warning of a deteriorating situation for crisis prevention. In recent years, a variety of research groups have also sprung up to provide conflict early warning based on data mining of social media and other publically available information. Some CSOs now routinely use commercial reconnaissance satellites to monitor at-risk areas for early warning purposes and to mobilize their constituencies.[51] Similarly, a burgeoning group of U.S. research and analysis organizations provide helpful policy advice to the U.S. government for managing such risks. Meanwhile, CSOs are becoming increasingly active in crisis prevention around the world; this includes monitoring elections for fraud and abuse, facilitating dialogue between groups in conflict, advocating for nonviolent solutions, and offering their services in mediation efforts on the part of international organizations.

Over the long term, CSOs should prove helpful—even critical—to advancing most of the U.S. preventive engagement goals—notably, helping to defend basic international norms, generating public support for new global regulatory agreements, promoting free trade and sustainable development, and continuing to push for democracy and human rights around the world. A vibrant civil society contributes to the defining pillars of good governance: strengthening institutions, demanding rule of law, furthering freedom of speech and expression, encouraging inclusion, and serving as a watchdog for government accountability, among other aspects.

THE BUSINESS SECTOR

Last but by no means least, corporate actors can contribute in important ways to the U.S. preventive engagement agenda. Businesses play a largely underappreciated role in promoting peace by simply being active in the marketplace. In furthering international trade and economic development, they clearly help reduce known risk factors for both interstate and intrastate conflict. They provide employment, encourage capital formation, and develop a direct stake in the creation of stable, functioning societies. Businesses, furthermore, help in the vital process of state building by creating a stable tax base for public revenues and advocating for infrastructure, education, health care, and other essential services. Yet left unregulated and supervised, corporate actors can also undermine political stability and increase the risk of conflict through corrupt practices, discriminatory employment, exploitative wages, and environmentally unsustainable development.

Besides the indirect and mostly long-term impact of corporate actors, specific business sectors often play a more visible role in crisis prevention and mitigation efforts. The extraction industries (for oil, gas, minerals, etc.) are now part of a global regulatory effort to prevent the diversion of profits into illegal and potentially destabilizing activities. Likewise, the activities of arms manufacturing industries as well as private security services are often restricted through sanctions regimes and other controls in support of diplomatic efforts toward a specific country or region. Similarly, the banking, insurance, commercial transportation, and travel industries, among others, are among the first to be involved in coercive efforts to pressure countries to desist from engaging in destabilizing activities. The same actors are also at the forefront of efforts to restrict the activities of armed nonstate actors, including those involved in organized crime.

Though clearly important in so many areas relevant to the preventive engagement agenda, the United States lacks a systematic approach for engaging corporate actors in various diplomatic initiatives. Instead, to the extent they are actively engaged, it is largely on an ad hoc basis.

* * *

How well the United States is able to encourage and harness the multitude of actors able to support preventive engagement across the three levels of activity will ultimately depend on the commitment of policy makers in Washington and in particular whether the relevant agencies and departments within the federal bureaucracy are appropriately oriented toward this end. In other words, preventive engagement must begin at home. What this should entail is the subject of the next and final chapter.

8

REORIENTING THE UNITED STATES

Neither a wise man nor a brave man lies down on the tracks of history to wait for the train of the future to run over him.

—DWIGHT D. EISENHOWER

A persistent and repeated error through the ages has been the failure to understand the preservation of peace requires active effort, planning, the expenditure of resources, and sacrifice, just as war does.

—DONALD KAGAN

THERE ARE GOOD reasons to be concerned about the direction of current global trends. Tensions have been steadily increasing among the major powers while several regions have grown more unstable and violent. New sources of insecurity and areas of rivalry are also emerging as a result of the breakdown of order in several countries, the rise of dangerous nonstate actors, and the acquisition of advanced military capabilities by regional powers, to name just some of the leading causes. At the same time, faith in the effectiveness of international institutions to mediate cooperative solutions to these challenges is seemingly waning. In short, the international order that has prevailed for many decades is fraying with potentially profound consequences for global peace and security.[1]

How the United States responds to these developments will, to a large extent, determine the direction the world takes over the next several decades if not the rest of the century. No other country has more power and influence to shape the course of events—certainly with the help of like-minded partners. Whether the United States will choose to play such a role in the coming years is a matter of growing concern, however. With his

"America First" pronouncements, President Trump has articulated a very narrow, self-interested, and short-sighted vision of how the United States will henceforth interact with world. By often openly expressing doubts about the continued value of many of America's long-standing security and trading arrangements, he has also sowed seeds of doubt about whether the United States remains committed to promoting international peace and prosperity. These actions along with the Trump administration's decision to drastically reduce funding for United Nations, withdraw from the Trans-Pacific Partnership trade deal, and no longer abide by the Paris accord to curb global warming, all signal a fundamental retrenchment of U.S. global engagement.

All of this amounts to a very unwise turn in U.S. foreign and security policy, which over time will surely have serious implications for America's influence in the world and, moreover, the future of the liberal international order it has worked so long and hard to create. Doubtless many Americans will continue to believe that what happens in distant areas of the world is of little concern to them or that the United States can get along just fine by itself. Possessing bountiful resources and blessed with friendly nations to the north and south and large oceans to the east and west, foreign threats can be kept at bay. Such sentiments are understandable, but they are fundamentally misguided. Challenges to international order cannot be ignored or wished away in the belief that the United States will remain unaffected—certainly not for very long. Geographical distance and self-sufficiency in certain areas can be beneficial, but for some potential threats—nuclear-armed ballistic missiles, cyberattacks, or pandemic outbreaks, to name just some—it is irrelevant. America's economic prosperity, moreover, is deeply entwined with the fortunes of many other countries, near and far. That could change should the forces of deglobalization gather momentum, but it clearly makes no sense to welcome that eventuality in the interests of greater U.S. autonomy.

Building up U.S. defenses and military capabilities to deter potential adversaries and dissuade others from doing things inimical to U.S. interests, as the Trump administration has declared its intention to do, will not suffice either. This may work for some threats, but not all. As we know from previous experience, America's military preponderance provides no such as-

224

surances. Similarly, developing more discrete and less costly coercive instruments—whether military or economic in form—to avoid the dilemmas of deeper and riskier entanglements can buy time and defer difficult decisions, but they are unlikely to provide long-term solutions. For all these reasons, this book has argued that the United States should adopt a deliberate preventive strategy to manage the risks of a more turbulent world before they manifest themselves in ways that confront America with difficult and potentially very costly choices about the use of military force to maintain international order. As discussed above, this requires sustaining over the long term various risk reduction initiatives to promote strategic stability among the major powers, bolster the norms and institutions that enhance world order, boost international trade, stimulate global development, foster democratic governance, and inhibit the effects of climate change. In the medium term it requires taking active measures to avert several crises that could very easily trigger U.S. military engagement in East Asia, eastern Europe, the Middle East, and elsewhere. And in the short term, the United States should manage various current sources of instability and conflict before they pose a greater risk.

Preventive engagement will only be possible, however, if the leadership of the United States—the president, his most senior advisors, and members of Congress—accepts its core imperative and fundamentally reorients the way in which the country approaches the management of foreign affairs and, more specifically, the risk of growing international disorder. Without a clear commitment by senior officials to the rationale and goals of preventive engagement, the rest of the government is unlikely to respond in the required fashion. Simply declaring preventive engagement to be the new national security strategy of the United States will not suffice, therefore. In effect, a strong and unambiguous signal needs to be transmitted throughout the U.S. government that "business as usual" is not sufficient or acceptable.

The good news is that wholesale institutional reform is not required. While there is merit to the argument that the United States continues to rely on national security structures and practices that were established to manage a very different world, replacing them with something entirely new is neither likely nor very practical. Short of another major national crisis that exposes critical failings in the current system and would in turn provide the necessary impetus for real reform, it is unrealistic to expect any administration to expend precious political capital on such an endeavor. What is needed instead is a steady reorientation of existing institutions and processes to make the United States less short-sighted and reactive to events and more forward-looking and forward-acting in minimizing current and potential risks to the nation.

This will only happen if those tasked with implementing preventive engagement receive the necessary resources, particularly budgetary support. The good news again is that a massive new infusion of funding is not required. Rather, existing funds should be progressively redirected and repurposed to support the strategy. Each of these steps to reorient the United States will be discussed in turn below.

REORIENTING U.S. LEADERSHIP

Since at least the end of the Cold War, every U.S. president has at some point declared the importance to the United States of preventing deadly conflict.[2] Such statements of intent have, however, usually come in the aftermath of a particularly costly humanitarian tragedy that was viewed in hindsight to have been eminently avoidable. The Obama administration was different in that from the outset it emphasized its intention to think and act more proactively. Very soon after taking office, for example, Vice President Joe Biden, in a speech clearly designed to distinguish the new administration's approach from that of its predecessor, openly declared, "We'll strive to act preventively, not preemptively, to avoid whenever possible or wherever possible the choice of last resort between the risks of war and the dangers of inaction. We'll draw upon all the elements of our power— military and diplomatic; intelligence and law enforcement; economic and cultural—to stop crises from occurring before they are in front of us."[3] Similarly, General James L. Jones, in his first speech as Obama's national security adviser, echoed many of the same intentions, saying, "We need to be able to anticipate the kind of operations that we should be thinking about six months to a year ahead of time in different parts of the world to bring the necessary elements of national and international power to bear to prevent future Iraqs and future Afghanistans."[4] And in a major speech to the Veterans of Foreign Wars just seven months into his first term, President Obama also declared that "one of the best ways to lead our troops wisely is to prevent the conflicts that cost American blood and treasure tomorrow."[5]

These statements were also backed up by some notable initiatives. In particular, the first Quadrennial Diplomacy and Development Review (QDDR) in 2010—a joint State Department and U.S. Agency for International Development (USAID) assessment of future goals and policies—declared conflict prevention to be a "core foreign policy goal" of the United States and established a Bureau for Conflict and Stabilization Operations (CSO) toward this end at the State Department. Besides enjoying the support and imprimatur of the secretary of state as well as regular funding from Congress—something its predecessor, the Office of the Coordinator for Reconstruction and Stabilization (S/CRS), never received—CSO was also clustered with several other bureaus under the nominal charge of a new undersecretary for civilian security, democracy, and human rights with the intention of giving it more institutional standing within the State Department.

In April 2012 the White House also stood up the Atrocities Prevention Board (APB) following the promulgation of Presidential Study Directive 10, which unambiguously declared "preventing mass atrocities and genocide" to be "a core national security interest and a core moral responsibility of the United States."[6] The APB—essentially an interagency committee—was tasked with developing whole-of-government responses to warnings of potential mass atrocities. To support its work, the intelligence community was directed to conduct a National Intelligence Estimate of the threat of mass atrocities and provide the APB more in-depth assessments on a regular basis. At the same time, the director of national intelligence was also instructed to make such assessments a regular part of his annual worldwide threat briefing to Congress. Various procedures, moreover, were instituted to permit relevant warning information to reach the highest levels of the U.S. government without delay.

By and large, however, the early emphasis given to preventive action tapered off as the Obama administration became increasingly consumed with managing a succession of crises and conflicts. The new organizational entities also struggled to gain traction. CSO found it difficult to gain the respect and support of other bureaus at the State Department, much less other departments in the interagency process. Multiple efforts to reinvent CSO's mission to demonstrate that it added value to U.S. conflict prevention and stabilization efforts only served to reinforce the general perception that it was a weak and marginal player. The APB fared better, as least initially, but once it became clear that it was not going to exert much influence in how the United States responded to mass atrocities in Syria and elsewhere, its institutional standing inevitably waned and never recovered. With no dedicated resources of its own or real authority to direct others, the role of the APB has inevitably remained modest.[7]

The lesson here is that public declarations of interest in supporting preventive action have to be backed up with a much stronger *demonstration of intent* to make this a core operating principle. A good place to start is with the formulation of the National Security Strategy of the United States. Since the 1986 Goldwater-Nichols Act, the White House is obliged to produce a National Security Strategy (NSS) on a regular basis. In theory at least, the NSS provides the overarching strategic framework for the National Military Strategy of the United States, which is produced every two years by the chairman of the Joint Chiefs of Staff for the secretary of defense and to provide general guidance for the Pentagon's Quadrennial Defense Review and the QDDR. The opportunity exists, therefore, to use the NSS process to lay out the broad goals and principal elements of a preventive engagement strategy in a coherent manner.

The strategy laid out in the NSS can in turn be reinforced not only by the various departmental strategy and quadrennial planning documents but also in regular interactions with Congress, whether it be testifying to various committees or submitting budget requests. Just as important, however, will be the explicit and implicit demands that the White House and senior leaders make of the rest of the government on a daily basis. This is especially true of intelligence requests and policy planning requirements. As several current and former U.S intelligence officials have pointed out, the demand signal is critical. If there is seemingly little interest or appetite from the White House and other senior policy makers for what is often classified as strategic analysis (as distinct from current intelligence), then there is little incentive to provide it to them.[8] The same is just as true for policy planning. Current and former government officials have also repeatedly acknowledged that only when there is a special request to focus on a medium- to long-term question and time is carved out of their daily schedule to do so will attention be devoted to discussing such issues. Otherwise, what is in the inbox drives policy.

REORIENTING THE U.S. BUREAUCRACY

Reorienting the U.S. bureaucracy will not necessitate major institutional changes but it must still be carried out in a comprehensive and systemic fashion. So often government reforms consist of haphazard and piecemeal efforts that almost invariably fail. A common tactic, for example, is to give specific individuals new powers to oversee or coordinate the work of others in a policy area considered either underserved or worthy of greater priority. Another is to establish a new office or program to perform the desired task, which typically ends up as either independent entities or being grafted onto an existing department. Thus have many White House "czars" or "special coordinators" been born and numerous bureaucratic "add-ons" emerged on the "org chart" of official Washington. These initiatives rarely work or last, usually because the relevant individuals or bureaus do not receive the necessary authorities and appropriate resources to match their nominal responsibilities. As a result, they become stymied and marginalized—bureaucratically orphaned—by the offices and agencies that they are supposed to manage or coordinate.

The process of bureaucratic reorientation proposed here applies to four areas critical to preventive engagement:

- Fostering preventive foresight and risk assessment
- Promoting preventive policy planning

- Enhancing crisis preparedness and management
- Resourcing preventive engagement

FOSTERING PREVENTIVE FORESIGHT AND RISK ASSESSMENT

The United States currently spends over $70 billion per year on intelligence gathering and analysis to provide early warning and day-to-day assistance for senior policy makers and to support the operational needs of U.S. field commanders.[9] Very little of this vast enterprise, however, is dedicated to what can generally be termed forward-looking strategic analysis. Rather, the overwhelming focus of the intelligence community is on satisfying short-term requirements. Nothing epitomizes this more than the huge effort devoted to the production of the President's Daily Brief and other similar intelligence products delivered every day to an exclusive group of senior U.S. policy makers to warn them of immediate threats and keep them informed of current developments around the world.[10]

By comparison, there is little demand for (and thus little incentive to produce) more detailed and lengthy assessments of emerging concerns—including National Intelligence Estimates, which used to be the signature product of the National Intelligence Council (NIC).[11] These are now rarely commissioned.[12] The one exception to the otherwise very short-sighted focus of the U.S. intelligence community is the NIC's unclassified Global Trends report that is produced every four years to assess potential developments over a twenty-year time horizon. Though generally well regarded for their analytical rigor, these reports have a very limited readership and make almost no impression on policy making.[13]

While parts of the U.S. intelligence community actively monitor specific threats—notably, the activities of known terrorist organizations and the status of foreign nuclear forces—for early warning purposes there is no routinized and systematic effort to "scan the horizon" for incipient sources of instability and conflict that could threaten U.S. interests. The NIC used to house the National Warning Staff (NWS) with a dedicated national intelligence officer for warning, but this was discontinued in 2008. Besides being responsible for issuing warning notices of threatening military activities to the whole of the U.S. government, the NWS also produced the Internal Instability Watchlist every year. This comprised a list of countries at risk of various forms of political instability and conflict along with an assessment of potential triggering events and a rating of their potential severity and impact on the United States.[14]

The warning function of the NWS is now formally the responsibility of each of the regional national intelligence officers at the NIC. Their ability to perform this role, however, is severely limited by their daily responsibilities supporting and briefing interagency meetings, and this leaves them little time to look and think ahead, much less carry out detailed assessments. The closest the intelligence community now seemingly comes to doing this is the Worldwide Threat Assessment briefing delivered each year to Congress by the director of national intelligence. These reports, however, have very little value for policy planning purposes because they more or less comprise a catalog of threats rather than a proper net assessment. Similarly, USAID produces its annual Alerts List of countries considered to be at risk of instability, but this is intended primarily to help its own staff apportion development assistance rather than serve as a general warning product for the U.S. government. Likewise, the CIA maintains its quarterly Atrocity Watchlist of "countries where there is evidence of, or the potential for, significant political repression or systematic human rights abuses," but this, too, is for a very narrow audience.[15]

The weak demand signal for forward-looking strategic analysis is reinforced by the intelligence community's own hesitancy to do such work for fear it will be criticized for overstepping the limits of its formal role. Assessing the significance of potential developments for the United States by definition requires making assumptions about U.S. interests and likely policy preferences, all of which risks analysis straying into sensitive territory. The reluctance to support any work that could be construed as speculative—or, worse, politicized—has grown even stronger as a result of the widespread recriminations caused by the flawed 2003 National Intelligence Estimate on Iraq's weapons of mass destruction programs. Although the intelligence community has taken commendable steps to address potential criticisms about the quality of its analysis through, among other things, better sourcing protocols and more rigorous tradecraft, the level of interest in forward-looking assessments has apparently declined.[16]

Other institutional reforms may also have inadvertently contributed to the short-term orientation of the intelligence community. The desire to break down unhelpful organizational compartments or "silos" to promote information sharing and coordination has led to creation of specialized teams of intelligence officers that focus on relatively discrete targets or mission areas. This approach was initially pioneered in the counterterrorism area by the director of national intelligence and extended to other specific and regional concerns. It has since been adopted by the CIA to guide its recent reforms.[17] Though the reasoning behind these reforms is compelling, it has made the intelligence community more focused on supporting daily operational requirements and less interested in what could be brewing just over the horizon.

Rectifying these shortcomings would not require a major reform effort or significantly new resources. But there must be a clear demand for a dedicated and properly resourced strategic foresight and risk assessment process to inform senior policy makers about current and plausible threats to the United States. Ideally, this should be performed in a way that would support the kinds of long-, medium-, and short-term preventive policy initiatives advocated in part 2 of this book. Such an effort, therefore, would logically call for three different but interrelated work streams, each focused on a different policy time frame and each operating according to a different production schedule. Each stream, however, should rationally proceed from a common baseline assessment and, moreover, be harmonized in the sense that common terminology, definitions, and analytical methods are employed to guide those performing this function and to avoid confusing those consuming its products. A notional U.S. strategic foresight and risk assessment process would have the following elements.

- At the beginning of every new administration or second term, the national security adviser would commission a baseline assessment of extant and plausible national security risks to the United States.[18] The assessment would be overseen by a new Strategy and Assessments Directorate at the National Security Council (NSC) and carried out by an interagency team made up of representatives of the intelligence community and senior officials from the relevant departments and agencies. This study would employ risk assessment techniques that are now commonly employed by several U.S. government agencies and numerous international organizations and foreign governments.[19] The most compelling model to emulate, however, is Britain's National Security Risk Assessment (NSRA) of external threats and contingencies, which the UK Cabinet Office periodically commissions to review national security strategy.[20] As described in the 2012 review, "The NSRA process compared, assessed and prioritized all major disruptive risks to our national interest, which are of sufficient scale or impact so as to require action from government and/or which have an ideological, international or political dimension."[21]

Using a similar approach, the staff of the NSC would oversee a comparable assessment that, when completed, would be briefed to the president and the full National Security Council. Logically, the Quadrennial National Security Risk Assessment (QNSRA) should inform the production of the U.S. National Security Strategy, which would also be produced by the new Strategy and Assessment Directorate. It would also be used to help set intelligence collection and analysis priorities as well as policy planning efforts that will be discussed below.

■ Every six months, the same interagency strategic assessments team would review and update a watchlist of prioritized short- to medium-term risks identified in the QNSRA that meet specific criteria for inclusion. This would cover, for example, notable changes to the assessed intent and capabilities of known terrorist groups, the status of identified and potentially new international flash points, and countries at risk of serious internal instability that could threaten American interests and potentially trigger U.S. military engagement. The foresight time horizon would be no more than twenty-four months, again to make the assessment more relevant to the political interests of most senior policy makers.

The Integrated National Security Watchlist (INSW) would draw on traditional sources of intelligence but also take advantage of new the open-source forecasting techniques described in chapter 2 that show considerable promise.[22] Each of the identified concerns on the watchlist would be coded or tagged (preferably using the same risk assessment terminology of the QNSRA) to indicate their relative significance and changing status for busy policy makers to more readily appreciate. As also discussed in chapter 2, policy makers have to be alerted not only to the likelihood of an emerging threat but also to that threat's potential negative implications, particularly how it might evolve and grow more serious. In a similar way to the QNSRA, the INSW should also be used to direct and prioritize the tasking of U.S. intelligence collection efforts. For this reason, updates of the INSW should be aligned with the National Intelligence Priorities Framework process, which is reviewed every six months and signed by the president.[23] Moreover, the addition of new concerns or contingencies onto the watchlist should trigger related policy planning if this is not already taking place.

- An independent government agency should also be established to carry out medium- to long-term horizon scanning and strategic assessments for the U.S. government. This would be made up of a multidisciplinary group of experts capable of assessing specific trends and plausible future developments at the request of the U.S. Congress and the executive branch of the government. Its scope would not be confined to national security concerns but rather be broadly relevant to the national interest. Some of its work would as a consequence be classified, while other products would be publically accessible. The time frame for its work would be variable, but no shorter than five years. This could absorb the Global Trends work of the NIC Strategic Futures Group, thereby freeing it up to carry out more focused strategic analysis.

PROMOTING PREVENTIVE POLICY PLANNING

To the extent that forward-looking planning is conducted within the U.S. government, it is largely on an ad hoc and, moreover, highly fragmented basis rather than the product of a regular and systematic process that incorporates all the relevant agencies. As Aaron Friedberg bluntly concluded after having served in the George W. Bush administration, "The U.S. government has lost the capacity to conduct serious, sustained national strategic planning. Although offices and bureaus scattered throughout the executive branch perform parts of this task for their respective agencies, no one place brings all the pieces together and integrates them into anything resembling a coherent, comprehensive whole."[24] The small policy planning bureau at the State Department was originally established for this purpose, but long ago became used primarily to draft speeches for the secretary of state and to carry out special projects on issues of current concern. The even smaller strategic planning directorate at the NSC performs more or less the same functions for the national security adviser in addition to being responsible for producing the NSS. Occasionally the State Department or the NSC will lead a forward-looking policy review that is focused on a specific country or region. These are typically for the purpose of generating broad policy guidance rather than considering how to avert potentially dangerous or harmful contingencies.[25]

These efforts should not be confused with the planning carried out by the Defense Department in conjunction with the U.S. military, which is by far the most extensive and elaborate effort of this kind within the U.S. government. In addition to preparing for a variety of contingencies short of war, detailed operational plans are also maintained and regularly updated to respond to potentially aggressive actions by known adversaries in various regional contexts. By their very nature, however, these efforts represent *contingency* planning rather than *preventive* planning exercises; they are essentially about being prepared for the worst rather than lessening the likelihood of it happening in the first place.[26] The Department of Homeland Security, especially through its Federal Emergency Management Agency, conducts similar planning, though obviously for domestic contingencies.

Attempts to improve strategic planning in recent years have achieved only modest success. During George W. Bush's second term, for example, a small planning effort was initiated to improve higher-level interagency strategic planning. This began initially as a mostly informal process whereby the Joint Chiefs of Staff, the NIC, and representatives from the principal planning components at the Departments of State, Defense, Treasury, Justice, and Homeland Security would meet irregularly to discuss potential contingencies and possible "strategic shocks."[27] In the waning months of the Bush administration, this was formalized with the creation of a National Security Policy Planning Committee. However, like many initiatives of a preceding administration, this body was never constituted by the Obama White House. Although a strategic planning directorate was retained at the NSC, its primary function was to draft the NSS and carry out special projects for the national security adviser. It performed no serious planning function for the NSC, nor did it provide real strategic guidance for the rest of the executive branch.[28]

Various proposals have been made to significantly upgrade strategic planning at the NSC. These range from the ambitious (reestablishing the Eisenhower administration Planning Board or creating a deputy national security adviser for strategic planning) to the more modest (maintaining a small planning cell at the NSC to carry out limited contingency planning).[29] The basic challenge to all these suggestions is that unless those responsible for formulating and executing day-to-day policy willingly accept or are directed to accept the deliberations of the planners, the proposed initiatives are unlikely to have any real impact on influencing the actions of the rest of the NSC, much less the principal government departments. For this reason, planning has to be carried out not by a separate and essentially disconnected body within the NSC but by the very bureaus and offices responsible for mainline policy making.

This approach to strategic planning is actually not so novel. Earlier U.S. administrations explicitly empowered the NSC to carry out not only contingency planning but also what we are describing here as preventive planning. Thus, the administration of Richard Nixon formally directed the Interdepartmental Regional Groups convened by the NSC to produce "contingency papers on potential crisis areas for review by the NSC."[30] Similarly, the Regional Interagency Groups of the NSC under President Ronald Reagan were instructed to "prepare contingency plans pertaining to potential crises in their respective areas of responsibility."[31] The Special Situation Group at the Reagan NSC was also directed to "formulate contingency planning *in anticipation* of a crisis," while a more working-level Crisis Pre-Planning Group was established to "develop options and recommendations concerning actions to mitigate and *successfully prevent* or resolve crisis situations."[32]

This commitment to preventive planning and crisis management continued under George H. W. Bush and the subsequent Clinton administration.

Each designated the NSC Deputies Committee "to focus on crisis prevention—including contingency planning for major areas of concern."[33] In almost all these cases, it is important to emphasize, the planning function was performed by the agencies and departments responsible for chairing and backstopping the work of the specific interagency committees rather than by designated officials at the NSC. Only with the Obama administration did the practice of having senior NSC officials chair all the interagency committees below the formally constituted National Security Council begin.[34]

With these precedents in mind, a more systematic and deliberate preventive planning process should be instituted within the U.S. government in the following manner:

- Designate and empower the NSC Deputies Committee and specifically the principal regional interagency committees to carry out crisis prevention planning for their areas of responsibility. This effort should be informed by the strategic risk assessment process described earlier in this chapter that would require the relevant committees to plan around the specific contingencies and concerns identified in both the QNSRA and the INSW.
- Restore chairmanship of the principal regional and functional interagency committees to the relevant government agencies and departments. The leading agency or department would in turn be responsible for drafting preventive plans for subsequent review by the interagency committee. Their in-house planning capacities should be augmented where necessary and suitably aligned to support this process. Completed plans would be regularly submitted for approval to the Deputies Committee.
- Coordinate strategic planning in support of longer term preventive engagement goals through the Strategy and Assessments Directorate at the NSC, but have it be carried out by the principal agencies involved in the relevant interagency committees.

ENHANCING CRISIS PREPAREDNESS AND MANAGEMENT

Well-established arrangements exist to apprise senior government officials of an imminent or breaking crisis and convene them at short notice. Protocols for managing major national emergencies have also been developed to allow rapid decision making in such circumstances and maintain continuity of government operations. From time to time, moreover, senior officials will also engage in tabletop or command post exercises to practice these procedures and also familiarize themselves with the challenges of crisis management. Despite all these efforts, however, the United States is often caught unprepared to manage sudden or unforeseen events with predictable results. As the 2010 QDDR candidly acknowledged, "Too often our reaction [to conflict and crises] has been post hoc and ad hoc. We have not defined and resourced the problems of conflict and crisis as a central mission of our civilian toolkit or developed adequate operational structures to support U.S. and multi-partner responses. We have responded to successive events without learning lessons and making appropriate institutional changes to provide continuity and support."[35] With the exception of civil emergency planning and some disaster relief planning, the level of effort devoted to training and preparing for major national security crises remains remarkably low.[36] Even the Pentagon's extensive preparations to manage a multitude of crises has its limitations. In particular, it is largely carried out with little input from other agencies and departments that are likely to play a role in specific contingencies.

Efforts since the end of the Cold War to improve U.S. management of what became known as complex contingency operations have also been pursued in an erratic fashion. Thus, only after having to carry out several costly foreign interventions did the Clinton administration establish clear guidance and procedures for the Deputies Committee to manage future crises of this nature.[37] But the incoming Bush administration never adopted these crisis management arrangements or developed ones of its own until the setbacks in Afghanistan and Iraq forced it to see the value of being better prepared. With National Security Presidential Directive 44, "Management of Interagency Efforts Concerning Reconstruction and Stabilization," promulgated in 2005, it stood up a new office at the State Department—the Office of the Coordinator for Reconstruction and Stabilization (S/CRS)—with the responsibility (among others) to "Coordinate interagency processes to identify states at risk of instability, lead interagency planning to prevent or mitigate conflict, and develop detailed contingency plans for integrated United States Government reconstruction and stabilization efforts for those states and regions and for widely applicable scenarios, which are integrated with military contingency plans, where appropriate."[38] From its inception, however, the S/CRS struggled to gain traction within the government. The lack of vocal and sustained support from the White House, persistent underfunding from a skeptical Congress, and bureaucratic resistance from within and outside the State Department collectively hobbled its effectiveness. While it managed to carry out some contingency planning, it ultimately represented a very spotty and modest effort.[39]

Similarly, the crisis management system developed by the S/CRS known as the Interagency Management System (IMS) was never used despite many instances when it could have been activated during the George W. Bush administration. The general perception of the IMS as being overly rigid and bureaucratic, along with the general reticence to cede management of a crisis to a new and unproven entity, largely explain this.[40] Not surprisingly, the Obama administration chose to let the IMS wither away and instead relied on Interagency Policy Committees and the Deputies Committee for crisis management.

Given these prior efforts to develop dedicated mechanisms and procedures to manage complex contingency crises, any effort to improve future U.S. preparedness and performance has to go *with* rather than *against* the grain of established decision-making practices. Although there are merits to establishing something equivalent to the British crisis management system known as COBR (for Cabinet Office Briefing Room), which has well-established and regularly rehearsed protocols for responding to short-notice or no-notice national emergencies, it is not clear that this approach can be transplanted onto the Washington policy making landscape, and certainly not without strong support from the president and enthusiastic buy-in from all the major departments.[41] Instead, the focus should be on how to facilitate better and faster responses within existing institutions and frameworks. More specifically, the following initiatives should be pursued:

- Complement interagency preventive planning with a comparable crisis contingency planning process overseen by the NSC Deputies Committee and also carried out by the principal regional interagency committees. This planning effort should also be informed by the QNSRA and the INSW.

Ideally it should also be invested with the kind of authorities that help motivate the Defense Department in developing its war plans—known overall as Guidance for Employment of the Force. This is a statutory requirement under title 10 of the U.S. Code. The selection of contingencies for planning must be approved by the secretary of defense and the president under a set schedule. A similar process, such as amending the relevant section of the U.S. code that pertains to the National Security Council (title 22), could be employed to drive wider civilian contingency planning.

- Improve the capacity to rapidly stand up interagency task forces or decision support groups in response to a crisis. Although there are advantages to developing formal procedures and responsibilities to facilitate decision making and government coordination in crisis situations, these cannot be overly rigid or bureaucratic as they are unlikely to ever be activated when needed. Senior policy makers typically prefer to make decisions within small groups of trusted aides—certainly in situations when information about the crisis is not yet public and when potential U.S. actions are likely to be politically sensitive for a variety of reasons. Policy makers still need assistance to reach decisions and execute them, however, so the flexibility to stand up a special support group or task force to backstop their deliberations is required. These should be more than just hastily constituted groupings; rather, they should draw on a roster of experienced officials versed in crisis management strategies and techniques.

- Improve the capacity to generate policy options rapidly in a crisis. Given that prior contingency planning may not accurately anticipate a specific crisis, it is desirable that those supporting senior-level decision making have the ability to amend extant plans or create new ones upon short notice. An NSC-led interagency task force should develop the means (using advanced decision support technologies) to generate rapidly different policy response packages for commonly occurring types of foreign crises. These generic policy packages or playbooks should be established on the basis of prior operational knowledge and regularly updated as new lessons are learned.

One can imagine, for example, templates being developed for a range of potential interstate crises that involve territorial or resource-related disputes and where there are already militarized borders with forces in confrontational postures. Equivalent templates can be developed for intrastate disputes. Obvious candidates would be the threat of coups and political succession disputes, including electoral violence, popular uprisings, religious and ethnic tensions, and resource-related disputes. Similar crisis management templates can be developed for other commonly recurring incidents such as terrorist incidents, hostage taking, and humanitarian contingencies.[42]

- Develop a crisis management database on countries of concern. In addition to ensuring that up-to-date intelligence reaches the appropriate decision makers in a form that is digestible and usable, having accurate and relevant information on U.S interests and available assets in a crisis-stricken area can also be invaluable. This includes accurate information on U.S. nationals at risk, commercial interests, and military and disaster response assets either close by or within operational reach. This database should be maintained and updated as part of the contigency planning process. Similarly, known personal connections between senior U.S. leaders (civil and military) and their foreign counterparts in those countries that could conceivably be harnessed in a variety of ways in a crisis should also be recorded and regularly updated. Relevant information on comparable allied or partner interests and assets should likewise be maintained.

RESOURCING PREVENTIVE ENGAGEMENT

Reorienting the United States to support preventive engagement in the manner outlined in this chapter should not require a significant increase in budget outlays. It will, however, require redirecting resources from some countries to others in accordance with changing preventive priorities and giving more support to some programs and less to others depending on their relative effectiveness. Current priorities and programs will all have to be reviewed on a case-by-case basis. Furthermore, as indicated in chapter 1, the costs of many preventive engagement initiatives can be shared with partner countries and international organizations.

A common lament of many engaged in operational conflict prevention and mitigation activities is the lack of flexible funding that can be repurposed as needs change or unobligated contingency funds that can be drawn upon on short notice for emergency situations. Appropriators have traditionally been wary of setting aside crisis contingency funds, especially for nonmilitary activities, out of concern that they will be used to cover other expenses. Thus, only a modest amount was initially appropriated for the Complex Crisis Fund established for this purpose in 2010, and it has declined steadily ever since. For this reason, the proposal made by Robert Gates when he was still secretary of defense to establish a pooled fund for conflict prevention and stabilization efforts should be seriously considered. Clearly inspired by the British precedent of creating Conflict Prevention Pools shared across the Department for International Development, the Foreign and Commonwealth Office, and the Ministry of Defence (initially for sub-Saharan Africa and then more generally), Gates proposed a joint Department of Defense and Department of State fund of approximately $2 billion that could be used on relatively short notice by both departments, preferably in a coordinated fashion.[43] The suggestion, however, never went very far, apparently because of unease within the State Department that the Defense Department was encroaching on the role traditionally carried out by the State Department and USAID. Given today's more austere funding environment, there is now an even more compelling need to revisit the idea of a pooled crisis prevention and stabilization fund that could conceivably also include USAID.

Funding should also be found from existing accounts to support many of the activities proposed above, including the new strategic foresight products and planning processes. Some offices and bureaus should receive additional funding as a consequence—though, again, overall appropriations may remain more or less the same. The funding of CSO at the State Department in particular deserves to be increased to support it playing a more important preventive role. Although its initial ambitions to maintain a civilian response corps to be deployed overseas upon short notice to help in stabilization efforts has now been abandoned for being largely duplicative of USAID capabilities (particularly those employed by its Office of Transitional Initiatives), CSO should also cease other overseas programming of this kind. Instead it should focus on three core areas of work: carrying out conflict risk assessments, supporting the preventive and contingency planning efforts of the State Department, and developing niche skills and capabilities to support *diplomatic* efforts for crisis prevention and conflict stabilization. The latter includes supporting mediation efforts, the work of special envoys, and backstopping crisis management task forces. It is also logical for it to lead cross-government efforts to prevent mass atrocities, and this should be coordinated through a regular interagency policy committee rather than an Atrocities Prevention Board. In doing all this, it should be moved from the "J" cluster at the State Department and relocated within the "P" grouping of regional bureaus under the direction of the undersecretary for political affairs to make it directly supportive of their planning and day-to-day needs.[44]

More generally, the amount of resources devoted to professional learning and training in support of the skill sets required for various areas of preventive engagement needs to be increased. This includes a systematic effort to record operational lessons and incorporate them into planning and training.

A FINAL WORD

The institutional reforms proposed in this final chapter to facilitate the larger shift in U.S. strategy will doubtless strike some readers as overly ambitious if not wholly impractical. Constructive criticism of these recommendations and, moreover, the larger argument of the book is certainly welcome, but summary rejection—especially if it is not accompanied by an alternative and, better still, superior strategy for how America can avoid war, stay strong, and keep the peace in the years ahead—is indefensible. It is tantamount to accepting that there is little or nothing that the United States can do to shape the future in a way that lessens the risks it faces. In effect, we should just hope for the best and cope with whatever challenges come our way, as well as we can.

Resignation to the forces of fate is simply irresponsible, however—not just for those Americans alive today but also for future generations to come. It also puts in jeopardy the international order that America has done so much to create, that so many benefit from today, and that many will benefit from tomorrow—the longer it is maintained and extended. To be clear, the strategy of preventive engagement that this book has set out to advance will not absolutely preclude America from being blindsided by unforeseen events, having to use military force, or becoming drawn into costly conflicts in the future. Clearly, no plan is infallible. But to paraphrase what Alexander Hamilton wrote long ago about government, shouldn't the course of America's future depend less on "accident and force" and more on "reflection and choice"?

ACKNOWLEDGMENTS

F OR GIVING ME the opportunity to write this book, I must begin by thanking the Council on Foreign Relations (CFR) and its president Richard N. Haass. Surprisingly few foreign policy research organizations can claim to have a program of work dedicated to the prevention of deadly conflict, and the Council is one of them. As its General John W. Vessey Senior Fellow for Conflict Prevention and director of the Center for Preventive Action (CPA), I have attempted to rectify what has long struck me as an illogical disconnect between "mainstream" foreign and security policy experts who largely view conflict prevention as something pursued primarily for humanitarian reasons in areas of marginal strategic interest to the United States and the "peacebuilding" community who see their efforts as mostly distinct from traditional notions of strategy and statecraft. Much of the work of the Center has therefore been directed at elevating the strategic importance of conflict prevention to the United States while also treating its pursuit as a strategic endeavor that necessarily entails the use of all elements of American statecraft. This book draws on that work and very much encapsulates CPA's core ethos and guiding principles.

Many colleagues, friends, and members of my immediate family have provided me with invaluable support at various stages in the writing of the book, for which I am profoundly grateful. At CFR, James Lindsay, senior vice president for the Studies Program, deserves special recognition. Jim provided important guidance and backing throughout the project. Other CFR colleagues in the Studies Program—notably, Ted Alden, Liz Economy, Laurie Garrett, Rob Kahn, Charles Kupchan, Stewart Patrick, Carla Robbins, Scott Snyder, and Micah Zenko—have likewise provided substantive input as well as much appreciated encouragement at various times.

I have also been blessed with an extraordinary set of research associates. Besides the substantial contribution they have made to the intellectual content of this book, I cannot imagine how I would have managed the day-to-day task of running the Center without them; they are, in chronological order, Jamie Ekern, Elise Vaughan, Sophia Yang, Steve Wittels, Andrew Miller, Alex Noyes, Rebecca Lissner, Amelia Wolf, Helia Ighani, Anna Feuer, Sarah Collman, James West, and Jennifer Wilson. I owe so much to their hard work, dedication, and (no less important) general good humor when my spirits sagged. Finally, some others at CFR also need to be acknowledged as they, too, have made my life so much easier. In particular, Amy Baker, Betsy Gude, Suzanne Helm, Bob McMahon, Jean-Michel Oriol, Anya Schmemann, Lisa Shields, and especially Trish Dorff have been simply exceptional. I could not have asked for a more professional and supportive group of colleagues.

I would be remiss if I did not also recognize here the extraordinary generosity of various funders to the work of the Center for Preventive Action and, by extension, the completion of this book. Patrick Byrne, who along with his father endowed the Vessey Chair at the Council, has been a constant source of encouragement and support. The Carnegie Corporation of New York has also funded the work of CPA from its inception, and thus so much of what we have accomplished would not have been possible without them. I am especially indebted to Deanna Arsenian and Stephen Del Rosso, who have been wonderfully supportive over the years.

As most authors will attest, books are almost always the result of many conversations with friends and colleagues who act as sounding boards for embryonic ideas while later giving generously with more substantive feedback on various manuscript drafts. Gordon Barrass, Chuck Call, Chet Crocker, Janine Davidson, Joshua Epstein, Suzanne Fry, Matt Hodes, Tori Holt, George Joulwan, Ken Knight, Scott Lasenksy, Matt Levinger, Tod Lindberg, Robert Litwak, Andrew Loomis, Princeton Lyman, Dan

Markey, Thomas McNaugher, Bridget Moix, Janne Nolan, Michael O'Hanlon, John Pike, Nicolas Regaud, James Schear, Mark Schneider, Daniel Serwer, Sarah Sewall, Tara Sonenshine, Joanna Spear, Jay Ulfelder, Karin von Hippel, Jonathan Winer, Joel Wit, Lawrence Woocher, Mona Yacoubian, and Cas Yost are all especially deserving here. I would also like to thank the anonymous peer reviewers of the completed manuscript for their many useful comments and suggestions. In the same vein, I have also benefited from the encouragement and editorial support of the exceptionally gifted professionals at Columbia University Press—notably, Anne Routon and Stephen Wesley—as well as Deborah Masi from Westchester Publishing Services.

Sadly, during the course of writing this book, several extraordinary people who had a profound impact on my life and intellectual development passed away. In addition to my brother Peter, to whom this book is in part dedicated, I will always be indebted to three others that at various times I had the honor and privilege to work for: John Steinbruner, Tadashi Yamamoto, and Richard Solomon. John instilled awe and admiration in everyone who had the good fortune to orbit his sun. His intellectual creativity and, above all else, courage when it came to proposing innovative policy solutions for tough challenges left an enduring mark on me. Tadashi inspired me in a different way. His infectious enthusiasm and boundless energy as he pursued his lifetime mission to nurture civil society in Japan and build intellectual exchange networks throughout Asia and between Asia and the rest of the world to promote reconciliation and mutual understanding was not just literally breathtaking but also deeply humbling. In contrast, Dick taught me to take the long view and, moreover, think strategically about the world. I would like to believe they would have all approved of this book.

Finally, I would like to thank my wife Sonni. As a foreign affairs practitioner, analyst, and first-rate editor, Sonni has made many valuable contributions to the book. But most of all it has been her unstinting love, patience, and encouragement that I have appreciated the most. Our three children Nick, Justin, and Isabel, to whom this book is also dedicated, deserve a lot of credit for never complaining about my frequent absences and general grumpiness while I toiled away on the manuscript. I just hope the worst outcomes discussed herein never come to pass in their lifetimes.

NOTES

PREFACE

1. See Jonathan Schell, *The Unfinished Twentieth Century* (London: Verso, 2001), 4; and Eric Hobsbawm, *The Age of Extremes: The Short Twentieth Century, 1914–1991* (London: Abacus, 1994).

2. See Roger Cohen, "The Great Unraveling," *New York Times*, September 15, 2014; George Packer, "The Birth of the New Century: What the World Lost in 2014," *Foreign Policy* 209 (2014): 53–55; Richard Gowan, "For the West, Freezing 2014's Conflicts Will Top Agenda in 2015," *World Politics Review*, December 1, 2014, http://www.worldpoliticsreview .com/articles/14544/for-the-west-freezing-2014-s-conflicts-will-top-agenda-in-2015; and Richard N. Haass, *A World in Disarray: American Foreign Policy and the Crisis of the Old Order* (New York: Penguin, 2017).

3. David Brooks, "The View from Trump Tower," *New York Times*, November 11, 2016.

4. Nicholas N. Eberstadt, "Our Miserable 21st Century," *Commentary*, February 2017, https://www.commentarymagazine.com/articles/our-miserable-21st-century/.

5. A Pew Research Center public opinion poll taken in May 2016, for example, found that 57 percent of Americans believed the United States should "deal with our own problems/ let others deal with theirs as best they can"—the highest response recorded for this question in fifty years of polling and 20 percentage points higher than a decade earlier. Pew Research Center, "Public Uncertain, Divided Over America's Place in the World," May 5, 2016, http://www.people-press.org/2016/05/05/public-uncertain-divided-over-americas -place-in-the-world/. Similarly, a preelection poll of Donald Trump supporters also indicated that 54 percent felt the United States "does too much to solve the world's problems." Pew Research Center, "Trump Supporters Differ from Other GOP Voters on Foreign Policy, Immigration Issues," May 11, 2016, http://www.pewresearch.org/fact -tank/2016/05/11/trump-supporters-differ-from-other-gop-voters-on-foreign-policy -immigration-issues/.

6. For arguments rebutting the inevitability of America's decline, see Joseph S. Nye Jr., "The Future of American Power: Dominance and Decline in Perspective," *Foreign Affairs* 89, no. 6 (2010): 2–12; Robert Kagan, *The World America Made* (New York: Knopf, 2012); and Robert J. Lieber, *Power and Willpower: Why the United States Is Not Destined to Decline* (Cambridge: Cambridge University Press, 2012).

7. For example, Paul K. McDonald and Joseph M. Parent, in "Graceful Decline? The Surprising Success of Great Power Retrenchment," *International Security* 35, no. 4 (2011): 40; refer to post–World War II British policy makers as "supple strategists" who "ruthlessly shifted and shed burdens when it was plain that resources were inadequate." See also George Friedman, "Britain Adapts to Decline," Realclear World, May 1, 2012, http://www.realclearworld.com/articles/2012/05/01/britain_adapts_to_decline_100031.html; and Gideon Rachman, "America Must Manage Its Decline," *Financial Times*, October 17, 2011.

8. See Paul Kennedy, *The Rise and Fall of the Great Powers* (New York: Random House, 1989).

9. The First World War started the downward descent. Although Britain emerged victorious, and with an even larger empire as part of the spoils, the exertion of fighting the war left it profoundly diminished. No country spent more of its national wealth on the war than Britain. Besides the human cost of over 750,000 men killed (one in sixteen males between the ages of fifteen and fifty), as well as other substantial material loses, Britain was forced to liquidate a large proportion of its overseas financial holdings and also seek hugely burdensome loans from the United States to pay for the war effort. The United States, meanwhile, went from being a debtor to a creditor nation almost overnight and took full advantage of the wholesale sell-off of British assets, particularly in Latin America, as well as the sharp decline in British exports during the war years to expand its economic power and influence. By November 1918, Britain owed the U.S. government and private lenders nearly £1 billion, which in turn limited its capacity to invest elsewhere. Moreover, the huge amount of domestic borrowing (government debt rose tenfold from 1913 to 1919, with the interest on it consuming close to half of total central government spending by the mid-1920s) meant higher taxation and interest rates in the postwar period, imposing yet another burden on the British economy.

By the time international trade picked up in the late 1920s, Britain was not well positioned to take advantage of it. Its domination of the international banking system and the freedom of maneuver this afforded had also ended. As the historian John Darwin notes, "London could no longer control interest rates across the world as it had before 1914, nor draw in the gold it needed by an upward shift in its own bank rate. And by the 1920s, the City's prime international asset, the collateral for any future crisis, was leaking away. By 1931, of the great treasure trove of dollar securities built up before 1914, scarcely one-tenth remained. The war chest of the British system was almost empty." The onset of the Second World War compounded the economic consequences of the First World War and sealed Britain's demise as a true world power. Before the war, "Britain was the only global power with interests in every continent and, in theory, the means to defend them." By the time the guns fell silent—and certainly following military demobilization—this was no longer the case. See John Darwin, *The Empire Project: The Rise and Fall of the British World System, 1830–1970* (Cambridge: Cambridge University Press, 2009), 323, 327. As economist Stephen Broadberry argues, "The two wars go some way to explaining Britain's decline relative to the USA during the twentieth century." Broadberry, "The Impact of the World Wars on the Long Run Performance of the British Economy," *Oxford Review of Economic Policy* 4, no. 1 (1988): 33. Though the human costs were less grievous than those of the First World War, the destruction of property, including nearly a third of its pre-1939 stock of merchant shipping, was much higher. Of greater impact, however, is that the war effectively bankrupted Britain. The British government was forced to deplete most of its reserves of dollar holdings and gold to pay for the war effort and then accept Lend-Lease assistance from the United States on terms distinctly disadvantageous to Britain's long-term economic interests. Britain in effect was required to cut down its exports and withdraw from many overseas markets as a condition for being bailed out financially, which, along with the interest on the debt, would hamper its postwar recovery. As a consequence, the "pre-war balance of commercial power between London and Washington shifted for good and erased Britain's century-old status as a (and, for much of the time, *the*) dominant force in the world's trading economy." Darwin, *Empire Project*, 511.

The sudden termination of U.S. Lend-Lease assistance in 1945 came as an economic shock to a Britain, which by then had become dependent on subsidized imports of many basic commodities. A new Anglo-American loan soon afterward would ease the blow, but not without there being major repercussions for Britain's financial independence and general freedom of maneuver. In addition to the added debt to be serviced—which would take until 2006 for Britain to finally pay off—Washington insisted that the British pound be convertible into the U.S. dollar within twelve months. Soon after this took effect, nations with sterling balances began a calamitous run on the Bank of England's reserves. As Niall Ferguson notes, this was "the first of a succession of sterling crises that punctuated Britain's retreat from Empire." See Niall Ferguson, *Empire: The Rise and Demise of the British World Order and the Lessons for Global Power* (New York: Basic Books, 2002), 300.

By the late 1940s Britain's economic weakness had already caused it to cut back its initial postwar security commitments in southeast Europe and hand them off to the United States. But the need to rearm as the Cold War intensified—and, in particular, to contribute to the United Nations' "police action" in Korea (something Britain could not buck if it was to uphold its status as a permanent member of the UN Security Council)—would contribute to yet another balance of payments crisis in 1951–1952, causing London to impose a new set of painful austerity measures. What pretensions remained of Britain's ability to act as a great power and "regional guardian" of the Middle East was shattered with the disastrous Suez Crisis in 1956. The Anglo-French invasion of Egypt to repossess the Suez Canal was strongly condemned by the United States and precipitated another ruinous run on sterling. When London pleaded for financial assistance from the International Monetary Fund to avoid having to devalue the pound, Washington made its approval of a billion-dollar rescue package conditional on Britain's complete withdrawal from Egypt, punctuating an already humiliating diplomatic climb down.

The Suez debacle certainly marked a psychological turning point for Britain, but it would take more than a decade of high defense expenditures and costly imperial rearguard actions in various parts of the world before its pretensions of maintaining a significant global presence would really come to an end. By one calculation, Britain carried out over thirty military interventions in more than twenty countries between 1949 and 1970—more than any other major state. Only with the decision in 1968 to withdraw its military presence "east of Suez" by 1971 did Britain finally acknowledge its diminished status as a second-rank power. With the exception of its ten-week campaign to retake the Falkland Islands and other possessions in the South Atlantic that had been occupied by Argentina in 1982, Britain's subsequent projections of military power overseas, and certainly the major ones, were all essentially carried out as adjuncts to those of the United States and, moreover, largely dependent on its capabilities—in Iraq in 1991, the former Yugoslavia in 1995, Afghanistan in 2001, and Iraq again in 2003.

10. The painful experience of the 2003 military intervention in Iraq arguably marked the final act in Britain's descent. The Iraq and, to a lesser extent, Afghanistan campaigns have had a profound effect on public attitudes toward the use of military power. The capacity of Britain to engage in overseas expeditionary campaigns has shrunk to the point where anything above a very modest level is now considered impractical. See "The Iraq War: Britain, Ten Years On," *Economist*, March 19, 2013, http://www.economist.com /blogs/blighty/2013/03/iraq-war; and Philip Saunders, "A Ruinous War Set the Path for British Retreat," *Financial Times*, July 8, 2016. Moreover, one can also draw a line between the eventual public disillusionment with both wars and, in particular, anger over the subsequently discredited official rationale for the Iraq campaign with the large levels of support for Scottish independence in 2015 and the majority vote in favor of Britain withdrawing from the European Union in 2016 (which could precipitate the dissolution of the United Kingdom). See Calum McMillan, "From Iraq to Indyref: How the 2003 War Influenced a Scottish Youth Which Came of Age in September 2014," Common Space, https://www.commonspace.scot/articles/1790/iraq-indyref-how-2003 -war-influenced-scottish-youth-which-came-age-september-2014.

11. Tristan Abbey, quoted in Dave Dilegge, "The Myth of Britain's 'Managed Decline,'" *SWJ Blog, Small Wars Journal*, February 15, 2012, http://smallwarsjournal.com/blog/the -myth-of-britain%E2%80%99s-%E2%80%9Cmanaged-decline%E2%80%9D. Darwin, *Empire Project*, 604, also refers to the myth of managed British decline as a "fanciful tale" and a "sanctimonious legend."

12. Theodore Roosevelt, speech at Capitol Square, Richmond, Virginia, October 18, 1905, http://www.theodore-roosevelt.com/images/research/txtspeeches/149.txt.

1. AMERICA'S PREDICAMENT

1. As far as can be determined, the term "preventive engagement" was first used by the European Union to describe the security strategy that it launched in 2003—and more specifically its call for "a strategic culture that fosters early, rapid, and when necessary,

robust intervention." See Council of the European Union, *European Security Strategy: A Secure Europe in a Better World*, December 12, 2003, http://www.consilium.europa.eu /uedocs/cmsUpload/78367.pdf. The terminology has since been dropped by the European Union. Others have used similar terms, with similar ends in mind; for example, "preventive defense," "preventive statecraft," and the more common "preventive diplomacy." These terms were or are used in more narrow ways than how preventive engagement is conceived here. See Ashton B. Carter and William James Perry, *Preventive Defense: A New Security Strategy for America* (Washington, D.C.: Brookings Institution, 1999); Michael S. Lund, *Preventing Violent Conflicts: A Strategy for Preventive Diplomacy* (Washington, D.C.: United States Institute of Peace, 1996); Bruce W. Jentleson, "The Realism of Preventive Statecraft," in *Conflict Prevention: Path to Peace or Grand Illusion?*, ed. David Carment and Albrecht Schnabel (New York: United Nations University Press, 2003), 26–46.

2. The term "Long Peace" was coined by John Lewis Gaddis in "The Long Peace: Elements of Stability in the Postwar International System," *International Security* 10, no. 4 (1986): 99–142.

3. The most comprehensive discussion of how the world has become a more peaceful place can be found in Stephen Pinker, *The Better Angels of Our Nature: Why Violence Has Declined* (New York: Viking, 2011). See also Joshua S. Goldstein, *Winning the War on War: The Decline of Armed Conflict Worldwide* (New York: Dutton, 2011).

4. See "Why the Global Arms Trade Is Booming," *Economist*, March 7, 2017, http://www .economist.com/blogs/economist-explains/2017/03/economist-explains-4.

5. For a discussion on the relative merits of nuclear proliferation, see Scott D. Sagan and Kenneth N. Waltz, *The Spread of Nuclear Weapons* (New York: Norton, 2012).

6. Richard N. Haass, "The New Thirty Years' War," Project Syndicate, July 21, 2014, https:// www.project-syndicate.org/commentary/richard-n—haass-argues-that-the-middle -east-is-less-a-problem-to-be-solved-than-a-condition-to-be-managed?barrier =accessreg.

7. See Peter Bergen and Jennifer Rowland, "Al Qaeda Controls More Territory than Ever in Middle East," CNN, January 7, 2014, http://www.cnn.com/2014/01/07/opinion/bergen -al-qaeda-territory-gains; Sam Jones, Borzou Daragahi, and Simeon Kerr, "Al-Qaeda: On the March," *Financial Times*, January 19, 2014, http://www.ft.com/intl/cms/s/2 /d8662d86-8124-11e3-95aa-00144feab7de.html#slide0; and Daniel L. Byman, "The Resurgence of al Qaeda in Iraq," Brookings Institution, http://www.brookings.edu/research /testimony/2013/12/12-resurgence-al-qaeda-iraq-byman.

8. See Halvard Buhaug and Ida Rudolfsen, *A Climate of Conflicts?*, http://file.prio.no /publication_files/prio/Buhaug,%20Rudolfsen%20-%20A%20Climate%20of%20 Conflicts,%20Conflict%20Trends%2005-2015.pdf.

9. See Peter Brecke, "The Long-Term Patterns of Violent Conflict in Different Regions of the World," paper prepared for the Uppsala Conflict Data Conference, Uppsala, Sweden, June 8–9, 2001, http://citeseerx.ist.psu.edu/viewdoc/download?doi=10.1.1.15 .9141&rep=rep1&type=pdf.

10. See Bear Braumoeller, "Is War Disappearing?," paper presented at the meeting of the American Political Science Association, Chicago, August 29–September 1, 2013, http://

papers.ssrn.com/sol3/papers.cfm?abstract_id=2317269; and Pasquale Cirillo and Nassim Nicholas Taleb, "What Are the Chances of a Third World War?," working paper, Real World Risk Institute, October 2015, http://www.fooledbyrandomness.com/longpeace .pdf.

11. "Lippmann Gap" was coined by political scientist Samuel P. Huntingdon. See Samuel P. Huntingdon, "Coping with the Lippmann Gap," *Foreign Affairs* 66, no. 3 (1987): 453–77.

12. Samantha Rich, "Trump Supporters Differ from Other GOP Voters on Foreign Policy, Immigration Issues," Pew Research Center, May 11, 2016, http://www.pewresearch.org /fact-tank/2016/05/11/trump-supporters-differ-from-other-gop-voters-on-foreign -policy-immigration-issues/.

13. See U.S. Defense Casualty Analysis System, "U.S. Military Casualties—Operation Enduring Freedom (OEF) Casualty Summary by Month and Service," https://www.dmdc .osd.mil/dcas/pages/report_oef_month.xhtml.

14. This includes the direct costs of the military operations as well as the huge reconstruction effort in Afghanistan and Iraq. Neta C. Crawford, "US Budgetary Costs of War Through 2016: $4.79 Trillion and Counting," Watson Institute, Brown University, September 2016, http://watson.brown.edu/costsofwar/files/cow/imce/papers/2016 /Costs%20of%20War%20through%202016%20FINAL%20final%20v2.pdf.

15. According to the CBO, the level of federal debt in 2016 caused by successive budget deficits is equivalent to 75 percent of the economy's GDP. This percentage is higher than at any time in the nation's history, with the exception of the brief period needed to finance U.S. involvement in the Second World War, when it reached 106 percent. See Congressional Budget Office, *The 2016 Long-Term Budget Outlook*, July 2016, https://www.cbo .gov/sites/default/files/114th-congress-2015-2016/reports/51580-ltbo-2.pdf.

16. On the implications of high debt ratios for economic growth, see Manmohan Kumar and Jaejoon Woo, *Public Debt and Growth*, Working Paper 10/174, International Monetary Fund, Washington, D.C., 2010, http://citeseerx.ist.psu.edu/viewdoc/download?doi =10.1.1.170.8959&rep=rep1&type=pdf; and Cristina Checherita and Philipp Rother, *The Impact of High and Growing Government Debt on Economic Growth: An Empirical Investigation for the Euro Area*, Working Paper Series no. 1237, European Central Bank, August 2010, https://www.ecb.europa.eu/pub/pdf/scpwps/ecbwp1237.pdf. On the implications of U.S. dependence on foreign capital inflows, see Wayne M. Morrison and Marc Labonte, *China's Holdings of U.S. Securities: Implications for the U.S. Economy*, Congressional Research Service, August 19, 2013, https://www.fas.org/sgp/crs/row /RL34314.pdf.

17. See Steve Sestanovich, *Maximalist: America in the World from Truman to Obama* (New York: Knopf, 2014).

18. The aphorism "You may not be interested in war, but war is interested in you" is widely attributed to Bolshevik leader Leon Trotsky, but such attribution is now thought to be apocryphal.

19. Barry R. Posen, *Restraint: A New Foundation for U.S. Grand Strategy* (Ithaca, N.Y.: Cornell University Press, 2014); Bruce W. Jentleson, "Strategic Recalibration: Framework

for a 21st-Century National Security Strategy," *Washington Quarterly* 37 (2014): 115–36; David A. Shlapak, "Towards a More Modest American Strategy," *Survival* 57, no. 2 (2015): 59–78.

20. See Richard N. Haass, *Foreign Policy Begins at Home: The Case for Putting America's House in Order* (New York: Basic Books, 2013).

21. See ibid.; Barry R. Posen, "Pull Back: The Case for a Less Activist Foreign Policy," *Foreign Affairs* 92, no. 116 (2013): 116–29; and Patrick M. Cronin, *Restraint: Recalibrating American Strategy*, Center for a New American Security, June 6, 2010, https://www.cnas.org/publications/reports/restraint-recalibrating-american-strategy.

22. See Stephen M. Walt, *Taming American Power: The Global Response to U.S. Primacy* (New York: Norton, 2005); Christopher Layne, "From Preponderance to Offshore Balancing: America's Future Grand Strategy," *International Security* 22, no. 1 (1997): 86–124; and Peter Beinart, "Obama's Foreign Policy Doctrine Finally Emerges with 'Offshore Balancing,'" *Daily Beast*, November 28, 2011, http://www.thedailybeast.com/articles/2011/11/28/obama-s-foreign-policy-doctrine-finally-emerges-with-off-shore balancing.html.

23. See the discussion of "retrenchment" in Stephen G. Brooks, G. John Ikenberry, and William C. Wohlforth, "Lean Forward," *Foreign Affairs* 92, no. 1 (2013): 130–42; and Posen, "Pull Back," 116–29.

24. See the discussion of "deep engagement" in Stephen G. Brooks, G. John Ikenberry, and William C. Wohlforth, "Don't Come Home America: The Case Against Retrenchment," *International Security* 37, no. 3 (2012–2013): 7–51.

25. See U.S. Department of Defense, *Defense Planning Guidance, FY 1994–1999 (Draft)*, February 29, 1992, https://www.archives.gov/files/declassification/iscap/pdf/2008-003-doc1.pdf, which states that "future peace and stability will continue to depend in large measure upon our willingness to maintain forward presence and to retain high-quality forces that enable response to crises that threaten our interests. The future may also come to depend on others' perceptions of our will and capability to reconstitute forces and to deter or defend against strategic attack, should that prove necessary. Maintaining that posture will be absolutely crucial in heading off future crises and dissuading future aggressors from challenging our vital interests."

26. Michael O'Hanlon, "U.S. Military Must Do More with Less Money," *Washington Examiner*, November 11, 2013, http://www.brookings.edu/research/opinions/2013/11/11-us-military-budget-ohanlon.

27. The United States Department of Defense requested a base budget of $585.2 billion in defense expenditures for fiscal year 2016. This figure includes the Overseas Contingency Operations Funding request, which totaled $50.9 billion. Office of the Under Secretary of Defense (Comptroller), *Fiscal Year 2016 Budget Request*, February 2015, http://dcmo.defense.gov/Portals/47/Documents/Publications/Annual%20Performance%20Plan/FY2016_Performance_Budget.pdf.

28. See Shlapak, "Towards a More Modest American Strategy," 62.

29. Stockholm International Peace Research Institute, SIPRI Military Expenditure Database, November 3, 2015, http://www.sipri.org/research/armaments/milex/milex_database.

30. Juan Cole, "Think Again: 9/11," *Foreign Policy* 156 (2006): 30, notes Osama bin Laden's "outrage at the 'occupation of the three holy cities'—Mecca, Medina, and Jerusalem—by the U.S. military presence in Saudi Arabia (now ended) and the Israeli possession of Jerusalem." See also Kenneth Katzman, *Al Qaeda: Profile and Threat Assessment*, August 17, 2005, https://fas.org/sgp/crs/terror/RL33038.pdf, 3; and Michael Scott Doran, "Somebody Else's Civil War," *Foreign Affairs* 81, no. 1 (2002): 27–28.

31. See Stockholm International Peace Research Institute, SIPRI Military Expenditure Database; and North Atlantic Treaty Organization, "Defence Expenditures of NATO Countries (2009–2016)," NATO, July 4, 2016, http://www.nato.int/nato_static_fl2014/assets/pdf/pdf_2016_07/20160704_160704-pr2016-116.pdf.

32. This is true even for America's leading allies, as became apparent during the Libyan intervention in 2011. See Ivo H. Daalder and James G. Stavridis, "NATO's Victory in Libya," *Foreign Affairs* 91, no. 2 (2012): 2–7; and Christopher S. Chivvis, "Libya and the Future of Liberal Intervention," *Survival* 54, no. 6 (2012): 69–92.

33. Stephen Hadley, remarks at the Atlantic Council conference "Atlantic Council Strategy Initiative Launch: America's Role in the World," Atlantic Council, March 13, 2015, http://www.atlanticcouncil.org/news/transcripts/transcript-america-s-role-in-the-world.

34. See Rosa Brooks, "Obama Needs a Grand Strategy," *Foreign Policy*, January 23, 2012, http://www.foreignpolicy.com/articles/2012/01/23/obama_needs_a_grand_strategy.

2. THINKING AHEAD

1. Robert M. Gates, "Secretary of Defense Speech: As Delivered by Secretary of Defense Robert M. Gates, West Point, NY, Friday, February 25, 2011," U.S. Department of Defense, http://archive.defense.gov/Speeches/Speech.aspx?SpeechID=1539; emphasis added.

2. Robert M. Gates, quoted in "Gates Puts Cost of Libya Mission at $750 Million," *New York Times*, May 12, 2011.

3. Mary McCarthy, "The National Warning System: Striving for an Elusive Goal," *Defense Intelligence Journal* 3, no. 1 (1994): 5–19; Mary McCarthy, "The Mission to Warn: Disaster Looms," *Defense Intelligence Journal* 7, no. 2 (1998): 17–31. See also Richard J. Kerr, "The Track Record: CIA Analysis from 1950 to 2000," in *Analyzing Intelligence: Origins, Obstacles and Innovations*, ed. Roger Z. George and James B. Bruce (Washington, D.C.: Georgetown University Press, 2008), 46–47.

4. The best discussion can be found in Richard K. Betts, *Military Readiness: Concepts, Choices, Consequences* (Washington, D.C.: Brookings Institution, 1995). See also Ariel Levite, *Intelligence and Strategic Surprises* (New York: Columbia University Press, 1987).

5. This section draws on the work of Christoph O. Meyer, Florian Otto, John Brante, and Chiara de Franco, "Recasting the Warning-Response Problem: Persuasion and Preventive Policy," *International Studies Review* 12 (2010): 556–78; Michael Fitzsimmons, "The Problem of Uncertainty in Strategic Planning," *Survival* 48, no. 4 (2006–2007): 131–46; Alexander L. George and Jane E. Holl, *The Warning-Response Problem and Missed*

Opportunities in Early Warning: A Report to the Carnegie Commission on Preventing Deadly Conflict (New York: Carnegie Corporation of New York, 1997), https://www.carnegie.org/media/filer_public/33/6e/336e40fd-5176-42c2-bb9d-afd7b3b6550a/ccny_report_1997_warning.pdf; and Kenneth G. Lieberthal, *The U.S. Intelligence Community and Foreign Policy: Getting Analysis Right* (Washington, D.C.: Brookings Institution, 2009).

6. Lawrence Woocher, "The Effects of Cognitive Biases on Early Warning," paper presented at the International Studies Association's Forty-Ninth Annual Convention, "Bridging Multiple Divides," San Francisco, March 26–29, 2008; Richards J. Heuer Jr., *Psychology of Intelligence Analysis* (Washington, D.C.: Center for the Study of Intelligence, 1999).

7. Thomas C. Schelling, foreword to *Pearl Harbor: Warning and Indecision*, by Roberta Wohlstetter (Stanford, Calif.: Stanford University Press, 1962), vii.

8. See Micah Zenko, *Red Team: How to Succeed by Thinking Like the Enemy* (New York: Basic Books, 2015).

9. Woocher, "Effects of Cognitive Biases."

10. As Mary McCarthy, a former U.S. national intelligence officer for warning, has written, "The typical policymaker who is handling at least a half dozen complex foreign policy problems at once, has several more on deck, and is managing a large office with all the usual personnel and budget concerns. The last thing he or she wants to hear is that one of those policy items is on its way to becoming a crisis. The policymaker bias, therefore, is to hear the warning, but fixate on the evidence that points away from the possible crisis outcome" (McCarthy, "National Warning System," 16).

11. McCarthy, "National Warning System," 16, notes that "warning too early may be futile; few policymakers will focus on a possible outcome some 18 months in the future."

12. George and Holl, *Warning-Response Problem*.

13. See Kenneth Knight, "Focused on Foresight: An Interview with the US's National Intelligence Officer for Warning," by Drew Erdmann and Lenny Mendonca, McKinsey and Company, June 2009, http://www.mckinsey.com/industries/public-sector/our-insights/focused-on-foresight-an-interview-with-the-uss-national-intelligence-officer-for-warning.

14. See George Bush and Brent Scowcroft, *A World Transformed* (New York: Knopf, 1998); and Richard N. Haass, *War of Necessity, War of Choice: A Memoir of Two Iraq Wars* (New York: Simon and Schuster, 2009).

15. At the beginning of 1990, U.S. intelligence officials became increasingly concerned about the possibility of an Iraqi attack against Kuwait and Saudi Arabia. By June and early July 1990, these concerns had intensified to the point at which the level of attention given by various U.S. intelligence agencies to the threat had not only been significantly upgraded but the Joint Chiefs of Staff in the Pentagon and U.S. Central Command had both begun to review contingency plans for military action and even carry out some preliminary war gaming exercises. Charles E. Allen, "Warning and Iraq's Invasion of Kuwait: A Retrospective Look," *Defense Intelligence Journal* 7, no. 2 (1998): 33–44. See also Bush and Scowcroft, *World Transformed*.

16. The White House, "National Security Directive 26: U.S. Policy Toward the Persian Gulf," October 1989, http://www.fas.org/irp/offdocs/nsd/nsd26.pdf.

17. Haass, *War of Necessity*, 60. Regarding the initial discussions about what the United States should do, President Bush later recalled, "I had no idea what our options were." George H. W. Bush, quoted in Steve Sestanovich, *Maximalist: America in the World from Truman to Obama* (New York: Knopf, 2014), 250.

18. See Gregory F. Treverton and Renanah Miles, *Unheeded Warning of War: Why Policy Makers Ignored the 1990 Yugoslavia Estimate* (Washington, D.C.: Center for the Study of Intelligence, 2015). The National Intelligence Estimate of October 18, 1990 (NIE 15–90), was remarkably prescient: "Yugoslavia will cease to function as a federal state within a year, and will probably dissolve within two. Economic reform will not stave off the breakup. . . . A full-scale interrepublic war is unlikely, but serious intercommunal conflict will accompany the breakup and will continue afterward. The violence will be intractable and bitter. There is little the United States and its European allies can do to preserve Yugoslav unity." See Office of the Historian, U.S. Department of State, "The Breakup of Yugoslavia, 1990–1992," https://history.state.gov/milestones/1989-1992/breakup-yugoslavia; and C. Thomas Fingar, *From "National Communism" to National Collapse: U.S. Intelligence Community Estimative Products on Yugoslavia 1948–1990* (Washington, D.C.: Government Printing Office, 2006).

19. See Mathew Levinger, "Why the U.S. Government Failed to Anticipate the Rwandan Genocide of 1994: Lessons for Early Warning and Prevention," *Genocide Studies and Prevention* 9 (2016): 33–58. Some UN officials in Rwanda did issue warnings to the headquarters of the United Nations in New York, but these do not appear to have been shared with U.S. officials.

20. See Jeffrey Richelson, ed., "U.S. Intelligence and the Indian Bomb," a collection of declassified documents and commentary assembled by the National Security Archive, http://nsarchive.gwu.edu/NSAEBB/NSAEBB187/.

21. See Peter L. Bergen, *Manhunt: The Ten-Year Search for Bin Laden from 9/11 to Abbottabad* (New York: Broadway, 2013).

22. Two former (anonymous) senior U.S. intelligence officials, interview with the author, Washington, D.C., 2013. See also *The 9/11 Commission Report: Final Report of the National Commission on Terrorist Attacks Upon the United States* (New York: Norton, 2004), 121, 194, 203, 341, 344, 349; and Steve Coll, *Ghost Wars* (New York: Penguin, 2004), 421, 564, 566.

23. Damon Wilson, quoted in Eli Lake, Noah Shachtman, and Christopher Dickey, "Ex-CIA Chief: Why We Keep Getting Putin Wrong," *Daily Beast*, March 3, 2014, http://www.thedailybeast.com/articles/2014/03/02/ex-cia-chief-why-we-get-putin-wrong.html. See also Helene Cooper, C. J. Chivers, and Clifford J. Levy, "U.S. Watched as Squabble Turned Into a Showdown," *New York Times*, August 18, 2008; and "The Chronicle of a Caucasian Tragedy," *Spiegel Online*, August 25, 2008, http://www.spiegel.de/international/world/road-to-war-in-georgia-the-chronicle-of-a-caucasian-tragedy-a-574812.html. Other accounts attribute the surprise to other factors: U.S. distraction with the war in Iraq and the tasking of key intelligence assets to cover other regions. See Ronald D. Asmus, *A Little War That Shook the World: Georgia, Russia, and the Future of the West* (New York: St. Martin's, 2010), 2.

24. Peter Baker, *Days of Fire: Bush and Cheney in the White House* (New York: Doubleday, 2013), 603.

25. Angela Stent, *The Limits of Partnership: U.S.-Russian Relations in the Twenty-First Century* (Princeton, N.J.: Princeton University Press, 2014), 172.

26. Michael Morrell, *The Great War of Our Time: The CIA's Fight Against Terrorism from Al Qai'da to ISIS* (New York: Twelve, 2015), 73.

27. Some maintain that warnings were given but the Obama administration was either distracted by other crises or chose to dismiss them. See Peter Baker and Eric Schmitt, "Many Missteps in Assessment of ISIS Threat," *New York Times*, September 29, 2104.

28. Burgess Everett and Josh Gerstein, "Why Didn't the U.S. Know Sooner?," *Politico*, March 4, 2014, http://www.politico.com/story/2014/03/united-states-barack-obama-ukraine-crimea-russia-vladimir-putin-104264; Eli Lake and Christopher Dickey, "U.S. Spies Said No Russian Invasion of Ukraine—Putin Disagreed," *Daily Beast*, February 28, 2014, http://www.thedailybeast.com/articles/2014/02/28/u-s-spies-said-no-invasion-putin-disagreed.html.

29. Morrell, *Great War of Our Time*, 73.

30. See Mark Hosenball, Phil Stewart, and Matt Spetalnick, "Exclusive: Congress Probing U.S. Spy Agencies' Possible Lapses on Russia," Reuters, October 8, 2015, http://www.reuters.com/article/us-mideast-crisis-intelligence-exclusive-idUSKCN0S20CZ20151008.

31. Some formulations of risk also include vulnerability.

32. For example, in the area of crime prevention, law enforcement agencies increasingly use the equivalent of epidemiological assessment techniques to focus police resources on high crime areas. This has been credited with helping to bring down rates of crimes in many cities of the United States. See John Tierney, "Prison Population Can Shrink When Police Crowd Streets," *New York Times*, January 25, 2013. For a skeptical view of the role of new policing techniques and a broader discussion of declining urban crime rates in the United States, see Steven D. Levitt, "Understanding Why Crime Fell in the 1990s: Four Factors That Explain the Decline and Six That Do Not," *Journal of Economic Perspectives* 18, no. 1 (2004): 163–90.

33. Thucydides, *Outbreak of the Peloponnesian War*.

34. See Donald Kagan, "Our Interests and Our Honor," *Commentary* 103, no. 4 (1997): 42–45.

35. Edward D. Mansfield and Brian M. Pollins, eds., *Economic Interdependence and International Conflict* (Ann Arbor: University of Michigan Press, 2003); Håvard Hegre, John R. Oneal, and Bruce Russett, "Trade Does Promote Peace: New Simultaneous Estimates of the Reciprocal Effects of Trade and Conflict," *Journal of Peace Research* 47, no. 6 (2010): 763–74; Edward D. Mansfield and Jon C. Pevehouse, "Trade Blocs, Trade Flows, and International Conflict," *International Organization* 54, no. 4 (2000): 775–808.

36. The marginal risk is not high, however. See Edward D. Mansfield and Jack Snyder, "Democratization and the Danger of War," *International Security* 20, no. 1 (1995): 5–38.

37. Human Security Research Group, *Human Security Report 2009/2010: The Causes of Peace and the Shrinking Costs of War* (New York: Oxford University Press, 2011), 31.

38. James Fearon, quoted in Human Security Research Group, *Human Security Report 2009/2010*, 51.

39. For a useful description of this and other modeling efforts, see Monty G. Marshall, "Fragility, Instability, and the Failure of States: Assessing Sources of Systemic Risk," Council on Foreign Relations, October 2008, http://www.cfr.org/conflict-prevention/fragility -instability-failure-states-assessing-sources-systemic-risk/p17638.

40. As one reviewer of this broad effort observed: "Because the events involved are so rare, it is extremely difficult to correctly distinguish the handful of countries that will suffer instability in a given month, quarter, or year from a larger set of countries that are similarly vulnerable. Even the most accurate statistical models of political instability will typically produce several to as many as a dozen false positives (warnings where no instability occurs) for each true positive (warning where instability does occur)." Jay Ulfelder, "Forecasting Political Instability," unpublished memorandum, Council on Foreign Relations, May 4, 2011.

41. Matthew Milan, "Backcasting 101," presentation to the Association for Information Science and Technology IA Summit Pre-Conference, April 10, 2008, http://www.slideshare .net/mmilan/backcasting-101-final-public?next_slideshow=1.

42. See Philip E. Tetlock and Daniel Gardner, *Superforecasting: The Art and Science of Prediction* (New York: Crown, 2015); and Nate Silver, *The Signal and the Noise: Why So Many Predictions Fail and Some Don't* (New York: Penguin, 2012).

43. Sherman Kent, "Words of Estimative Probability," *Studies in Intelligence*, Fall 1964, https://www.cia.gov/library/center-for-the-study-of-intelligence/csi-publications /books-and-monographs/sherman-kent-and-the-board-of-national-estimates -collected-essays/6words.html. See also Jeffrey A. Friedman and Richard Zeckhauser, "Handling and Mishandling Estimate Probability: Likelihood, Confidence, and the Search for Bin Laden," *Intelligence and National Security*, May 2014, 1–23.

44. See "Fact Sheet 2: National Security Risk Assessment," http://www.livreblancdefen seetsecurite.gouv.fr/pdf/factsheet2-national-security-risk-assessment.pdf.

3. ACTING AHEAD

1. Donald Rumsfeld to Paul Wolfowitz, memorandum, "Subject: Potential Outcomes," December 3, 2001, http://library.rumsfeld.com/doclib/sp/1651/2001-12-03%20to%20 Paul%20Wolfowitz%20re%20Potential%20Outcomes.pdf.

2. Besides the "bad things," Wolfowitz also listed some "good things"—one of which was that Saddam Hussein could be replaced "by a new thug." See Paul Wolfowitz to Donald Rumsfeld, e-mail memorandum, "9/13/02 Potential Outcomes of Things That Could Go Right and Things That Could Go Wrong," December 5, 2001, http://library.rumsfeld .com/doclib/sp/1651/2001-12-03%20to%20Paul%20Wolfowitz%20re%20Potential%20Outcomes.pdf.

3. Al Kamen, "Worldly Advice to Rumsfeld from, Gingrich, Wolfowitz & Co," *Washington Post*, March 4, 2001.

4. For the best discussion on political will in the context of preventive action, see Lawrence Woocher, "Deconstructing "Political Will": Explaining the Failure to Prevent Deadly Conflict and Mass Atrocities," *Journal of Public and International Affairs* 12 (2001): 179–206.

5. Gareth Evans, "Preventing Deadly Conflict and the Problem of Political Will," 2002 Montague Burton Professor of International Relations Lecture at the University of Oxford, October 17, 2002.

6. President Dwight D. Eisenhower may have been the first to note this problem, saying, "What is important is seldom urgent, and what is urgent is seldom important." Dwight D. Eisenhower, quoted in James Clear, "How to Be More Productive and Eliminate Time Wasting Activities by Using the 'Eisenhower Box,'" http://jamesclear.com/eisenhower -box.

7. Robert B. Semple Jr., "Men in the News: Negotiators of Paris Cease-Fire Agreement for Vietnam," *New York Times*, January 24, 1973, http://www.nytimes.com/1973/01/24 /archives/men-in-the-news-negotiators-of-paris-ceasefire-agreement for.html.

8. Brent Scowcroft, quoted in Bartholomew Sparrow, *The Strategist: Brent Scowcroft and the Call of National Security* (New York: Public Affairs, 2015), 487.

9. Condoleezza Rice, quoted in David Rothkopf, "National Insecurity: Can Obama's Foreign Policy Be Saved?," *Foreign Policy*, September 9, 2014, http://foreignpolicy.com/2014 /09/09/national-insecurity/.

10. For an excellent synthesis of the various cognitive biases that can encourage such thinking, see Lawrence Woocher, "The Effects of Cognitive Biases on Early Warning and Response," paper presented to the International Studies Association Forty-Ninth Annual Conference, March 26, 2008.

11. Henry Kissinger, quoted in Niall Ferguson, "The Meaning of Kissinger," *Foreign Affairs* 94, no. 5 (2015): 134–43.

12. Woocher, "Effects of Cognitive Biases," 410.

13. Alexander L. George and Jane E. Holl, *The Warning-Response Problem and Missed Opportunities in Early Warning: A Report to the Carnegie Commission on Preventing Deadly Conflict* (New York: Carnegie Corporation of New York, 1997), 10; emphasis in the original.

14. Ibid.

15. Woocher, "Effects of Cognitive Biases."

16. For a discussion of the evolution of the precautionary principle in the context of international relations, see Craig McLean and Alan Patterson, *The Precautionary Principle in International Relations: Constructing Foreign and Defense Policy in an Age of Uncertainty* (Lewiston, N.Y.: Mellen, 2012), chap. 2.

17. Jessica Stern and Jonathan B. Wiener, "Precaution Against Terrorism," in *Managing Strategic Surprise: Lessons in Risk Management and Risk Assessment*, ed. Paul Bracken, Ian Bremmer, and David Gordon (Cambridge: Cambridge University Press, 2008), 115. See also McLean and Patterson, *Precautionary Principle*, 32.

18. Rio Declaration on Environment and Development, quoted in Stern and Wiener, "Precaution Against Terrorism," 111.

19. European Commission, "Communication from the Commission on the Precautionary Principle," February 2, 2000, http://eur-lex.europa.eu/legal-content/EN/ALL/?uri =CELEX:52000DC0001.

20. Evans, "Preventing Deadly Conflict."

21. Something similar was proposed in a U.S. Defense Science Board study convened to consider ways to improve U.S. readiness for potential postconflict stabilization operations. It recommended that contingencies classified as "ripe and important" should trigger intensive planning by "joint interagency task forces." See U.S. Defense Science Board, *2004 Summer Study on Transition to and from Hostilities* (Washington, D.C.: Office of the Under Secretary of Defense for Acquisition, Technology, and Logistics, 2004), http:// cgsc.cdmhost.com/cdm/singleitem/collection/p4013coll11/id/1755, 13.

22. Stern and Wiener, "Precaution Against Terrorism," 144.

23. See Lawrence Woocher, *Preventing Violent Conflict: Assessing Progress, Meeting Challenges*, United States Institute of Peace Special Report 231, September 2009, http://www.usip .org/sites/default/files/preventing_violent_conflict.pdf, 11.

24. See Michèle A. Flournoy and Shawn Brimley, eds., *Finding Our Way: Debating American Grand Strategy*, Center for a New American Security, June 2008, https://s3 .amazonaws.com/files.cnas.org/documents/FlournoyBrimley_Finding-Our-Way _June08.pdf.

25. This also explains why there are so few training courses on policy planning and formulation. For example, the vast majority of the courses available at the U.S. State Department's Foreign Service Institute are oriented toward area studies, languages, technical services, and communication and leadership skills. See "Foreign Service Institute Course Schedule and Tuitions, October 1, 2013–September 30, 2015," George P. Schultz National Foreign Affairs Training Center, 2014–2015, https://permanent.access.gpo.gov/gpo52250 /2014-2015/FY2014-2015_Schedule_Tuitions.pdf.

26. See World Health Organization, "WHO Strategy for Prevention and Control of Chronic Respiratory Diseases," 2017, http://www.who.int/respiratory/publications/strategy/en /index5.html.

27. See Brandon C. Welsh and David P. Farrington, *The Future of Crime Prevention: Developmental and Situational Strategies*, December 11, 2010, University of Cambridge Institute of Criminology, http://www.crim.cam.ac.uk/people/academic_research/david _farrington/nijprev.pdf, 2–3.

28. This discussion draws on Welsh and Farrington, *Future of Crime Prevention*; Lawrence W. Sherman, Denise Gottfredson, Doris MacKenzie, John Eck, Peter Reuter, and Shawn Bushway, *Preventing Crime: What Works, What Doesn't, What's Promising. A Report to the United States Congress*, 1997, National Criminal Justice Reference Service, https://www .ncjrs.gov/works/; Australian Institute of Criminology, "Crime Prevention Approaches, Theory and Mechanisms," http://www.aic.gov.au/publications/current%20series/rpp /100-120/rpp120/07_approaches.html; World Health Organization, *Violence Prevention: The Evidence*, 2010, http://www.who.int/violence_injury_prevention/violence/4th _milestones_meeting/evidence_briefings_all.pdf; "Crime, Interrupted," *Economist*, November 19, 2008, http://www.economist.com/node/12574177.

29. See Robert V. Wolf, *Law Enforcement and Public Health: Sharing Resources and Strategies to Make Communities Safer*, http://ric-zai-inc.com/Publications/cops-p226-pub.pdf.

30. Indeed, others have drawn the parallels if not elaborated on the details. See William J. Perry, "Using Military Force When Deterrence Fails: Remarks to Aspen, CO, Institute Conference," *Defense Issues* 10, no. 80 (1995): 1–4. Secretary of Defense Perry and future secretary of defense Ashton Carter would later elaborate on this concept in Ashton B. Carter and William J. Perry, *Preventive Defense: A New Security Strategy for America* (Washington, D.C.: Brookings Institution, 2000). The disease prevention approach has also been invoked as a good template for counterterrorism. In a speech, Richard Haass, then director of policy planning at the U.S. State Department, argued, "The challenge of terrorism is thus akin to fighting a virus in that we can accomplish a great deal but not eradicate the problem. We can take steps to prevent it, protect ourselves from it, and, when an outbreak occurs, quarantine it, minimize the damage it inflicts, and attack it with all our power. Therefore, the ultimate goal of our campaign is progress through the steady accumulation of individual successes. Patience and persistence will be the watchwords for this campaign." Richard N. Haass, "The Bush Administration's Response to 9/11—and Beyond," remarks to the Council on Foreign Relations, October 15, 2001, http://2001-2009.state.gov/s/p/rem/5505.htm.

31. This section builds on and refines an earlier typology of preventive action proposed in Paul B. Stares and Micah Zenko, *Enhancing U.S. Preventive Action* (New York: Council on Foreign Relations, 2009).

32. Risk reduction measures are thus different from what are sometimes referred to as threat reduction measures, the latter intended for the most part to lower the dangers associated with *known or extant* national security threats rather than to prevent or inhibit their initial emergence. For a discussion of threat reduction measures in the U.S. and Russian context, see Ian Anthony, *Reducing Threats at the Source: A European Perspective on Cooperative Threat Reduction* (Stockholm: Stockholm International Peace Research Institute, 2004).

33. Douglas C. North, John Joseph Wallis, and Barry R. Weingast, *Violence and Social Orders: A Conceptual Framework for Interpreting Recorded Human History* (New York: Cambridge University Press, 2009), 13.

34. Rules can be defined as "expectations of right conduct in defined circumstances." See Raymond Cohen, *International Politics: The Rules of the Game* (New York: Longman, 1981), 8. Other basic order-inducing rules include ensuring that promises made and the agreements entered into by members of society will be honored and fulfilled, and that their personal possessions are secure from challenges that are persistent and limitless in nature. See Hedley Bull, *The Anarchical Society: A Study of Order in World Politics* (New York: Columbia University Press, 1977), 4–5.

35. For a useful overview of the theoretical literature on the role of states in reducing violence, see Sean Fox and Kristian Hoelscher, "Political Order, Development and Social Violence," *Journal of Peace Research* 49, no. 3 (2012): 433–34.

36. See Azar Gat, "Is War Declining–and Why?," *Journal of Peace Research* 50, no. 2 (2012): 150–51. According to Steven Pinker, violent mortality has dropped from an estimated

15 percent of the population in prestate societies to between 1 percent and 5 percent. See Steven Pinker, *The Better Angels of Our Nature: Why Violence Has Declined* (New York: Viking, 2011), 48–54.

37. See United Nations, Charter of the United Nations, http://www.un.org/en/sections/un -charter/chapter-i/index.html, chap. 1, art. 2.

38. John Mueller, "War Has Almost Ceased to Exist: An Assessment," *Political Science Quarterly* 123, no. 2 (2009): 300–302, 306–7; Pinker, *Better Angels of Our Nature*, 258.

39. Those making this argument are often associated with specific schools within inter-national relations theory—functionalists, constructivists, and neoliberal institution-alists. See Christian Reus-Smit and Duncan Snidal, eds., *The Oxford Handbook of International Relations* (New York: Oxford University Press, 2008). For good overviews of the literature on the relationship between international organizations and conflict, see Charles Boehmer, Erik Gartzke, and Timothy Nordstrom, "Do Intergovern-mental Organizations Promote Peace?," *World Politics* 57 (2004): 3–7; and Emilie Hafner Burton and Alexander H. Montgomery, "Power Positions: International Organizations, Social Networks, and Conflict," *Journal of Conflict Resolution* 50, no. 1 (2006): 5–7.

40. Boehmer, Gartzke, and Nordstrom, "Do Intergovernmental Organizations Promote Peace?," 28–30. See also Steve Chan, "Discerning the Causal Relationships Between Great Powers' Membership in Intergovernmental Organizations and Their Initiation of Militarized Disputes," *Conflict Management and Peace Science* 22 (2005): 239–56.

41. The Four Policemen idea eventually morphed into the system for the Permanent Five members of the UN Security Council (France being the additional power), while coop-eration among the informal "quad" grouping within NATO (made up of the United States, Great Britain, France, and West Germany) did much to manage alliance politics through the latter half of the Cold War.

42. John J. Mearsheimer, "Back to the Future: Instability in Europe After the Cold War," *International Security* 15, no. 1 (1990): 26–27. See also John Lewis Gaddis, "The Long Peace: Elements of Stability in the Postwar International System," *International Security* 10, no. 4 (1986): 99–142.

43. See John A Vasquez and Choong-Nam Kang, "How and Why the Cold War Became a Long Peace: Some Statistical Insights," *Cooperation and Conflict* 48, no. 1 (2012): 41.

44. See Sara Z. Kutchesfahani, "The Relevance of Historical Experience to Current Nu-clear Proliferation Challenges," in *A Collection of Papers from the 2009 PONI Conference Series*, ed. Mark Jansson (Washington, D.C.: Center for Strategic and International Studies, 2010), https://csis-prod.s3.amazonaws.com/s3fs-public/110921_Kutchesfahani2 .pdf?gMPBF5BSZb5BhTWzVMofp7w0ijgpBOfj.

45. It has been argued that alliances that are offensive in orientation or involve promises of nonintervention in the disputes of other powers are more prone to conflict since they are more threatening and permissive of aggressive behavior. See Brett Ashley Leeds, "Do Alliances Deter Aggression? The Influence of Military Alliances on the Initiation of Militarized International Disputes," *American Journal of Political Science* 47, no. 3 (2003): 437.

46. Bruce Russett, "The Democratic Peace," in Human Security Research Group, *Human Security Report 2009/2010: The Causes of Peace and the Shrinking Costs of War* (New York: Oxford University Press, 2011), 30.

47. Some do argue, nonetheless, that democracies are still inherently less likely to go to war than other types of states. See Sean Lynn-Jones, "Why the United States Should Promote Democracy," Belfer Center for Science and International Affairs, March 1998, http://www.belfercenter.org/publication/why-united-states-should-spread-democracy.

48. Russett, "Democratic Peace," 30.

49. Charles A. Kupchan, *How Enemies Become Friends: The Sources of Stable Peace* (Princeton, N.J.: Princeton University Press, 2010), 13.

50. Ibid., 31; Lynn-Jones, "Why the United States Should Promote Democracy," 6.

51. Håvard Hegre, Tanja Ellingsen, Scott Gates, and Nils Petter Gleditsch, "Toward a Democratic Civil Peace? Democracy, Political Change, and Civil War 1816–1992," *American Political Science Review* 95, no. 1 (2001): 16–33.

52. Jack Goldstone, Robert H. Bates, David L. Epstein, Ted Robert Gurr, Michael B. Lustik, Monty G. Marshall, Jay Ulfelder, and Mark Woodward, "A Global Model for Forecasting Political Instability," *American Journal of Political Science* 54, no. 1 (2010): 190–208.

53. I am very grateful to my Council on Foreign Relations colleagues Jamille Bigio and Rachel B. Vogelstein for bringing to my attention the considerable literature on the relationship between peace and women's empowerment. Jamille Bigio and Rachel B. Vogelstein, *How Women's Participation in Conflict Prevention and Resolution Advances U.S. Interests* (New York: Council on Foreign Relations, 2016).

54. See, for example, Thomas Carothers, "Democracy Assistance: Political vs. Developmental," *Journal of Democracy* 20, no. 1 (2009): 5–19.

55. Goldstone et al., "Global Model for Forecasting Political Instability," 205.

56. See Kupchan, *How Enemies Become Friends*.

57. See Human Security Research Group, *Human Security Report 2009/2010*, 29; Edward D. Mansfield and Brian M. Pollins, "Interdependence and Conflict: An Introduction," in *Economic Interdependence and International Conflict: New Perspectives on an Enduring Debate*, ed. Edward D. Mansfield and Brian M. Pollins (Ann Arbor: University of Michigan Press, 2003), 1–28; Erik Gartzke, Quin Li, and Charles Boehmer, "Investing in the Peace: Economic Interdependence and International Conflict," *International Organization* 55, no. 2 (2001): 391–438. There are some dissenters, however; see, for example, Katherine Barbieri, "Economic Interdependence: A Path to Peace or a Source of Interstate Conflict?," *Journal of Peace Research* 33, no. 1 (1996): 29–49.

58. See Gartzke, Li, and Boehmer, "Investing in the Peace."

59. Macartan Humphreys, *Economics and Violent Conflict* (Cambridge, Mass.: Harvard University, 2003), https://www.unicef.org/socialpolicy/files/Economics_and_Violent_Conflict.pdf; Gartzke, Li, and Boehmer, "Investing in the Peace."

60. See Gat, "Is War Declining?," 153; and, more specifically, see Stephen G. Brooks, "'Economic Actors' Lobbying Influence on the Prospects for War and Peace," *International Organization* 67 (2013): 863–88.

61. Human Security Research Group, *Human Security Report 2009/2010*, 51.

62. Lael Brainard and Derek Chollet, eds., *Too Poor for Peace? Global Poverty, Conflict, and Security in the 21st Century* (Washington, D.C.: Brookings Institution, 2007), 11–15.

63. For a graph on men who experienced violence when they were young that are more likely to act violently as adults, see World Bank, *World Development Report 2014: Risk and Opportunity—Managing Risk for Development* (Washington, D.C.: World Bank, 2013), 114.

64. James D. Fearon and David Laitin, "Ethnicity, Insurgency, and Civil War," *American Political Science Review* 97, no. 1 (2003): 75–90.

65. See Francis Fukuyama, *The Origins of Political Order: From Prehuman Times to the French Revolution* (New York: Farrar, Straus and Giroux, 2012); James A. Robinson and Daron Acemoglu, *Why Nations Fail: The Origins of Power, Prosperity, and Poverty* (New York: Crown Business, 2012); and North, Wallis, and Weingast, *Violence and Social Orders.*

66. For discussions of current state-building challenges and critiques of current approaches, see Stephen D. Krasner, "International Support for State-Building," *Prism* 2, no. 3 (2011): 65–74; Ashraf Ghani and Clare Lockhart, *Fixing Failed States: A Framework for Rebuilding a Fractured World* (New York: Oxford University Press, 2009); James Dobbins, Michele A. Poole, Austin Long, and Benjamin Runkle, *After the War: Nation-Building from FDR to George W. Bush* (Santa Monica, Calif.: RAND, 2008); Stewart Patrick, *Weak Links: Fragile States, Global Threats, and International Security* (New York: Oxford University Press, 2011); and Charles T. Call and Elizabeth M. Cousens, "Ending Wars and Building Peace: International Responses to War-Torn Societies," *International Studies Perspectives* 9 (2008): 1–21.

67. World Bank, *World Development Report 2011: Conflict, Security and Development* (Washington, D.C.: World Bank, 2011), 11.

68. Ibid., 12–13. See also Bruce Jones and Molly Elgin-Cossart, *Development in the Shadow of Violence: A Knowledge Agenda for Policy*, https://www.idrc.ca/sites/default/files/sp /Documents%20EN/Development-in-the-shadow-of-violence.pdf, 10–11.

69. See Stephen D. Krasner and Carlos Pascual, "Addressing State Failure," *Foreign Affairs* 84, no. 4 (2005): 153–63; "Unbundling the Nation State," *Economist*, February 7, 2014, http://www.economist.com/news/international/21595928-countries-have-started -outsource-public-services-each-other-unbundling-nation.

70. See Jack L. Snyder, *From Voting to Violence: Democratization and Nationalist Conflict* (New York: Norton, 2000); and Richard Ned Lebow, *Between Peace and War* (Baltimore: Johns Hopkins University Press, 1984).

71. See Malcolm N. Shaw, "Case Concerning the Land, Island and Maritime Frontier Dispute (El Salvador/Honduras: Nicaragua Intervening), Judgment of 11 September 1992," *International and Comparative Law Quarterly* 42, no. 4 (1993): 929–37; Gino J. Naldi, "Case Concerning the Territorial Dispute (Libyan Arab Jamahiriya/Chad)," *International and Comparative Law Quarterly* 44, no. 3 (1995): 683–90; International Court of Justice, "Maritime Delimitation and Territorial Questions Between Qatar and Bahrain," September 11, 1992, http://www.icj-cij.org/docket/index.php?sum=443&p1 =3&p2=3&case=87&p3=5; and United Nations, "UN Court Rules in Maritime Dis-

pute Between Singapore and Malaysia," May 23, 2008, http://www.un.org/apps/news /story.asp?NewsID=26780&Cr=icj&Cr1#.U1AjVPldXzg.

72. See Barnett R. Rubin and Bruce D. Jones, "Prevention of Violent Conflict: Tasks and Challenges for the United Nations," *Global Governance* 13 (2007): 395.

73. Tom Phillips, Oliver Holmes, and Owen Bowcott, "Beijing Rejects Tribunal's Ruling in South China Sea Case," *Guardian*, July 12, 2016, https://www.theguardian.com /world/2016/jul/12/philippines-wins-south-china-sea-case-against-china.

74. John Bray and Jean Devlin, "Trade, Investment, and Conflict" paper produced for Civil Society Dialogue Network, October 29, 2012, http://eplo.org/wp-content/uploads/2017 /02/CSDN_Policy-meeting_Private-Sector_Trade-Investment-Conflict.pdf; Martin Fackler, "China and Japan in Deal Over Contested Gas Fields," *New York Times*, June 19, 2008, http://www.nytimes.com/2008/06/19/world/asia/19sea.html?_r=0.

75. Oregon State University Program in Water Conflict Management and Transformation, "Case Studies—Water Conflict Resolution," http://www.transboundarywaters.orst .edu/research/case studies/index.html; Walter Gibbs, "Russia and Norway Reach Accord on Barents Sea," *New York Times*, April 27, 2010, http://www.nytimes.com /2010/04/28/world/europe/28norway.html; Arild Moe, Daniel Fjærtoft, and Indra Øverland, "Space and Timing: Why Was the Barents Sea Delimitation Dispute Resolved in 2010?," *Polar Geography* 34, no. 3 (2011): 145–62.

76. For examples, see Simon J. A. Mason and Matthias Siegfried, "Confidence Building Measures (CBMs) in Peace Processes," in *Managing Peace Processes: Process Related Questions*, vol. 1 (Addis Ababa: African Union and the Centre for Humanitarian Dialogue, 2013): 57–77.

77. For a concise description of the standard explanations of intrastate violence, see the World Bank, *World Development Report 2011*, 73–95.

78. Frances Stewart, ed., *Horizontal Inequalities and Conflict: Understanding Group Violence in Multiethnic Societies* (New York: Palgrave Macmillan, 2010); Frances Stewart, "Crisis Prevention: Tackling Horizontal Inequalities," *Oxford Development Studies* 28, no. 3 (2000): 245–62.

79. See Stef Vandeginste, "Power-Sharing, Conflict, and Transition in Burundi: Twenty Years of Trial and Error," *Africa Spectrum* 44, no. 3 (2009): 63–86; Barry Bearak, "Madagascar Political Rivals Agree to Power-Sharing Deal," *New York Times*, August 9, 2009, http://www.nytimes.com/2009/08/10/world/africa/10madagascar.html; John Young, "Regionalism and Democracy in Ethiopia," *Third World Quarterly* 19, no. 2 (1998): 191–204; Henry E. Alapiki, "State Creation in Nigeria: Failed Approaches to National Integration and Local Autonomy," *African Studies Review* 38, no. 2 (2005): 49–65; Augustus Richard Norton, "Lebanon After Ta'if: Is the Civil War Over?," *Middle East Journal* 45, no. 3 (1991): 457–73; and Faten Ghosn and Amal Khoury, "Lebanon After the Civil War: Peace or the Illusion of Peace?," *Middle East Journal* 65, no. 3 (2011): 381–97.

80. See Chetan Kumar and Jos De la Haye, "Hybrid Peacemaking: Building National 'Infrastructures for Peace,'" *Global Governance* 18 (2011): 13–20; World Bank, *World Development Report 2011*, 189.

81. See European Union External Action Service, "Strengthening National Capacities for Mediation and Dialogue: National Dialogue Platforms and Infrastructures for Peace," http://ecdpm.org/publications/national-dialogue-platforms-infrastructures -peace/.

82. See Lydia Polgreen, "World Bank Ends Effort to Help Chad Ease Poverty," *New York Times*, September 10, 2008, http://www.nytimes.com/2008/09/11/world/africa/11chad .html; Thierry Vircoulon, "Oil in Chad: The Fragile State's Easy Victory Over International Institutions," *In Pursuit of Peace*, International Crisis Group, September 9, 2010, http://blog.crisisgroup.org/africa/2010/09/09/oil-in-chad-the-fragile-states-easy -victory-over-international-institutions/; World Bank Chad-Cameroon Petroleum Development and Pipeline Project, "Management Statement on the Lessons from Evaluation of the Chad-Cameroon Oil Development and Pipeline Program," November 23, 2009, http://web.worldbank.org/archive/website01210/WEB/0__CO-19 .HTM; and George E. Mitchell, "Leveraging Project Finance for Development: The Chad-Cameroon Oilfield Development and Pipeline Project," *Journal of Civil Society and Social Transformation* 1 (2010): 14–25.

83. One example of a successful case is São Tomé and Principe, which has designed one of the most effective funds, governed by the 2004 Oil Revenue Management Law, in anticipation of future oil development. See Amber Linea Moreen, *Overcoming the "Resource Curse": Prioritizing Policy Interventions in Countries with Large Extractive Industries* (Santa Monica, Calif.: RAND, 2007).

84. J. Andrew Grant, "The Kimberly Process at Ten: Reflections on a Decade of Efforts to End the Trade in Conflict Diamonds," in *High-Value Natural Resources and Peacebuilding*, ed. Päivi Lujala and Siri Aas Rustad (London: Earthscan, 2012), 159–79; Scanteam, *Achievements and Strategic Options: Evaluation of the Extractive Industries Transparency Initiative*, https://eiti.org/sites/default/files/documents/2011-EITI-evaluation-report .pdf. The EITI has had mixed results in some places. See Nicholas Shaxson, *Nigeria's Extractive Industries Transparency Initiative: Just a Glorious Audit?* (London: Chatham House, 2009).

85. See Bruce Cronin, "Creating Stability in the New Europe: The OSCE High Commissioner on National Minorities and the Socialization of Risky States," *Security Studies* 12, no. 1 (2002): 132–63; and Walter A. Kemp, ed., *Quiet Diplomacy in Action* (New York: Springer, 2001).

86. See Ivana Djuric, "The Post-War Repatriation of Serb Minority Internally Displaced Persons and Refugees in Croatia—Between Discrimination and Political Settlement," *Europe-Asia Studies* 62, no. 10 (2010): 1639–60; and Viktor Koska, *The Evolution of the Croatian Citizenship Regime: From Independence to EU Integration*, CITSEE Working Paper Series 15, University of Edinburgh School of Law, 2011.

87. One example of a peace education initiative can be found in Mindanao, Philippines; see "Peace Education in Mindanao Schools & Communities," International Youth Foundation, http://www.iyfnet.org/library/peace-education-mindanao-schools-communities. On interfaith dialogues, see David Smock, *Interfaith Dialogue and Peacebuilding* (Washington, D.C.: United States Institute of Peace, 2002).

88. King Abdullah bin Abdulaziz International Dialogue Centre for Interreligious and Intercultural Dialogue, "United Against Violence in the Name of Religion: Supporting Diversity in Iraq and Syria," November 18–19, 2014, http://www.kaiciid.org/publications-resources/united-against-violence-name-religion-supporting-diversty-iraq-syria.

89. Dorina Bekoe, *Trends in Electoral Violence in Sub-Saharan Africa*, Peace Brief 13 (Washington, D.C.: United States Institute of Peace, 2010), https://www.usip.org/sites/default/files/PB13Electoral%20Violence.pdf.

90. United Nations Development Programme, *Elections and Conflict Prevention: A Guide to Analysis, Planning and Programming* (New York: United Nations Development Programme, 2009).

91. Mwangi S. Kimenyi, "Kenya: A Country Redeemed After a Peaceful Election," Brookings Institution, April 2, 2013, https://www.brookings.edu/blog/up-front/2013/04/02/kenya-a-country-redeemed-after-a-peaceful-election/.

92. Carter Center, *Final Report to the Guyana Elections Commission on the 2006 General and Regional Elections* (Atlanta: Carter Center, 2007), https://www.cartercenter.org/documents/guyanaelect%20rpt07_final.pdf; Bekoe, *Trends in Electoral Violence*.

93. See Richard Gowan, "'Less Bound to the Desk': Ban Ki-moon, the UN, and Preventive Diplomacy," *Global Governance* 18 (2012): 387–404. See also United Nations, *Preventive Diplomacy: Delivering Results* (New York: United Nations Department of Political Affairs, 2011), http://www.un.org/undpa/sites/www.un.org.undpa/files/SG%20Report%20on%20Preventive%20Diplomacy.pdf.

94. See the remarks by Lynn Pascoe in Andrew Solomon, Lynn Pascoe, Paul B. Stares, and David R. Smock, "Rediscovering Preventive Diplomacy," panel discussion, Brookings Institution, Washington, D.C., July 26, 2010, https://www.brookings.edu/wp-content/uploads/2012/04/20100726_UN_diplomacy.pdf.

95. See Dennis Blair, *Military Engagement: Influencing Armed Forces Worldwide to Support Democratic Transitions*, vol. 1, *Overview* (Washington, D.C.: Brookings Institution, 2013), 74, 91–92, and for useful guidance on how to develop potentially productive relationships for preventive engagement, 79–80.

96. See International Monetary Fund, "IMF Rapid Credit Facility (CRF)," http://www.imf.org/external/np/exr/facts/rcf.htm.

97. See Polly Nayak and Michael Krepon, *U.S. Crisis Management in South Asia's Twin Peaks Crisis* (Washington, D.C.: Stimson Center, 2006); Don Oberdorfer, *The Two Koreas: A Contemporary History* (Reading, Mass.: Addison-Wesley, 1997); Emery Brusset, *Evaluation of the Conflict Prevention Pools: Case Study Sudan* (London: UK Foreign and Commonwealth Office, Cabinet Office, Ministry of Defence, and Treasury, 2004); Bonnie Glaser, "Armed Clash in the South China Sea," Council on Foreign Relations, April 2012, http://www.cfr.org/asia-and-pacific/armed-clash-south-china-sea/p27883.

98. See Howard Wolpe, *Making Peace After Genocide: Anatomy of the Burundi Process*, Peaceworks no. 70 (Washington, D.C.: United States Institute of Peace, 2011), http://www.usip.org/sites/default/files/PW_Burundi.pdf; Charles J. Brown, "The Obama Administration and the Struggle to Prevent Atrocities in the Central African Republic: December 2012–September 2014," United States Holocaust Memorial Museum,

November 2016, https://www.ushmm.org/m/pdfs/20161116-Charlie-Brown-CAR
-Report.pdf. Although the DRC is still in the midst of a crisis, and it is too soon to tell
whether conflict prevention efforts will be successful or not, the U.S. special envoy has
conducted quiet diplomacy for more than a year with the government and regional
partners.

99. Barnett R. Rubin and Bruce D. Jones, "Prevention of Violent Conflict: Tasks and Challenges for the United Nations," *Global Governance* 13, no. 3 (2007): 395.

100. Rubin and Jones, "Prevention of Violent Conflict"; United Nations, *Preventive Diplomacy*; Gowan, "'Less Bound to the Desk'"; Kumar and De la Haye, "Hybrid Peacemaking."

4. RISK REDUCTION

1. McKinsey and Company, "No Ordinary Disruption: The Forces Reshaping Asia," September 2015, 5, http://www.mckinsey.com/~/media/mckinsey%20offices/singapore/pdfs/no_ordinary_disruption_the_forces_reshaping_asia.ashx.

2. Thomas Fingar, *National Intelligence Assessment on the National Security Implications of Global Climate Change*, statement to the House Permanent Select Committee on Intelligence and House Select Committee on Energy Independence and Global Warming, June 25, 2008, https://fas.org/irp/congress/2008_hr/062508fingar.pdf.

3. National Intelligence Council, *Global Trends 2030: Alternative Worlds*" (Washington, D.C.: National Intelligence Council, 2012), http://www.dni.gov/files/documents/Global Trends_2030.pdf.

4. For a discussion of what is often called the power transition theory of great power relations and its contemporary relevance to China, see Richard Ned Lebow and Benjamin Valentino, "Lost in Transition: A Critical Analysis of Power Transition Theory," *International Relations* 23, no. 3 (2009): 389–410; and M. Taylor Fravel, "International Relations Theory and China's Rise: Assessing China's Potential for Territorial Expansion," *International Studies Review* 12 (2010): 505–32.

5. See Robert S. Jervis, "Was the Cold War a Security Dilemma?," *Journal of Cold War Studies* 3, no. 1 (2001): 36–60, http://www.ou.edu/uschina/SASD/SASD2006/Jervis2001CWSecDil.pdf.

6. National Intelligence Council, *Global Trends 2030*, 19.

7. For a very provocative discussion of the effect of various technologies on deglobalization, see T. X. Hammes, "Will Technological Convergence Reverse Globalization?," Strategic Forum 297 (Washington, D.C.: National Defense University, 2016), http://ndupress.ndu.edu/Portals/68/Documents/stratforum/SF-297.pdf.

8. For a video and text transcript of Xi's speech, see C-SPAN, "U.S.-China Relations," recorded February 15, 2012, https://www.c-span.org/video/?304439-1/uschina-relations. See also David Lampton, "A New Type of Major Power Relationship: Seeking a Durable Foundation for U.S.-China Ties," *China-U.S. Focus*, September 21, 2013, http://www.nbr.org/publications/element.aspx?id=650.

9. See the Declaration on Principles for Relations and Comprehensive Cooperation Between the People's Republic of China and the Republic of India, June 25, 2003, http://china.usc.edu/declaration-principles-relations-and-comprehensive-cooperation-between-peoples-republic-china-and; and the Five Principles of Peaceful Coexistence (1954), which was recently reiterated on its sixtieth anniversary in 2014. See Xi Jinping, "Carry Forward the Five Principles of Peaceful Coexistence to Build a Better World Through Win-Win-Cooperation," Ministry of Foreign Affairs of the People's Republic of China, speech given on June 28, 2017, http://www.fmprc.gov.cn/mfa_eng/wjdt_665385/zyjh_665391/t1170143.shtml.

10. This was arguably the case with the initial breakthrough Shanghai communiqué between the United States and China in 1972 for the subsequent normalization of relations, as well as the agreement between the United States and the Soviet Union in the same year that set out basic principles of peaceful coexistence for strategic arms limitation.

11. Several proposals have been made along these lines. See for example, Gregory D. Koblentz, *Strategic Stability in the Second Nuclear Age* (New York: Council on Foreign Relations, 2014); and James Steinberg and Michael E. O'Hanlon, *Strategic Reassurance and Resolve: U.S.-China Relations in the Twenty-First Century* (Princeton, N.J.: Princeton University Press, 2014).

12. See David C. Gompert and Philip C. Saunders, *The Paradox of Power: Sino-American Strategic Restraint in the Age of Vulnerability* (Washington, D.C.: National Defense University, 2011), 89. See also Steinberg and O'Hanlon, *Strategic Reassurance and Resolve*, 156; Robert A. Manning and Barry Pavel, "How to Stop the Scary Slide in U.S.-China Ties," *National Interest*, July 14, 2014, http://nationalinterest.org/feature/how-stop-the-scary-slide-us-china-ties-10865.

13. Hans M. Kristensen and Mathew McKinzie, *Reducing Alert Rates of Nuclear Weapons* (Geneva: United Nations Institute for Disarmament Research, 2012).

14. Steinberg and O'Hanlon, *Strategic Reassurance and Resolve*, 197–201.

15. Ibid., 109–10, 112. See also Micah Zenko, "Dangerous Space Incidents," Council on Foreign Relations, April 2014, http://www.cfr.org/space/dangerous-space-incidents/p32790.

16. See Benjamin Brake, "Strategic Risks of Ambiguity in Cyberspace," Council on Foreign Relations, May 2015, http://www.cfr.org/cybersecurity/strategic-risks-ambiguity-cyberspace/p36541; and Steinberg and O'Hanlon, *Strategic Reassurance and Resolve*, 178–79.

17. Steinberg and O'Hanlon, *Strategic Reassurance and Resolve*, 211.

18. U.S. Department of Defense, *Nuclear Posture Review Report*, April 2010, http://www.defense.gov/Portals/1/features/defenseReviews/NPR/2010_Nuclear_Posture_Review_Report.pdf.

19. As will be discussed in chapter 5, this would have implications for NATO deployments to the Baltic states and the future configuration of U.S. forces on the Korean Peninsula following reunification.

20. See Edward Luck, "The Responsibility to Protect: Growing Pains or Early Promise?," *Ethics and International Affairs* 24, no. 4 (2010): 349–65.

21. Mark Mazower, *Governing the World: The History of an Idea, 1815 to the Present* (New York: Penguin, 2013), 395.

22. See Page Fortna, "Enough with the Pessimism About Peacekeeping," September 24, 2015, http://politicalviolenceataglance.org/2015/09/24/enough-with-the-pessimism -about-peacekeeping/; and Kyle Beardsley, David Cunningham, and Peter B. White, "How the UN Contributes to Conflict Prevention," September 11, 2015, https:// politicalviolenceataglance.org/2015/09/11/how-the-un-contributes-to-conflict -prevention/.

23. Kara C. McDonald and Stewart M. Patrick, *UN Security Council Enlargement and U.S. Interests* (New York: Council on Foreign Relations, 2010).

24. Ibid., 26.

25. See Laurent Fabius, "A Call for Self-Restraint at the U.N.," *New York Times*, October 4, 2013, http://www.nytimes.com/2013/10/04/opinion/a-call-for-self-restraint-at-the-un .html.

26. McDonald and Patrick, *UN Security Council Enlargement*, 28–29.

27. Council on Foreign Relations, *U.S. Trade and Investment Policy* (New York: Council on Foreign Relations, 2011), 6.

28. Some more modest agreements were reached, however, in Bali in 2013. See James McBride, "The World Trade Organization (WTO)," Council on Foreign Relations, September 12, 2016, http://www.cfr.org/international-organizations-and-alliances /world-trade-organization-wto/p9386.

29. See Richard Baldwin, "21st Century Regionalism: Filling the Gap Between 21st Century Trade and 20th Century Trade Rules," Staff Working Paper ERSD-2011- 08, World Trade Organization, 2011, https://www.wto.org/english/res_e/reser_e /ersd201108_e.pdf; and Gabriel Siles-Brugge, "Global Trade Politics and the Transatlantic Trade and Investment Partnership," E-International Relations, May 5, 2014, http://www.e-ir.info/2014/05/05/global-trade-politics-and-the-transatlantic-trade-and -investment-partnership/.

30. One estimate from the Peterson Institute for International Economics reckons that the TPP could generate an additional $77 billion per annum in real income for the United States and add an additional $123.5 billion to U.S. exports by 2015. See Brad Glosserman, *America's TPP Dilemmas*, PacNet 20, Center for Strategic and International Studies, April 2, 2015, https://csis-prod.s3.amazonaws.com/s3fs-public/legacy_files/files /publication/Pac1520.pdf.

31. See Jagdish Bhagwati, Pravin Krishna, and Arvind Panagariya, "Where Is the World Trade System Heading?," in *Power Shifts and New Blocs in the Global Trading System*, ed. Sanjaya Baru and Suvi Dogra (London: Routledge, 2015), 17–37.

32. See Mireya Solis, "The Geopolitical Importance of the Trans-Pacific Partnership: At Stake, a Liberal Economic Order," Brookings Institution, March 13, 2015, https://www .brookings.edu/blog/order-from-chaos/2015/03/13/the-geopolitical-importance-of-the -trans-pacific-partnership-at-stake-a-liberal-economic-order/. See especially Ashley J. Tellis, "The Geopolitics of the TTIP and TPP," in *Power Shifts and New Blocs in the Global Trading System*, 93–120.

33. See Michael B. Froman, "The Strategic Logic of Trade," *Foreign Affairs* 93, no. 6 (2014), https://www.foreignaffairs.com/articles/americas/strategic-logic-trade; and Thomas Donilon, "The United States and the Asia-Pacific in 2013," speech delivered to the Asia Society, March 11, 2013, http://asiasociety.org/new-york/complete-transcript-thomas-donilon-asia-society-new-york.

34. See Oli Brown, Faisal Haq Shaheen, Shaheen Rafi Khan, and Moeed Yusuf, *Regional Trade Agreements: Promoting Conflict or Building Peace?*, International Institute for Sustainable Development, October 2005, https://www.iisd.org/sites/default/files/publications/security_rta_conflict.pdf.

35. "Global Trade After the Doha Round," *New York Times*, January 1, 2016, http://www.nytimes.com/2016/01/01/opinion/global-trade-after-the-failure-of-the-doha-round.html.

36. For a discussion of this reform proposal, see Jaime Zabludovsky Kuper and Sergio Gómez Lora, "The High Stakes in Regional Trade Talks," Council on Foreign Relations, November 23, 2013, http://www.cfr.org/councilofcouncils/global_memos/p32417.

37. See Mustapha Rouis and Steven R. Tabor, *Regional Economic Integration in the Middle East and North Africa: Beyond Trade and Reform* (Washington, D.C.: World Bank, 2013), xix, xxii.

38. Ibid., xxi.

39. Ibid.

40. See Robert Z. Lawrence, "Recent US Free Trade Initiatives in the Middle East: Opportunities but No Guarantees," Faculty Research Working Paper RWP06-050, Harvard University, December 2006, http://www.iie.com/publications/papers/lawrence1206.pdf.

41. See Shayerah Ilias Akhtar, Mary Jane Bolle, and Rebecca M. Nelson, *U.S. Trade and Investment in the Middle East and North Africa: Overview and Issues for Congress* (Washington, D.C.: Congressional Research Service, 2013), https://www.fas.org/sgp/crs/misc/R42153.pdf.

42. See Daniel S. Markey, *Reorienting U.S. Pakistan Strategy: From Af-Pak to Asia* (New York: Council on Foreign Relations, 2014), 24–26.

43. See Gordon Adams and Richard Sokolsky, "Savaging State and USAID Budgets Could Do Wonders for Results," *Foreign Policy*, March 9, 2017, http://foreignpolicy.com/2017/03/09/savaging-state-and-usaid-budgets-could-do-wonders-for-results-tillerson-development-diplomacy-cuts/.

44. In March 2017, the Trump administration released a preliminary budget proposal from the Office of Management and Budget requesting "$25.6 billion in base funding for the Department of State and USAID, a $10.1 billion or 28 percent reduction from the 2017 annualized CR level." See "America First: A Budget Blueprint to Make America Great Again," Office of Management and Budget, March 16, 2017, 39, https://www.whitehouse.gov/sites/whitehouse.gov/files/omb/budget/fy2018/2018_blueprint.pdf.

45. For an excellent overview, see "The U.S. Foreign Aid Budget, Visualized," *Washington Post*, October 18, 2016. See also Charles Call, "The Lingering Problem of Fragile States," *Washington Quarterly* 39, no. 4 (2017): 193–209.

46. UK Cabinet Office official, interview with the author, London, 2015.

47. See UK Foreign and Commonwealth Office, Department for International Development, and Ministry of Defence, *Conflict Pool Strategic Guidance* (London: UK Foreign and Commonwealth Office, Department for International Development, and Ministry of Defence, 2013), https://www.gov.uk/government/uploads/system/uploads/attachment _data/file/200169/Conflict_Pool_Strategic_Guidance_FINAL.pdf.

48. See John Norris, "A Better Approach to Fragile States: The Long View," Center for American Progress, June 22, 2016, https://www.americanprogress.org/issues/security /reports/2016/06/22/139897/a-better-approach-to-fragile-states/.

49. Sean Lynn-Jones, *Why the United States Should Spread Democracy*, Belfer Center for Science and International Affairs Discussion Paper 98-07, March 1998, http://www .belfercenter.org/publication/why-united-states-should-spread-democracy.

50. See writing on democratic recession. Joshua Kurlantzick, *Democracy Retreat: The Revolt of the Middle Class and the Worldwide Decline of Representative Government* (New Haven, Conn.: Yale University Press, 2013); Larry Diamond, "Facing Up to the Democratic Recession," *Journal of Democracy* 26 (January 2015): 141–55.

51. Thomas Carothers, "Prospects for U.S. Democracy Promotion Under Trump," Carnegie Endowment for International Peace, January 2017, http://carnegieendowment.org /2017/01/05/prospects-for-u.s.-democracy-promotion-under-trump-pub-66588. See also Carothers, "Does Democracy Promotion Have a Future?," Carnegie Endowment for International Peace, June 2008, http://carnegieendowment.org/2008/06/23/does -democracy-promotion-have-future-pub-20247.

52. United Nations Framework Convention on Climate Change, "Paris Agreement— Status of Ratification," http://unfccc.int/paris_agreement/items/9444.php.

53. See Joeri Rogelj, Michel den Elzen, Niklas Hohne, Taryn Fransen, Hanna Fekete, Harald Winkler, Roberto Schaeffer, Fu Sha, Keywan Riahi, and Malte Meinshausen, "Paris Agreement Climate Proposals Need a Boost to Keep Warming Well Below 2C," *Nature* 534, no. 7609 (2016): 631–39, doi:10.1038/nature18307; and Chris Mooney, "The World Has the Right Climate Goals—but the Wrong Ambition Levels to Achieve Them," *Washington Post*, June 29, 2016.

54. See Melanie Hart, "3 Things Americans Should Know About China and the Paris Climate Agreement," Center for American Progress, February 9, 2017, https://www .americanprogress.org/issues/green/news/2017/02/09/414850/3-things-americans -should-know-about-china-in-the-paris-climate-agreement/.

5. CRISIS PREVENTION

1. See, for example, James R. Clapper, *Statement for the Record: Worldwide Threat Assessment of the US Intelligence Community* (Washington, D.C.: Office of the Director of Intelligence, 2016), http://www.armed-services.senate.gov/imo/media/doc/Clapper_02-09-16.pdf.

2. The 2015 *National Military Strategy of the United States of America* states, "Today, the probability of U.S. involvement in interstate war with a major power is assessed to be

low but growing." See U.S. Joint Chiefs of Staff, *National Military Strategy of the United States of America* (Washington, D.C.: U.S. Department of Defense, 2015), 4, http://www.jcs.mil/Portals/36/Documents/Publications/2015_National_Military_Strategy.pdf.

3. Michael D. Swaine, "Testimony by Dr. Michael D. Swaine," in *China's Maritime Disputes in the East and South China Seas: Hearing Before the U.S.-China Economic and Security Review Commission* (Washington, D.C.: United States–China Economic and Security Review Commission, 2013), 25, https://www.uscc.gov/sites/default/files/transcripts/USCC%20Hearing%20Transcript%20-%20April%204%202013.pdf.

4. Sheila Smith, "A Sino-Japanese Clash in the East China Sea," Council on Foreign Relations, April 2013, 1; Michael McDevitt, "The East China Sea; The Place Where Sino-U.S. Conflict Could Occur," *American Foreign Policy Interests* 36, no. 2 (2014): 100–110.

5. The White House, "Joint Statement from President Donald J. Trump and Prime Minister Shinzo Abe," February, 10, 2017, https://www.whitehouse.gov/the-press-office/2017/02/10/joint-statement-president-donald-j-trump-and-prime-minister-shinzo-abe.

6. Barack Obama, "Joint Press Conference with President Obama and Prime Minister Abe of Japan," April 24, 2014, http://www.whitehouse.gov/the-press-office/2014/04/24/joint-press-conference-president-obama-and-prime-minister-abe-japan.

7. The treaty states that "an armed attack on either of the Parties would be dangerous to its own peace and safety and declares that it would act to meet the common dangers in accordance with its constitutional processes." U.S. Department of State, "U.S. Collective Defense Arrangements," http://www.state.gov/s/l/treaty/collectivedefense/.

8. Glaser, "Armed Clash in the South China Sea," 2; see also Hugh White, *The China Choice: Why America Should Share Power* (Oxford: Oxford University Press, 2012), 126.

9. Terri Moon Cronk, "Pacom Chief: China's Land Reclamation Has Broad Consequences," *DoD News*, July 24, 2015. See also Patrick Cronin, ed., *Cooperation from Strength: The United States, China and the South China Sea* (Washington, D.C.: Center for a New American Security, 2012).

10. Brendan Taylor, "The South China Sea Is Not a Flashpoint," *Washington Quarterly* 37, no. 1 (2014): 99–111.

11. For a thorough discussion of U.S.-Taiwan relations, see Shirley A. Kan and Wayne M. Morrison, *U.S.-Taiwan Relationship: Overview of the Issues* (Washington, D.C.: Congressional Research Service, 2014).

12. In 2008, during another period of heightened cross-strait tensions over a referendum on Taiwan's membership in the UN, the United States once again sent aircraft carriers close to Taiwan but not into the strait.

13. "Big Brother Comes Wooing," *Economist*, July 2, 2014, http://www.economist.com/blogs/banyan/2014/07/china-taiwan-relations-0.

14. Richard K. Betts, *American Force: Dangers, Delusions and Dilemmas in National Security* (New York: Columbia University Press, 2012), 184.

15. Aaron L. Friedberg, *A Contest for Supremacy: China, America, and the Struggle for Mastery in Asia* (New York: Norton, 2011), 219–21.

16. Betts, *American Force*, 186.

17. For an interesting discussion of various scenarios from a Chinese perspective, see Wu Xiinbo, "Managing Crisis and Sustaining Peace Between China and the United States," *Peaceworks* 61 (2008): 29–30.

18. Bonnie S. Glaser and Jacqueline Vitello, *Tough Times Ahead If the DPP Returns to Power?*, PacNet 41, Center for Strategic and International Studies, July 21, 2015, https://www.csis.org/analysis/pacnet-41-tough-times-ahead-if-dpp-returns-power.

19. For an insightful discussion of the dynamics of a Taiwan crisis, see Michael D. Swaine, "Sino-American Crisis Management and the U.S.-Japan Alliance: Challenges and Implications," in *The Japan-U.S. Alliance and China-Taiwan Relations*, ed. Akikazu Hashimoto, Mike Mochizuki, and Kurayoshi Takara (Washington, D.C.: Sigur Center for Asian Studies, George Washington University), 94, http://carnegieendowment.org/files/Swaine_Chapter.pdf.

20. See Paul B. Stares, "Assessing the Risk of Regime Change in North Korea," *38 North*, December 16, 2016, http://38north.org/2016/12/nkinstability121616/.

21. For a lengthier discussion, see Paul B. Stares and Joel S. Wit, *Preparing for Sudden Change in North Korea* (New York: Council on Foreign Relations, 2009).

22. Ulrike Demmer and Ralf Neukirch, "Fear of Russia: NATO Developed Secret Contingency Plans for Baltic States," *Spiegel Online*, December 7, 2010, http://www.spiegel.de/international/europe/fear-of-russia-nato-developed-secret-contingency-plans-for-baltic-states-a-733361.html.

23. For an excellent analysis of Russia's weaknesses and sense of insecurity, see Eugene Rumer, "Russia—a Different Kind of Threat," Carnegie Endowment for International Peace, July 20, 2015, http://carnegieendowment.org/2015/07/20/russia-different-kind-of-threat/idml.

24. The agreement also includes a phased but conditional reduction in international sanctions on Iran in return for its compliance. On the threat of a preventive military attack, see Jeffrey Goldberg, "Obama to Israel—Time Is Running Out," *Bloomberg View*, March 2, 2014, http://www.bloombergview.com/articles/2014-03-02/obama-to-israel-time-is-running-out.

25. Peter Kenyon, "Did Iran's Ballistic Missile Test Violate a UN Resolution?," NPR, February 3, 2017, http://www.npr.org/sections/parallels/2017/02/03/513229839/did-irans-ballistic-missile-test-violate-a-u-n-resolution.

26. Karen de Young, "Trump Administration Says It Is Putting Iran 'on Notice' Following Missile Test," *Washington Post*, February 1, 2017.

27. Mathew Kroenig, "Time to Attack Iran," *Foreign Affairs* 91, no. 1 (2012): 76–86.

28. There is already speculation that Israel and Saudi Arabia are discussing operational collaboration for an attack on Iran. See "Report: Mossad Working with Saudis on Contingency Plans for Potential Attack on Iran," *Jerusalem Post*, November 17, 2013.

29. Colin H. Kahl, "Not Time to Attack Iran," *Foreign Affairs*, March–April 2012, https://www.foreignaffairs.com/articles/iran/2012-01-17/not-time-attack-iran; Kris Michaud, Joe Buccino, and Stephen Chenelle, "The Impact of Domestic Shale Oil Production on

U.S. Military Strategy and Its Implications for U.S.-China Maritime Partnership," *Small Wars Journal*, March 14, 2014, http://smallwarsjournal.com/jrnl/art/the-impact -of-domestic-shale-oil-production-on-us-military-strategy-and-its-implications-fo.

30. "Pakistan's Nuclear Scenarios, U.S. Solutions," *Room for Debate*, *New York Times*, May 5, 2009, http://roomfordebate.blogs.nytimes.com/2009/05/05/pakistan-scenarios -us-solutions/.

31. Jeffrey Goldberg and Marc Ambinder, "The Pentagon's Secret Plans to Secure Pakistan's Nuclear Arsenal," *National Journal*, November 9, 2011.

32. Some also worry about Moldova and, more specifically, actions by the ethnically Russian breakaway province of Transnistria to agitate for closer ties with Moscow as also being a potentially dangerous flash point. While the potential clearly exists for heightened tensions in Moldova, the risk of it leading to a U.S.-Russia crisis are much lower than for Georgia given Moldova's closer ties to the West. See Neil Buckley, "Transnistria Shapes Up as the Next Ukraine-Russian Flashpoint," *Financial Times*, June 3, 2015.

33. See David Kramer, "Renewed Confrontation in Georgia," Council on Foreign Relations, March 2016, http://cfr/org/report/renewed-confrontation-georgia.

34. See Michael McDevitt, *The South China Sea: Assessing U.S. Policy Options for the Future*, Center for Naval Analyses, November 2014, https://www.cna.org/cna_files/pdf/IOP -2014-U-009109.pdf; and Jeffrey Bader, Kenneth Lieberthal, and Michael McDevitt, *Keeping the South China Sea in Perspective*, Brookings Institution, September 2, 2014, https://www.brookings.edu/research/keeping-the-south-china-sea-in-perspective/.

35. See McDevitt, *South China Sea*, viii.

36. With regard to the Sino-Japanese dispute, see Smith, *Sino-Japanese Clash*; James L. Schoff, "Obama's Quiet Priority in Japan: The East China Sea," Carnegie Endowment for International Peace, April 10, 2014, http://carnegieendowment.org/2014/04/10 /obama-s-quiet-priority-in-japan-east-china-sea-pub-55311; Michael O'Hanlon, "A Six Point Plan to Solve the Senkaku Dispute," *National Interest*, December 29, 2014, http://nationalinterest.org/feature/six-point-plan-solve-the-senkaku-island-dispute -11925; and Wu Xinbo, "America Should Step Back from the East China Sea," *New York Times*, April 23, 2014.

37. McDevitt, *South China Sea*, viii–ix.

38. See Thomas Frear, Ian Kearns and Łukasz Kulesa, *Preparing for the Worst: Are Russian and NATO Military Exercises Making War in Europe More Likely?* (London: European Leadership Network, 2015), 6, http://www.europeanleadershipnetwork.org/medialibrary/2015 /08/07/ea2b8c22/Preparing%20for%20the%20Worst.pdf.

39. Fiona Hill and Steven Pifer, "Putin's Risky Game of Chicken," *New York Times*, June 15, 2015.

40. See Rumer, "Russia."

41. Anthony Cordesman, *The Iran Nuclear Agreement: The Need for a Full U.S. Implementation Plan* (Washington, D.C.: Center for Strategic and International Studies, 2015), http://csis.org/files/publication/150824_iran.pdf.

42. Kenneth Katzman and Paul K. Kerr, coordinators, *Iranian Nuclear Agreement: Selected Issues for Congress*, CRS 7-5700 (Washington, D.C.: Congressional Research Service, 2015), 13.

43. David Ignatius, "Calming the Waters in the Gulf," *Washington Post*, April 6, 2007.

44. National Iranian American Council, "Memo: Iran's Ballistic Missile Testing," March 10, 2017, https://www.niacouncil.org/memo-irans-ballistic-missile-testing/.

45. For a discussion of these arguments, see Richard C. Bush III, "Uncharted Strait," Brookings Institution, January 14, 2013, https://www.brookings.edu/wp-content/uploads/2016/06/14-taiwan-bush.pdf; and "From Keystone to Millstone?," *Economist*, March 3, 2011, http://www.economist.com/node/21016515/comments.

46. Bonnie S. Glaser, *Building Trust Across the Taiwan Strait: A Role for Military Confidence-Building Measures* (Washington, D.C.: Center for Strategic and International Studies, 2010).

47. See, for example, Richard Haass, "Time to End the North Korean Threat," *Wall Street Journal*, December 23, 2014.

48. See Paul B. Stares, *Allied Rights and Legal Constraints on German Military Power* (Washington, D.C.: Brookings Institution, 1990).

49. Barack Obama and Lee Myung-bak, "Joint Vision for the Alliance of the United States of America and the Republic of Korea," White House Press Release, June 16, 2009, http://obamawhitehouse.archives.gov/the-press-office/joint-vision-alliance-united-states-america-and-republic-korea.

50. See Daniel S. Markey, *No Exit from Pakistan: America's Tortured Relationship with Islamabad* (Cambridge: Cambridge University Press, 2013), 225–31.

51. Nuclear Threat Initiative, "Pakistan," http://ntiindex.org/countries/pakistan/. See also Mark Fitzpatrick, *Overcoming Pakistan's Nuclear Dangers* (London: Routledge, 2014), 121.

52. Fitzpatrick, *Overcoming Pakistan's Nuclear Dangers*, 123–24.

53. On the need for nuclear normalization or "mainstreaming," see Toby Dalton and Michael Krepon, *A Normal Nuclear Pakistan* (Washington, D.C.: Carnegie Endowment for Peace and Stimson Center, 2015), http://carnegieendowment.org/files/Normal NuclearPakistan.pdf.

54. This discussion draws heavily on Kramer, "Renewed Confrontation in Georgia."

55. See Robert Satloff and David Schenker, "Growing Stress on Jordan," Council on Foreign Relations, March 2016, http://www.cfr.org/jordan/growing-stress-jordan/p37635. For an extensive set of recommendations, see Mona Yacoubian, "Renewed Conflict in Lebanon," Council on Foreign Relations, June 2014, http://cfr.org/report/renewed-conflict-lebanon.

56. See Paul B. Stares and Helia Ighani, "How Stable is Saudi Arabia?," Council on Foreign Relations, May 15, 2017, https://www.cfr.org/expert-brief/how-stable-saudi-arabia.

57. Madeleine Albright and William Cohen, *Preventing Genocide: A Blueprint for U.S. Policymakers* (Washington, D.C.: United States Holocaust Memorial Museum, 2008).

6. CONFLICT MITIGATION

1. See James R. Clapper, *Statement for the Record: Worldwide Threat Assessment of the US Intelligence Community* (Washington, D.C.: Office of the Director of Intelligence, 2014), https://www.dni.gov/files/documents/SASC_Unclassified_2016_ATA_SFR_FINAL.pdf.

2. See Seth G. Jones, *A Persistent Threat: The Evolution of al Qa'ida and Other Salafi Jihadists* (Santa Monica, Calif.: RAND, 2014), 40; *Terrorist Threat to the U.S. Homeland— Al-Qaeda in the Arabian Peninsula (AQAP): Hearing Before the Subcommittee on Counterterrorism and Intelligence of the Committee on Homeland Security, House of Representatives*, 112th Cong., March 2, 2011 (statements by Christopher Boucek, Jarrett Brachman, and Barak Barfi), https://www.gpo.gov/fdsys/pkg/CHRG-112hhrg72216/html/CHRG-112hhrg72216.htm; and *Understanding the Threat to the Homeland from AQAP: Hearing Before the Subcommittee on Counterterrorism and Intelligence of the Committee on Homeland Security, House of Representatives*, 113th Cong., September 18, 2013 (statement by Brian Katulis), https://www.gpo.gov/fdsys/pkg/CHRG-113hhrg86483/pdf/CHRG-113hhrg86483.pdf.

3. See Stephen Tankel, "A Pakistan-Based Terrorist Attack on the U.S. Homeland," Council on Foreign Relations, August 2011, http://cfr.org/report/pakistan-based-terrorist-attack-us-homeland; and *Protecting the Homeland Against Mumbai-Style Attacks and the Threat from Lashkar-e-Taiba: Hearing Before the Subcommittee on Counterterrorism and Intelligence of the Committee on Homeland Security, House of Representatives*, 113th Cong., June 12, 2013 (statement by Stephen Tankel), https://www.gpo.gov/fdsys/pkg/CHRG-113hhrg85686/html/CHRG-113hhrg85686.htm.

4. See Rolf Mowatt-Larrsen, *Al Qaeda Weapons of Mass Destruction Threat: Hype or Reality? A Timeline of Terrorist Efforts to Acquire WMD* (Cambridge, Mass.: Belfer Center for Science and International Affairs, 2010).

5. See James R. Clapper, *Statement for the Record: Worldwide Threat Assessment of the US Intelligence Community* (Washington, D.C.: Office of the Director of Intelligence, 2016), http://www.armed-services.senate.gov/imo/media/doc/Clapper_02-09-16.pdf.

6. Don Oberdorfer, *The Two Koreas: A Contemporary History* (Reading, Mass.: Addison-Wesley, 1997), 315.

7. See Rick Newman, "How a Second Korean War Would Harm the U.S. Economy," *U.S. News*, April 3, 2013, http://www.usnews.com/news/blogs/rick-newman/2013/04/03/how-a-second-korean-war-would-harm-the-us-economy.

8. Choe Sang-Hun, "South Korea and U.S. Make Plans for Defense," *New York Times*, March 23, 2013.

9. See Paul B. Stares, "Military Escalation in Korea," Council on Foreign Relations, November 2010, http://cfr.org/report/military-escalation-korea; and Paul B. Stares, "On Escalation in Korea," 38 North, January 13, 2010, http://38north.org/2011/01/on-escalation-in-korea/.

10. This growing concern was reportedly raised as a "core U.S. national security interest" by U.S. secretary of defense Robert Gates in his meeting with Chinese president Hu Jintao in January 2011 and, most probably, President Obama at the Washington summit soon

after. See Elisabeth Bumiller and David E. Sanger, "Gates Warns of North Korea Missile Threat to U.S.," *New York Times*, January 11, 2011, http://www.nytimes.com/2011/01/12 /world/asia/12military.html?_r=0.

11. Stares, "Military Escalation in Korea," 3.

12. See Daniel S. Markey, "Terrorism and Indo-Pakistani Escalation," Council on Foreign Relations, January 2010, http://cfr.org/report/terrorism-and-indo-pakistan-escalation.

13. See Bruce Riedel, *Avoiding Armageddon: America, India, and Pakistan to the Brink and Back* (Washington, D.C.: Brookings Institution, 2013).

14. See Toby Dalton and George Perkovich, "Is a Pakistan-India War Just One Terrorist Attack Away?," *Herald*, January 24, 2017, http://herald.dawn.com/news/1153648.

15. See Samarjit Ghosh, *Two Decades of Indo-Pak CBMs: A Critique from India*, IPCS Issue Brief 132 (New Delhi: Institute of Peace and Conflict Studies, 2009), http://www.ipcs .org/pdf_file/issue/IB132-Ploughshares-Samarjit.pdf; "Indo-Pak Border CBMs to Be Implemented in 15 Days," *Hindu*, September 13, 2015; Faculty of Social Sciences, Graduate School of Public and International Affairs, University of Ottawa, "The Ottawa Dialogue," http://socialsciences.uottawa.ca/dialogue/.

16. Thomas E. Ricks, "The Most Likely Apocalypse in Our Future: An Indian-Pakistani Nuclear Exchange," *Foreign Policy*, March 8, 2011, http://ricks.foreignpolicy.com /posts/2011/03/08/the_most_likely_apocalypse_in_our_future_an_indian_pakistani _nuclear_exchange. The only other imaginable case of a nuclear exchange between two such adversaries is war between the United States and North Korea, but it is not immediately obvious that the United States would feel compelled to use nuclear weapons if attacked.

17. For a comprehensive review of Pakistan and Indian nuclear capabilities, see Mark Fitzpatrick, *Overcoming Pakistan's Nuclear Dangers* (London: International Institute for Strategic Studies, 2014).

18. Dalton and Perkovich, "Is a Pakistan-India War Just One Terrorist Attack Away?"

19. Anthony H. Cordesman, *Red Lines, Deadlines, and Thinking the Unthinkable: India, Pakistan, Iran, North Korea, and China* (Washington, D.C.: Center for Strategic and International Studies, 2013), 4.

20. See Natural Resources Defense Council, *The Consequences of Nuclear Conflict Between India and Pakistan* (Washington, D.C.: Natural Resources Defense Council, 2002).

21. See Alan Robock and Owen Brian Toon, "Self-Assured Destruction: The Climate Impacts of Nuclear War," *Bulletin of the Atomic Scientists* 68, no. 5 (2012): 66–74; and Ricks, "Most Likely Apocalypse."

22. Jamal Afridi and Jayshree Bajoria, "China-Pakistan Relations," Council on Foreign Relations, July 6, 2010, http://www.cfr.org/china/china-pakistan-relations/p10070.

23. Daniel S. Markey, *No Exit from Pakistan: America's Tortured Relationship with Islamabad* (Cambridge: Cambridge University Press, 2013), 189–92.

24. Ibid.

25. Anne Barnard, "Death Toll from War in Syria Now 470,000, Group Finds," *New York Times*, February 11, 2016, http://www.nytimes.com/2016/02/12/world/middleeast/death -toll-from-war-in-syria-now-470000-group-finds.html?_r=0.

26. Barbara F. Walter, "The Four Things We Know About How Civil Wars End (and What This Tells Us About Syria)," Political Violence at a Glance, October 8, 2013, http:// politicalviolenceataglance.org/ 2013/10/18/the-four-things-we-know-about-how-civil-war s-end-and-what-this-tells-us-about-syria/.

27. In April 2014, Secretary of Homeland Security Jeh Johnson stated that "Syria has become a matter of homeland security" because of the threat posed by militants in Syria targeting the United States. Jeh Johnson, quoted in Elliott Abrams, "Syria: Humanitarian Disaster—and Security Threat," Council on Foreign Relations, June 13, 2014, http://www.cfr.org/syria/syria-humanitarian-disaster-security-threat /p33082.

28. See Yaroslav Trofimov, "After Mosul, Will U.S.-Iran Rivalry Undermine Iraq?," *Wall Street Journal*, March 16, 2017.

29. "Quarterly Report to the United States Congress," Special Inspector General for Afghanistan Reconstruction, April 30, 2017, https://www.sigar.mil/pdf/quarterlyreports /2017-04-30qr.pdf.

30. See Seth G. Jones, "Strategic Reversal in Afghanistan," Council on Foreign Relations, June 2016, http://www.cfr.org/afghanistan/strategic-reversal-afghanistan/p37947.

31. To some even the risk of nuclear war cannot be dismissed. See Loren Thomson, "Four Ways the Ukraine Crisis Could Escalate to Use of Nuclear Weapons," *Forbes*, April 24, 2014, https://www.forbes.com/sites/lorenthompson/2014/04/24/four-ways-the-ukraine -crisis-could-escalate-to-use-of-nuclear-weapons/#6f373a41232a.

32. "Yemen's Brutal Conflict Pushing One Million Displaced to Return to Danger," Joint UNHCR-IOM Press Release, United Nations High Commissioner for Refugees, February 2017, http://www.unhcr.org/afr/news/press/2017/2/58ac0b170/yemens-brutal -conflict-pushing-million-displaced-return-danger-joint-unhcr.html.

33. Izza Leghtas, "'Hell on Earth': Abuses Against Refugees and Migrants Trying to Reach Europe from Libya," Refugees International, June 2017, https://static1.squarespace.com /static/506c8ea1e4b01d9450dd53f5/t/592f37468419c2ac554b4c9f/1496266580341/2017 .6.1+Libya.pdf.

34. Carla Babb, "VOA Exclusive: Dozens More US Troops Deployed to Somalia," Voice of America, April 14, 2017, https://www.voanews.com/a/dozens-more-us-troops-deployed -somalia-voa-exclusive/3809351.html.

35. Jacey Fortin, "Riek Machar, South Sudan Opposition Leader, Returns as Part of Peace Deal," *New York Times*, April 26, 2016.

36. "Under Fire: The July 2016 Violence in Juba and UN Response," Center for Civilians in Conflict, October 5, 2016, http://civiliansinconflict.org/uploads/files/publications /CIVIC_-_Juba_Violence_Report_-_October_2016.pdf.

37. "Famine Declared in Region of South Sudan—UN," United Nations News Center, February 20, 2017, http://www.un.org/apps/news/story.asp?NewsID=56205#.WTXM7 vnyu70.

38. Katherine Almquist Knopf, *Ending South Sudan's Civil War* (New York: Council on Foreign Relations, 2017), http://www.cfr.org/south-sudan/ending-south-sudans-civil -war/p38510.

39. For a discussion of the logic and principal elements of this approach, see Robert S. Litwak, *Preventing North Korea Nuclear Breakout* (Washington, D.C.: Woodrow Wilson Center for International Scholars, 2017).

40. For a good overview of this dispute, see Ken E. Gause, "Dealing with North Korean Provocations Around the Northern Limit Line," in *CNA Maritime Asia Project, Workshop One: The East China and Yellow Seas*, ed. Michael A. McDevitt and Catherine E. Lea (Alexandria, Va.: CNA, 2010), 19–34.

41. See Terence Roehrig, "Korean Dispute Over the Northern Limit Line: Security, Economics, or International Law," *Maryland Series in Contemporary Asian Studies* 2008, no. 3 (2008): 54–56.

42. See Matthew Bunn, Martin B. Malin, Nickolas Roth, and William H. Tobey, *Advancing Nuclear Security: Evaluating Progress and Setting New Goals* (Cambridge, Mass.: Belfer Center for Science and International Affairs, 2014), http://www.belfercenter.org/sites/default/files/files/publication/advancingnuclearsecurity.pdf.

43. See Gigi Kwik Gronvall, *Mitigating the Risks of Synthetic Biology* (New York: Council on Foreign Relations, 2015).

44. Some terrorism experts have long maintained that the motive of many militant groups is essentially defensive (to repel the presence of U.S. forces), or to function as modern-day "crusaders" from their homelands (especially in religiously sensitive areas), while to others the goal initially is seen to have been the opposite: to draw the United States into costly conflicts that weaken its support for secular regimes they wish to overthrow. See, for example, Michael Scott Duran, "Somebody Else's Civil War: Ideology, Rage and the Assault on America," in *How Did This Happen? Terrorism and the New War*, ed. James Hoge Jr. and Gideon Rose (New York: Public Affairs: 2001), 31–52; and Robert Pape, *Dying to Win: The Strategic Logic of Suicide Terrorism* (New York: Random House, 2006).

45. Pew Research Center, "Public Sees U.S. Power Declining as Support for Global Engagement Slips," December 3, 2013, http://www.people-press.org/2013/12/03/public-sees-u-s-power-declining-as-support-for-global-engagement-slips/.

46. For an extensive discussion of U.S. policy to prevent a Pakistan-based terrorist attack against the United States, see Tankel, "Pakistan-Based Terrorist Attack."

47. See Paul B. Stares and Mona Yacoubian, "Rethinking the 'War on Terror': New Approaches to Conflict Prevention and Management in the Post-9/11 World," in *Leashing the Dogs of War: Conflict Management in a Divided World*, ed. Chester A. Crocker, Fen Osler Hampson, and Pamela Aall (Washington, D.C.: United States Institute of Peace, 2007), 425–36.

48. Donald Rumsfeld, "Global War on Terrorism," memorandum, October 16, 2003, http://www.globalsecurity.org/military/library/policy/dod/rumsfeld-d20031016sdmemo.htm.

49. See Max Abrams, "What Terrorists Really Want: Terrorist Motives and Counterterrorism Strategy," *International Security* 32, no. 4 (2008): 78–105.

50. See Audrey Kurth Cronin, "ISIS Is Not a Terrorist Group," *Foreign Affairs* 94, no. 2 (2015): 93–94.

51. Abrams, "What Terrorists Really Want," 104.

52. Max Fisher, "Political Science Says Syria's Civil War Will Probably Last at Least Another Decade," *Washington Post*, October 23, 2013.

53. See Dick Krickus, "America Can't End Syria's Civil War," *National Interest*, August 30, 2014, http://nationalinterest.org/feature/america-cant-end-syrias-civil-war-11166.
54. Probably the most well thought out is the peace plan proposed by James Dobbins, Jeffrey Martini, and Philip Gordon. See Dobbins, Martini, and Gordon, *A Peace Plan for Syria III* (Santa Monica, Calif.: RAND, 2017).
55. See Seth G. Jones and Keith Crane, *Afghanistan After the Drawdown* (New York: Council on Foreign Relations, 2013); and Dobbins, Martini, and Gordon, *Choices for America in a Turbulent World*, 109.
56. See Stephen J. Hadley and Andrew Wilder, "Four Steps to Afghan Reconciliation," *Washington Post*, August 12, 2015, https://www.washingtonpost.com/opinions/four-steps-to-afghan-reconciliation/2015/08/12/55c6930c-3eb0-11e5-9443-3ef23099398b_story.html.
57. For a discussion of one such proposal see "Study of the Benefits of Establishing a Pakistan-India Cross Border Special Economic Zone (SEZ)," paper prepared by the Transnational Strategy Group, Washington, D.C., November 2014.
58. See Markey, "Terrorism and Indo-Pakistani Escalation," 3–5.
59. See "Confidence Building and Nuclear Risk-Reduction Measures in South Asia," Stimson Center, June 14, 2012, https://www.stimson.org/content/confidence-building-and-nuclear-risk-reduction-measures-south-asia.
60. See Knopf, *Ending South Sudan's Civil War*.
61. Wendy R. Sherman, "U.S. Foreign Policy in Somalia," United States Institute of Peace, https://www.usip.org/events/us-foreign-policy-somalia.
62. See Adel Abdel Ghafar and Mattia Toaido, "Does the Road to Stability in Libya Pass Through Cairo?," Brookings Institution, June 1, 2017, https://www.brookings.edu/blog/markaz/2017/06/01/does-the-road-to-stability-in-libya-pass-through-cairo/.

7. PARTNERS IN PREVENTION

1. This chapter draws on Paul B. Stares and Micah Zenko, *Partners in Preventive Action* (New York: Council on Foreign Relations, 2011).
2. There are three treaties pertaining to nuclear terrorism that the United States, China, Russia, and India are party to: the Convention on the Physical Protection of Nuclear Material, the International Convention on the Suppression of Acts of Nuclear Terrorism, and the Global Initiative to Combat Nuclear Terrorism.
3. Russia had also been invited to these meetings (to make it the G-8), but since its annexation of Ukraine, these meetings have been suspended indefinitely. Some G-7 or G-8 summits have made conflict prevention a specific part of the agenda. See John Kirton and Dr. Ella Kokotsis, "Compliance with G8 Commitments: The Peace and Security and Conflict Prevention Agenda, from Okinawa 2000–Genoa 2001," paper prepared for the Department of Foreign Affairs and International Trade Canada Policy Planning Division in Preparation for the Canadian Presidency of the G-8 Foreign

Ministers' Process in 2002, October 24, 2001, http://www.g8.utoronto.ca/scholar
/kirton2001/kirton-kokotis.pdf.

4. In particular, the International Network on Fragility and Conflict—a subsidiary body
of the OECD Development Assistance Committee founded in 2009—issues regular
reports on best practices for foreign assistance programs. See Organisation for Economic
Co-operation and Development, "Conflict, Fragility and Resilience," http://www.oecd
.org/dac/governance-peace/conflictfragilityandresilience/#d.en.253929.

5. See Abbās Varij Kāzemi and Xiangming Chen, "China and the Middle East: More
than Oil," *World Financial Review*, November 26, 2014, http://www.worldfinancialreview
.com/?p=3177.

6. See Nidhi Verma, "TABLE—India's Country-Wise Crude Oil Imports Since 2001/02,"
Reuters India, August 6, 2012, http://in.reuters.com/article/2012/08/06/india-crude
-import-idINL4E8IU4HI20120806.

7. James Chen, *The Emergence of China in the Middle East*, Strategic Forum no. 271 (Washington, D.C.: Institute for National Strategic Studies, National Defense University,
2011), http://ndupress.ndu.edu/Portals/68/Documents/stratforum/SF-271.pdf.

8. International Trade Center, "Trade Map Database," http://www.trademap.org/(X(1)
S(1zcdb155vrlrka452svjwyee))/Index.aspx.

9. More active Chinese diplomatic efforts in Afghanistan began in 2014, with the recognition that security in China's restive western provinces depend on Afghan stability. Foreign Minister Wang Yi visited Kabul in February 2014, urging the Afghan leadership to
embrace a "broad-based and inclusive political reconciliation," saying that "peace and stability in [Afghanistan] has an impact on the security of western China . . . and affects
the tranquility and development of the entire region" and pledging Chinese support
toward political reconciliation. Wang Yi, quoted in Mirwais Harooni, "Top Official Says
Chinese Security Depends on Afghan Stability," Reuters, February 22, 2014, http://www
.reuters.com/article/2014/02/22/us-afghanistan-china-idUSBREA1L0D720140222.
In July 2014 China appointed Sun Yuxi as special envoy for Afghanistan, tasked with
maintaining "close communication" with Afghanistan and other relevant parties to
help "ensure lasting peace, stability, and development for Afghanistan and the region."
See "China Appoints Special Envoy for Afghanistan," Reuters, July 18, 2014, http://
www.reuters.com/article/us-china-afghanistan-idUSKBN0FN11Z20140718. China is
also a member of the Quadrilateral Coordination Group (along with Afghanistan,
Pakistan, and the United States), which was formed in early 2016 to promote the
peace process and negotiations between Kabul and the Taliban. See Edward Wong,
"China Urging Afghanistan to Restart Peace Talks with Taliban," *New York Times*,
January 27, 2016, http://www.nytimes.com/2016/01/28/world/asia/china-afghanistan
-taliban-talks.html?_r=0.

10. This includes a $2.87 billion investment in the Mes Aynak copper mine and oil explora-
tion rights to the Amu Darya River basin. Development of both projects has stalled
over security concerns and contract disputes. See Lynne O'Donnell, "China's MCC
Turns Back on US$3b Mes Aynak Afghanistan Mine Deal," *South China Morning Post*,
March 20, 2015, http://www.scmp.com/news/world/article/1453375/chinas-mcc-turns

-back-us3b-mes-aynak-afghanistan-mine-deal; Jessica Donati, "Missing Refinery Deal Halts Landmark China-Afghan Oil Project," Reuters, August 18, 2013, http://www .reuters.com/article/afghanistan-china-idUSL4N0GJ05G20130818.

11. See recent high-level UN reports such as "Uniting Our Strengths for Peace—Politics, Partnership and People. Report of the High-Level Independent Panel on United Nations Operations," United Nations, June 2015, http://peaceoperationsreview.org/wp-content /uploads/2015/08/HIPPO_Report_1_June_2015.pdf; "The Challenge of Sustaining Peace," Report of the Advisory Group of Experts for the 2015 Review of the United Nations Peacebuilding Architecture, June 2015, http://www.un.org/en/peacebuilding/pdf /150630%20Report%20of%20the%20AGE%20on%20the%202015%20Peacebuild-ing%20Review%20FINAL.pdf; "Preventing Conflict, Transforming Justice, Securing the Peace: A Global Study on the Implementation of United Nations Security Council resolution 1325," http://www.peacewomen.org/sites/default/files/UNW-GLOBAL -STUDY-1325-2015%20(1).pdf.

12. "Can the Security Council Prevent Conflict?," Security Council Report, February 2017, http://www.securitycouncilreport.org/atf/cf/%7B65BFCF9B-6D27-4E9C-8CD3 -CF6E4FF96FF9%7D/research_report_conflict_prevention_2017.pdf.

13. The UN Department of Political Affairs (DPA) produces analytical reports and briefing notes warning of incipient crises for its director—the undersecretary-general for political affairs—and transmits information to the UN Executive Committee on Peace and Security. The undersecretary-general also participates in the secretary-general's policy committee, "a cabinet-style decision-making mechanism" that provides strategic guidance to the UN Secretariat. In addition, the undersecretary-general can report warnings of potential conflict directly to the secretary-general, who can raise matters informally with Security Council members at monthly working lunches or formally through the council's scheduled work program. The DPA works closely with the UN Development Programme, and in particular, its Bureau of Crisis Prevention and Recovery, to manage the UN's informal interagency coordination mechanism—the UN Framework for Coordination on Preventive Action. See Stares and Zenko, *Partners in Preventive Action*, 13–14.

14. See Bruce D. Jones, "The UN Security Council and Crisis Management: Still Central After All These Years," in *Managing Conflict in a World Adrift*, ed. Chester A. Crocker, Fen Osler Hampson, and Pamela Aall (Washington, D.C.: United States Institute of Peace, 2007), 312–13.

15. See High-Level Independent Panel on United Nations Peace Operations, *Uniting Our Strengths for Peace—Politics, Partnerships and People* (New York: United Nations, 2015), http://peaceoperationsreview.org/wp-content/uploads/2015/08/HIPPO_Report_1 _June_2015.pdf.

16. North Atlantic Treaty Organization, *Strategic Concept for the Defence and Security of the Members of the North Atlantic Treaty Organization* (Brussels: NATO Public Diplomacy Division, 2014), http://www.nato.int/nato_static_fl2014/assets/pdf/pdf_publications /20120214_strategic-concept-2010-eng.pdf. Since 2012, NATO has established the Comprehensive Crisis and Operations Management Center for this purpose.

17. This is not to overlook or underestimate the role NATO played in building confidence among its European members through mutual transparency and defense cooperation, and particularly its integrated command system; this undoubtedly contributed to Europe becoming the most peaceful region in the world.

18. Kimberly Marten, *Reducing Tensions Between Russia and NATO* (New York: Council on Foreign Relations, 2017).

19. Reinhart Rummel, "The EU's Involvement in Conflict Prevention—Strategy and Practice," in *Conflict Prevention: Is the European Union Ready?*, ed. Jan Wouters and Vincent Kronnenberger (Brussels: Asser, 2004), 67–92; Emma J. Stewart, *The European Union and Conflict Prevention*, Kiel Peace Research Series (Berlin: Lit Verlag, 2006).

20. The watchlist is created using a combination of quantitative and qualitative methodologies with inputs from the Directorate-General for External Relations as well as the EU Joint Situation Centre, which monitors day-to-day events around the world, and the Intelligence Division of the EU Military Staff, which is tasked with assessing "current and emerging areas of instability." Information for the watchlist and other related assessments comes from multiple sources: intelligence inputs from member states, reports for EU delegations, EU special representatives in the field, and also the European Satellite Center. As a result of partnership agreements, the EU also exchanges information with the UN, the OSCE, and other international bodies. NATO, however, reportedly contributes little of value to the EU Joint Situation Centre, and this is the source of some frustration. Major General João Nuno Jorge Vaz Antunes, "Developing an Intelligence Capability," *Studies in Intelligence* 49, no. 4 (2005): 65–70.

21. "Military and Civilian Missions and Operations," European Union External Action, https://eeas.europa.eu/topics/military-and-civilian-missions-and-operations/430/military-and-civilian-missions-and-operations_en.

22. Ibid.

23. Treaty of Lisbon Amending the Treaty on European Union and the Treaty Establishing the European Community, December 13, 2007, http://eur-lex.europa.eu/legal-content/en/TXT/?uri=CELEX%3A12007L%2FTXT.

24. See A. E. Juncos, *A More Coherent and Effective European Foreign Policy?* (London: Federal Trust for Education and Research, 2009), 12–13.

25. Since adopting the Petersberg Tasks in 1992, the EU has expanded the spectrum of missions it has collectively committed to perform—using military means, if necessary. The Lisbon Treaty further refines these tasks to include "joint disarmament operations . . . military advice and assistance tasks . . . conflict prevention and peacekeeping tasks . . . peace-making and post-conflict stabilisation" and also to contribute to combating terrorism "by supporting third countries . . . in their territories." See Treaty of Lisbon, article 28B, para. 1. Responsibility for maintaining these national and multinational constituted battle groups is rotated every six months within the EU. See European Union, "The EU Battlegroups and the EU Civilian and Military Cell," http://www.consilium.europa.eu/uedocs/cmsUpload/Battlegroups.pdf.

26. "Military and Civilian Missions and Operations."

27. The OSCE has no institutionalized conflict risk assessment or watchlist system because it has no mandate to monitor events either within or beyond the territorial limits of its member states. The seven-person OSCE Situation/Communications Room in the Conflict Prevention Centre in Vienna produces a twice-daily compilation of open-source reports and internal communications from OSCE field missions for senior officials. These are also shared with the EU and NATO Situation Centres under a reciprocal arrangement. The Situation/Communications Room has also developed a short message service–based system to warn senior officials of breaking news. Similarly, the OSCE has no authority to carry out contingency planning for potential missions. The OSCE has institutional mechanisms to respond to emergency conflict-related situations and resolve them peacefully, including the Berlin Mechanism, whereby states are obliged to provide information within forty-eight hours following a request from another member for clarification of an evolving situation; the Valletta Mechanism, which lays out procedures for the peaceful resolution of disputes; and the OSCE Convention on Conciliation and Arbitration. Only the Berlin Mechanism has been implemented. OSCE Secretariat Conflict Prevention Centre, *OSCE Mechanisms and Procedures: Summary/Compendium* (Vienna: Organization for Security and Co-operation in Europe, 2008), http://www.osce.org/cpc/34427.

28. In response to rising tensions in Georgia, a group of OSCE ambassadors were dispatched there in July 2008 on a fact-finding mission. Once hostilities erupted, the chairman-in-office (the OSCE's most senior permanent official) engaged in personal shuttle diplomacy in the region, and an additional twenty military monitoring officers (out of eighty authorized) were sent within days to bolster the OSCE mission. Russia, however, vetoed continuation of the mission in December 2008. See "Statement by OSCE Secretary General Marc Perrin de Brichambaut at the Sixteenth OSCE Ministerial Council Meeting," Helsinki, December 4, 2008, http://www.osce.org/mc/35321 ?download=true.

29. See Center for Strategic and International Studies and Institute for New Democracies, *After the Astana Summit: More Questions than Answers*, Policy Brief no. 9 (Washington, D.C.: Center for Strategic and International Studies and Institute for New Democracies, 2010), https://csis-prod.s3.amazonaws.com/s3fs-public/legacy_files/files/publication /101217_CSIS-IND_PolicyBrief.Nr.9.pdf.

30. Oranization of American States (OAS) *IACHR Annual Report 2008*, "Chapter III: The Petition and Case System," 2009, http://www.cidh.org/annualrep/2008eng/TOC.htm. The Inter-American Commission on Human Rights (IACHR) also maintains eight rapporteurs for thematic issues who publish warnings of violations within OAS member states. In addition, the commission can refer cases to the autonomous IACHR, which has issued far-reaching provisional measures for action by member states, including in "cases of extreme gravity and urgency." See OAS, "Inter-American Convention on Human Rights," article 63(2), November 1969, http://www.cidh.oas.org/basicos /english/basic3.american%20convention.htm.

31. See Stares and Zenko, "Partners in Preventive Action." See also Andrés Serbin, *The Organization of American States, the United Nations Organization, Civil Society, and Conflict*

Prevention (Buenos Aires: Coordinadora Regional de Investigaciones Económicas y Sociales, 2009), http://www.cries.org/documentos_cries_old/documentos-cries11 -eng.pdf. There is a mandated dispute resolution mechanism used during crises through the Meeting of Consultation of Ministers of Foreign Affairs, held "in order to consider problems of an urgent nature and of common interest to the member states of the Organization of American States." See OAS, "Meetings of the Consultation of Ministers of Foreign Affairs," http://www.oas.org/en/about/meetings_foreign_affairs.asp. According to OAS officials, this has proven too slow and ineffective for the most pressing issues, as foreign ministers can only convene after a member state has appealed to the Permanent Council and the council votes to permit a meeting.

32. Serbin, *Organization of American States*, 7–12.

33. Over the past five years, ASEAN has entered into a number of agreements that promote greater integration and transparency in areas such as economic development, energy security, and education. In November 2007, at the Thirteenth ASEAN Summit, the heads of state put forth the long-term goal of creating an ASEAN Community by 2015 to consist of three components: the ASEAN Economic Community, which aims to promote economic integration through internal free trade; the ASEAN Political Security Community, which aspires to "promote political development in adherence to the principles of democracy, the rule of law and good governance, respect for and promotion and protection of human rights and fundamental freedoms as inscribed in the ASEAN Charter"; and the ASEAN Socio-Cultural Community, whose primary goal "is to contribute to realizing an ASEAN Community that is people-centered and socially responsible with a view to achieving enduring solidarity and unity among the nations and peoples of ASEAN." In 2009, the Secretariat published a framework and work plan for achieving an ASEAN Community by 2015. Association of Southeast Asian Nations, *Roadmap for an ASEAN Community: 2009–2015* (Jakarta: Association of Southeast Asian Nations, 2009), http://www.asean.org/wp-content/uploads/images /ASEAN_RTK_2014/2_Roadmap_for_ASEAN_Community_20092015.pdf.

34. Association of Southeast Asian Nations, *ASEAN Charter*, article 23, first published in 2007, adopted by all member states in 2008, http://asean.org/wp-content/uploads /images/archive/publications/ASEAN-Charter.pdf.

35. Herbert Wulf and Tobias Debiel, "Conflict Early Warning and Response Mechanisms: Tools for Enhancing the Effectiveness of Regional Organizations? A Comparative Study of the AU, ECOWAS, IGAD, ASEAN/ARF and PIF," Crisis States Research Centre, May 2009, http://eprints.lse.ac.uk/28495/1/WP49.2.pdf. For plans to create an early warning system, see Association of Southeast Asian Nations, *ASEAN Political-Security Blueprint* (Jakarta: Association of Southeast Asian Nations, 2009), 9.

36. "China, SE Asian Nations Agree on 'Code of Conduct' for South China Sea," Voice of America, May 18, 2017, https://www.voanews.com/a/china-and-southeast-asian-nations -agree-on-code-of-conduct-framework-for-south-china-sea/3856806.html.

37. For a useful essay on the problems and prospects for multilateralism in Asia, see Evan A. Feigenbaum and Robert A. Manning, *The United States in the New Asia* (New York: Council on Foreign Relations, 2009).

38. Smail Chergui, "Foreword," in *Meeting the Challenge of Conflict Prevention in Africa: Towards the Operationalization of the Continental Early Warning System*, African Union, 2008, 2, http://www.peaceau.org/uploads/meeting-the-challenge-of-conflict-prevention -in-africa.pdf.

39. Organisation of African Unity, "Constitutive Act of the African Union," July 11, 2000, article 4, https://www.au.int/web/sites/default/files/treaties/7758-treaty-0021 _-_constitutive_act_of_the_african_union_e.pdf.

40. Ibid., article 23; African Union, "Protocol Relating to the Establishment of the Peace and Security Council of the African Union," July 9, 2002, article 7(g), http://www .peaceau.org/uploads/psc-protocol-en.pdf.

41. African Union, "Protocol Relating to the Establishment of the Peace and Security Council," article 12. The Continental Early Warning System aims to consist of two components. The first is the twenty-four-hour Situation Room located within the Peace and Security Directorate's Conflict Management Division in Addis Ababa. The Situation Room has a staff of thirteen and serves as the point of contact between the commission and member states, Regional Economic Communities (RECs), and NGOs. It also collects data from open sources, AU field missions, and RECs for indicators of potential or ongoing conflicts, which is then screened and disseminated to analysts within the Peace and Security Council. See "African Regional Communities and the Prevention of Mass Atrocities," African Task Force on the Prevention of Mass Atrocities, October 2016, http://www.geno cideprevention.eu/wp-content/uploads/2016/10/African-Regional-Communities-and -the-Prevention-of-Mass-Atrocities-Final-Report-African-Task-Force.pdf.

42. The most developed is ECOWAS's Early Warning and Response Network (ECOW-ARN). Situated in the Office of the Commissioner for Political Affairs, Peace and Security, ECOWARN consists of four subregional zonal bureaus—located in Benin, Burkina Faso, Gambia, and Liberia—that collect and evaluate data based on ninety-four conflict indicators, primarily from open sources and NGOs but also from some member states, and an Observation and Monitoring Centre at the ECOWAS Commission in Abuja that produces analytical warning reports. See "The ECOWAS Conflict Prevention Framework," ECOWAS Commission, January 1, 2008, http:// documentation.ecowas.int/download/en/publications/Conflict%20Prevention%20 frmework.pdf; and Organisation for Economic Co-operation and Development, *SWAC News*, April-May 2009, 2–4, http://www.oecd.org/swac/swacnewsaprilmay 2009.htm. IGAD operates an early warning system based in Ethiopia, Kenya, and Uganda—the Committee on Early Warning and Response—focused primarily on pastoral conflicts. Economic Community of Central African States (ECCAS) operates the Early Warning Mechanism of Central Africa. The framework for harmonizing the early warning units of the subregional organizations with the AU's Continental Early Warning System failed to become fully operational by its set goal of 2009. See African Union, "Framework for the Operationalization of the Continental Early Warning System as Adopted by the Governmental Experts Meeting on Early Warning and Prevention," December 17–19, 2006, http://www.peaceau.org/uploads/early -warning-system-1.pdf.

43. African Union, "Protocol Related to the Establishment of the Peace and Security Council," article 11.

44. Ibid., article 13.

45. African Union, "Policy Framework for the Establishment of the African Standby Force and the Military Staff Committee," adopted by the Third Meeting of the African Chiefs of Defense Staff, May 15–16, 2003, http://www.peaceau.org/uploads /asf-policy-framework-en.pdf; African Union, "Roadmap for the Operationalization of the African Standby Force," March 22–23, 2005, http://reliefweb.int/sites/reliefweb .int/files/resources/C4BC0E63EEA32DBDC1256FE1004D4476-au-gen-23mar .pdf.

46. Jamila El Abdellaoui, *The Panel of the Wise: A Comprehensive Introduction to a Critical Pillar of the African Peace and Security Architecture*, ISS Paper no. 193 (Pretoria: Institute for Security Studies, 2009), 8; African Union, "Seventh Meeting of the Panel of the Wise," November 19, 2009, http://www.peaceau.org/uploads/5.-communique-of-the -7th-statutory-mtg-pow-addis-nov-11doc.pdf.

47. "The Outcome of the Council of the League of Arab States Meeting at the Ministerial Level in Its Extraordinary Session on the Implications of the Current Events in Libya and the Arab Position," March 12, 2011, http://responsibilitytoprotect.org/Arab%20 League%20Ministerial%20level%20statement%2012%20march%202011%20-%20 english(1).pdf.

48. For a comprehensive assessment of the role of the Arab League and the Gulf Cooperation Council for conflict mediation, see Marco Pinfari, "Nothing but Failure? The Arab League and the Gulf Cooperation Council as Mediators in Middle Eastern Conflict," Crisis States Research Centre Working Paper no. 45, London School of Economics, March 2009.

49. Some definitions will also suggest that they are generally interested in the greater good of society, but this ignores the extent to which civil society organizations (CSOs) are often narrowly focused and self-interested.

50. See Thania Paffenholz, "Civil Society and Conflict Management," in *Managing Conflict in a World Adrift*, ed. Chester A. Crocker, Fen Osler Hampson, and Pamela Aall (Washington, D.C.: United States Institute of Peace Press, 2007), 348. See also World Bank, "Defining Civil Society," http://web.worldbank.org/WBSITE/EXTERNAL /TOPICS/CSO/0,,contentMDK:20101499~menuPK:244752~pagePK:220503~piPK: 220476~theSitePK:228717,00.html.

51. For example, the Satellite Sentinel Project is a collaboration of CSOs that uses imagery captured from satellites passing over Sudan and South Sudan to identify "possible threats to civilians, detect bombed or razed villages, or note other evidence of pending mass violence." The images are analyzed and used to produce reports and press releases, and "sounds the alarm by notifying major news organizations and a mobile network of activists on Twitter and Facebook. Satellite Sentinel Project, "Our Story," http://www .satsentinel.org/our-story.

8. REORIENTING THE UNITED STATES

1. For an extensive discussion of these trends, see Richard N. Haass, *A World in Disarray: American Foreign Policy and the Crisis of the Old Order* (New York: Penguin, 2017).

2. Conflict prevention has been a recurring feature of declaratory U.S. foreign policy since the end of the Cold War, if not before.

3. Joseph R. Biden, "Remarks by Vice President Biden at 45th Munich Conference on Security Policy," February 7, 2009, https://obamawhitehouse.archives.gov/the-press -office/remarks-vice-president-biden-45th-munich-conference-security-policy.

4. James L. Jones, "Speech to the Atlantic Council," Washington, D.C., May 25, 2009, http://www.atlanticcouncil.org/news/transcripts/jones-james-5-27-09-transcript. In an interview with the *Washington Post*, Jones also indicated his intent to build a "21st Century NSC," one that can "look over the horizon to see what's coming at us" and deal with emerging threats "proactively." See David Ignatius, "National Security Facilitator," *Washington Post*, April 30, 2009.

5. Barack Obama, "Remarks by President Obama at the Veterans of Foreign Wars Convention in Phoenix, Arizona," August 17, 2009, https://obamawhitehouse.archives.gov /realitycheck/video/President-Obama-Speaks-to-the-Veterans-of-Foreign-Wars?page =23#transcript.

6. White House Office of the Press Secretary, "Fact Sheet: A Comprehensive Strategy and New Tools to Prevent and Respond to Atrocities," April 23, 2012, https:// obamawhitehouse.archives.gov/the-press-office/2012/04/23/fact-sheet-comprehensive -strategy-and-new-tools-prevent-and-respond-atro.

7. See James Finkel, *Atrocity Prevention at the Crossroads: Assessing the President's Atrocity Prevention Board After Two Years*, Center for the Prevention of Genocide Series of Occasional Papers no. 2 (Washington, D.C.: U.S. Holocaust Memorial Museum, 2014); and Elliott Abrams, "Obama's Atrocity Prevention Board—Abandoned but Not Forgotten," *National Review*, October 7, 2015, http://www.nationalreview.com/article /425179/obamas-atrocity-prevention-board-abandoned-not-forgotten-elliott-abrams.

8. Current senior intelligence official, interview with the author, Virginia, 2016. See also the remarks by current and former U.S. government officials at "CIA-GW Intelligence Conference: Panel on 21st Century Warning" (video), https://www.youtube.com/watch ?v=ApC-akErg7k.

9. "Intelligence Budget Data," Federation of American Scientists, https://fas.org/irp /budget/index.html.

10. Gregory F. Treverton, "First Callers: The President's Daily Brief Across Three Administrations," Center for the Study of Intelligence, Central Intelligence Agency, September 2013, https://www.cia.gov/library/center-for-the-study-of-intelligence/csi -publications/books-and-monographs/csi-intelligence-and-policy-monographs/pdfs /first-callers.pdf.

11. See Stephen Marrin, "Evaluating the Quality of Intelligence Analysis: By What (Mis) Measure?," *Intelligence and National Security* 27, no. 6 (2012): 896–912.

12. Current senior intelligence official, interview with the author, Virginia, 2016. The National Intelligence Council (NIC), which is formally part of the Office of the Director of

National Intelligence, does from time to time produce National Intelligence Assessments that do not require the consensus approval of the intelligence community.

13. These reports began as a self-initiated project rather than in response to a formal tasking. See Thomas Fingar, *Reducing Uncertainty: Intelligence Analysis and National Security* (Stanford, Calif.: Stanford University Press, 2011), 60.

14. Former senior U.S. intelligence official, interview with the author, Virginia, 2014.

15. See Director of Central Intelligence's Warning Committee, "Atrocities Watchlist," created May 1, 1999, https://www.cia.gov/library/readingroom/docs/DOC_0001381831.pdf.

16. Ibid.

17. See David Ignatius, "The CIA Gets a Makeover," *Washington Post*, April 9, 2015.

18. Informal exercises of this kind are almost always conducted during or immediately following the transition period between national elections in November and the swearing in of the president in January. President Obama, for example, requested at the beginning of his first term a study from the director of national intelligence on major countries at risk of experiencing serious instability. Former senior U.S. intelligence official, interview with the author, Virginia, 2014.

19. For example, the U.S. Department of Homeland Security conducts a comprehensive Strategic National Risk Assessment of "known threats and hazards that have the potential to significantly impact the Nation's homeland security." See U.S. Department of Homeland Security, *Strategic National Risk Assessment in Support of PPD 8: A Comprehensive Risk-Based Approach Toward a Secure and Resilient Nation* (Washington, D.C.: U.S. Department of Homeland Security, 2011), 1, https://www.dhs.gov/xlibrary/assets/rma-strategic-national-risk-assessment-ppd8.pdf.

20. See Government of the United Kingdom, *A Strong Britain in an Age of Uncertainty: The National Security Strategy* (London: Her Majesty's Stationery Office, 2010), https://www.gov.uk/government/uploads/system/uploads/attachment_data/file/61936/national-security-strategy.pdf.

21. See "Annex A: National Security Risk Assessment Methodology," in Government of the United Kingdom, *Strong Britain in an Age of Uncertainty*, 37.

22. See, in particular, the efforts of the Intelligence Advanced Research Projects Agency (IARPA) at "Aggregative Contingent Estimation (ACE)," https://www.iarpa.gov/index.php/research-programs/ace.

23. See "National Intelligence Priorities Framework," Intelligence Community Directive 204, https://fas.org/irp/dni/icd/icd-204.pdf.

24. Aaron L. Friedberg, "Strengthening U.S. Strategic Planning," *Washington Quarterly* 41, no. 1 (2007–2008): 47.

25. For example, in August 2010, the Obama administration conducted a classified review of the prospects for unrest and reform in the Arab world. While it identified various stress points in the Middle East and "evidence of growing citizen discontent within the region's regimes," its goal was to provide broad policy guidance rather than specific planning for plausible contingencies. Thus, when the Arab Spring erupted in 2011, it was caught unawares, not only by the popular uprising in Tunisia, where it started, but also by the major turmoil that ensued in Egypt and beyond. See Mark Landler, "Secret Report Ordered by Obama Identified Potential Uprisings," *New York Times*,

February 16, 2011; and David Ignatius, "Obama's Low-Key Strategy for the Middle East," *Washington Post*, March 6, 2011.

26. See Janine Davidson, "Making Government Work: Pragmatic Priorities for Inter-agency Coordination," *Orbis* 53, no. 3 (2009): 429. The major Combatant Commands have started to give more attention to how to "shape" the strategic environment and even prevent instability and conflict as part of their Theater Campaign Plans, but these are understandably focused on orchestrating military capacities rather than being part of a whole-of-government response.

27. Former senior U.S. policy maker, interview with the author, Washington, D.C., 2014. See also Peter Feaver and William Imboden, "A Strategic Planning Cell on National Security at the White House," in *Avoiding Trivia: The Role of Strategic Planning in American Foreign Policy*, ed. Daniel W. Drezner (Washington, D.C.: Brookings Institution, 2009), 108–9.

28. Much like its predecessor, the Obama administration did eventually create an informal interagency Strategic Planning Small Group made up of planners from the principal agencies, but this was essentially to discuss long-range trends and challenges rather than to perform a proper policy planning function. Interviews with senior Obama administration officials, 2015. Former senior U.S. policy maker, interview with the author, Washington, D.C., 2016.

29. See Paul Miller, "Organizing the National Security Council: I Like Ike's," *Presidential Studies Quarterly* 43, no. 3 (2013): 592–606; Bruce Jentleson, "An Integrative Executive Office Strategy for Policy Planning," in Drezner, *Avoiding Trivia*, 69–83. As Friedberg notes in "Strengthening U.S. Strategic Planning," 50, strategic planning's purpose would not be to "anticipate and analyze every conceivable contingency" but rather to "select a finite number that, because of their plausibility, their likely effects, or some combination of the two, would demand a significant response."

30. "Reorganization of the National Security Council System," National Security Decision Memorandum 2, January 20, 1969, 4.

31. "National Security Council Structure," National Security Decision Directive 2, January 12, 1982, 6.

32. "Crisis Management," National Security Decision Directive 3, December 14, 1981, 1, emphasis added; "Crisis Information and Management System (CIMS): Project Medusa," National Security Decision Directive 95, May 18, 1983, 3, emphasis added.

33. "Organization of the National Security Council," Presidential Decision Directive (PDD) 2, January 20, 1993, 4, https://fas.org/irp/offdocs/pdd/pdd-2.pdf.

34. See Karen DeYoung, "How the Obama White House Runs Foreign Policy," *Washington Post*, August 4, 2015.

35. U.S. Department of State and U.S. Agency for International Development, *Leading Through Civilian Power: The First Quadrennial Diplomacy and Development Review* (Washington, D.C.: U.S. Department of State and U.S. Agency for International Development, 2010), 123, http://www.state.gov/documents/organization/153108.pdf.

36. A revealing example of the gaps that sometimes occur as a consequence is provided by Robert Gates in his memoir as secretary of defense. As he recounts, despite considerable attention being devoted to preventing Iran from acquiring nuclear weapons, including

preparations to carry out military strikes against its research and development facilities if merited, remarkably little thought was given to the potential implications of an Israeli strike on Iran. Not until 2010, when Gates urgently requested that a special meeting of the principals be convened to discuss what the United States should do in the event Israel did attack Iran, was this considered. As he recalls,

> U.S. military leaders were increasingly worried that either the Israelis or the Iranians might take military action with little or no warning and that such action would require an immediate response from U.S. forces in the Gulf. There would be no time for protracted meetings in Washington or for the President to consult anyone but me, the next person in the chain of command. Other than the U.S. response to a small-scale Iranian "fast-boat" attack on one of our Navy ships, *there had been no discussion in either the Bush or the Obama administrations, other than private conversations I had with each president—about momentous decisions that might be required within minutes if serious shooting broke out in the Gulf.* Robert M. Gates, *Duty: Memoirs of a Secretary at War* (New York: Vintage, 2015), 391–92 (emphasis added)

37. "Managing Complex Contingency Operations," Presidential Decision Directive 56, May 1997. Among other things, the directive called for the Deputies Committee to constitute an Executive Committee to formulate policy, develop elaborate "pol-mil" plans, and oversee implementation. It also set up the Interagency Working Group for Contingency Planning. See Barnett R. Rubin, *Blood on the Doorstep: The Politics of Preventive Action* (New York: Century Foundation, 2002), 197.

38. For the full text of "Management of Interagency Efforts Concerning Reconstruction and Stabilization," National Security Presidential Directive 44, December 7, 2005, see http://fas.org/irp/offdocs/nspd/nspd-44.html.

39. See Paul B. Stares and Micah Zenko, *Enhancing U.S. Preventive Action* (New York: Council on Foreign Relations, 2009), 16.

40. The Interagency Management System (IMS) called for the establishment of an interagency Country Reconstruction and Stabilization Group cochaired by the S/CRS coordinator, the relevant assistant secretary from the State Department, and the NSC senior director. This group would be responsible for generating a strategic plan to respond to the crisis, which would be presented for approval to the Deputies Committee or higher if necessary. It would also oversee its subsequent implementation and coordinate where necessary with the relevant regional U.S. Combatant Commander.

41. For more information on how the COBR system works, see UK Cabinet Office, "Responding to Emergencies: The UK Central Government Response Concept of Operations," https://www.gov.uk/government/uploads/system/uploads/attachment_data/file/192425/CONOPs_incl_revised_chapter_24_Apr-13.pdf.

42. This discussion draws on sections drafted by the author for Madeleine K. Albright and William S. Cohen, *Preventing Genocide: A Blueprint for U.S. Policymakers* (Washington, D.C.: United States Holocaust Memorial Museum, 2008), 66–67.

43. See Mary Beth Sheridan and Greg Jaffe, "Gates Proposes $2 Billion in Funds to Aid Unstable Countries," *Washington Post*, December 24, 2009; and Robert M. Gates, "Helping Others Defend Themselves: The Future of U.S. Security Assistance," *Foreign Affairs*, May–June 2010, 2–6.
44. I am grateful to a former senior U.S. official for this suggestion. At the same time, it also makes sense for the Bureau of Counterterrorism Bureau and the Bureau of International Narcotics and Law Enforcement Affairs to move to the "T" cluster.

INDEX

Note: page numbers in italics refer to figures; those followed by *t* refer to tables; those followed by n refer to notes, with note number.

AMISOM. *See* African Union Mission in
Somalia
Ansar al-Sharia, 182
antisatellite capabilities, and major power
strategic stability, 110
APB. *See* Atrocities Prevention Board
APSA. *See* African Peace and Security
Architecture
Arab League, 216
Arab Spring, and U.S. early warning
system, 37, 292n25
armed rebellion: crisis prevention strategies
for, 81, 85; triggering events for, 81
arms control agencies, adequate funding
for, 117
arms control regimes: fate of, in event of
major power conflict, 101; importance of
strengthening, 117
ASEAN. *See* Association of Southeast
Asian Nations
Asia: regional organizations, and
preventive engagement, 213–14, 217–18.
See also East Asia; Northeast Asia;
South Asia
al-Assad, Bashar, 143
Association of Southeast Asian Nations
(ASEAN), 213, 218; and ASEAN
community as goal, 288n33; and
preventive engagement, 288n33
Atrocities Prevention Board (APB), 52, 227,
228, 243
AU. *See* African Union
Australia, U.S. alliance with, as stabilizing
force, 119

backcasting analysis, 45
Bahrain, risk of instability in, 150, 152*t*
Baltic region, potential sources of conflict
with Russia, 143–45; crisis prevention
measures, 154–56
Betts, Richard, 138
Biden, Joe, 226–28
bin Laden, Osama, 9, 168

Biological Weapons Convention,
importance of, 117
border disputes, UN and, 207
Bouazizi, Mohamed, 37
branch analysis, in assessing triggering
contingencies, *46*, 47
British Empire, collapse of, 250–52nn9–10;
as cautionary tale for U.S., xv–xvi; lack
of coherent strategy as cause of, xvi; U.S.
gains from, 250–51n9. *See also* Great
Britain
bureaucracy, federal: current and past
early warning programs, 230–31;
Obama administration preventive
engagement measures, 227–28;
strategic planning in, as fragmented,
234–35, 238, 293n36
bureaucracy, federal, reorienting toward
preventive engagement, 229–43;
adjustments to existing system as
sufficient for, 225–26, 232; critical areas
for, 229–30; enhancing crisis
preparedness and management, 230,
237–41; fostering preventive foresight
and risk assessment, 230–34; and
funding of preventive engagement
bureaucracy, 226; models for, 233;
necessary elements of, 232–34; new
agencies needed for, 233–34; piecemeal
efforts, inadequacy of, 229; promoting
preventive policy planning, 230, 234–37;
resources and funding for, 241–43; and
three work streams for three types of
preventive engagement, 232
bureaucratic silos: breakup of, and focus on
short-term intelligence, 232; early
warning systems and, 31–32
Bureau for Conflict and Stabilization
Operations (CSO), 227, 228, 242–43
Bush (George H. W.) administration: and
preventive planning, 236–37; and rush of
events as obstacle to preventive action,
58; and U.S. early warning system, 34

level of economic development, as predictive factor for conflict, 43

liberal international order: collapse of, and increased risk of costly military conflict, xv; defining characteristics of, xii; economic and environmental challenges and, 10–11; emerging challenges to, xii–xiv, 3–11, 223–24; potential for collapse of, xv; projected impact of severe recession on, 102; resilience of, xiv; stabilizing measures, as means of conflict risk reduction, 71–73; strategy to preserve, importance of, xvii–xviii; Trump administration and, xvii, 224; U.S. power to preserve, 223–24; value of, xv, 224–25

liberal international order, supply-side strategies for preserving: arguments for increasing U.S. military capacity, 11, 15–16; arguments for reduction of U.S. commitments, 11, 12–15; limitations of, 3, 11–16; tasks included in, 11–12

Libya: conflict mitigation strategies for, 199; refugees from, 182; and Responsibility-to-Protect violations of sovereignty, 112, 216; as short-term category 2 risk, 182, 185*t*

Lippmann Gap, supply side theories for closing, 3, 11–16

Lisbon Treaty (2009), 211, 286n25

Lithuania, fear of Russian aggression, 143–44

Long Peace: decline in conflict during, 3, *4*; potential for abrupt end to, 11; progressive globalization as key to preserving, 103; U.S. policies contributing to, 21

loss aversion, as obstacle to preventive action, 59

Machar, Riek, 183–84

major powers: and military forces balancing, as conflict risk reduction, 71–73; military forces upgrades, 5; partnerships with, and preventive engagement, 203–6; points of agreement and disagreement, 203, 204; policies to promote strategic stability among, 107–11; rising tensions between, 3–5, 223; and U.S. regional security guarantees, 120

Mandela, Nelson, 216

Markey, Daniel, 125

mass atrocities, crisis prevention measures for, 164–66

Mazower, Mark, 112

Mearsheimer, John, 72

MENA. *See* Middle East and North Africa (MENA) region

Mexico, risk of instability in, 151

Middle East: category 3 risks in, 150; China's economic ties to, 204–5; crisis prevention measures for, 163–64; increasing instability in, 99–100; India's economic ties to, 204–5; and NATO stabilization, 118; regional organizations, and preventive engagement, 216–17; risk of regional conflict in, 5, 7–8, 105; risk of U.S. military engagement in, 8, 100; and U.S. regional alliances as stabilizing force, 118, 119

Middle East and North Africa (MENA) region: efforts to encourage regional trade in, 124–25; Trade and Investment Partnership Initiative, 124

Middle East Free Trade Area, 124

military action, public support for: exhaustion of in Britain, 252n10; potential exhaustion of in U.S., xvi, 4; war on terror and, xii

military forces: and emerging technologies, 5; and intrastate conflict, crisis prevention strategies for, 86; major power balancing of, as means of conflict risk reduction, 71–73; major powers' upgrades in, 5; missile defense systems, and major power strategic stability, 109. *See also* cyberwarfare; force, use of; weapons

terrorists: goals of, 282n44; increase in lone wolf attacks, 169–70; increasing threat from, xiii–xiv, *8*, 8–10, *9*; likely long-term threat from, 10; motives of recruits to, 189; and nuclear weapons, 6 7, 10, 104, 188; U.S. military presence as incitement to, 16; and weapons of mass destruction, 169, 187, 188, 203, 284n2. *See also* counterterrorism; Islamist terrorists; war on terrorism

terrorists, attack on U.S. homeland by: as category 1 risk, 168–70; conflict mitigation measures, 187–90; counterterrorism efforts and, 169; and pressure to retaliate, 169–70. *See also* September 11th terrorist attacks

threat reduction, vs. risk reduction, 263n32

threats: as basis for early warning systems, 38; as binary concept, 38; calculating magnitude of, 38. *See also* early warning systems

tier I conflict mitigation priorities, 185*t*, 185–94

tier I crisis prevention measures, 152*t*, 152–54

tier II conflict mitigation priorities, 185*t*, 193–98

tier II crisis prevention measures, 152*t*, 157–62

tier III conflict mitigation priorities, 185*t*, 198–200

tier III crisis prevention measures, 152*t*, 162–66

TPP. *See* Trans-Pacific Partnership (TPP)

trade, international: and complex "behind the border" issues, 121–22; debate on, 120; and environmental goods, removal of tariffs on, 123; liberalization of, 120–22, *121*; promotion of, as long-term preventive strategy, 120–25; and regional trade agreements, 122–24; strategic value of, 120. *See also* economic interdependence

Trade Facilitation Agreement, 123

Transatlantic Trade and Investment Partnership (TTIP), 122–23

Trans-Pacific Partnership (TPP), 122–23, 272n30; U.S. withdrawal from, 224

Treaty on the Non-Proliferation of Nuclear Weapons, importance of, 117

triggering contingencies: commonly-occurring, development of preventive action templates for, 89, 240–41; high consequence, *see* category 1 risks; medium consequence, *see* category 2 risks; low consequence, *see* category 3 risks

triggering contingencies, assessing likelihood of: formal models for, 43; gaming exercises in, 48; long-term assessments, 44–45; medium-term assessments, 45–47, *46*, *47*; polling in, 47–48; pre-forensic analysis in, 46; ranking of likelihood, 48; risk of false confidence in results, 48; as second step in preventive foresight, 40; short-term assessments, 47–48; statistical analysis in, 42–46, 260n40

triggering contingencies, evaluating impact and consequences of: assessment criteria for, 48–49; focus on, as means of motivating preventive action, 63; ranking by category, 50–51, 51*t*; risk matrix in, 51, 51*t*, 52–53, *53*, 54*t*, 54; as third step in preventive foresight, 40

triggering contingencies, understanding of: basic principles for, 40–42; as first step in preventive foresight, 40

Trump administration: aid to Saudi coalition in Yemen, 197–98; challenges to liberal international order, xvii, 224; and Iran nuclear deal, 146; and relations with Russia, 143; as symptom of growing dissatisfaction with globalization, xiii, 249n5; and U.S. military forces, planned buildup of, xvii, 224–25

Tunisia, Arab Spring and, 37

Turkey: conflict with Kurds, potential U.S.
involvement in, 177–78; and Libyan peace
negotiations, 199; risk of instability in,
150, 152*t*; and Syrian civil war, 177

Ukraine, and crisis of 2004, 118–19
Ukraine, Russian meddling in: conflict
mitigation measures for, 195–96;
escalation of, as short-term category 2
risk, 180, 185*t*; EU and, 217; lack of
major power cooperation on, 205; and
NATO membership, 162, 195–96; and
relations with U.S., 143
unavoidable contingencies, tendency to
avoid preventive action for, 59
Union of South American Nations, 213
United Arab Emirates (UAE), and Libyan
peace negotiations, 199
United Nations (UN): and climate change,
206; and conflict risk reduction, 70; and
consensus for action, as issue, 208; and
economic development, 206; and
international norms, 206; and intrastate
conflict, crisis prevention strategies for,
85–86; and Libyan peace negotiations,
199; likely impact of major power
conflict on, 101, 105; likely impact of
progressive globalization on, 103; likely
impact of regressive globalization on,
101; number of state members, 95;
peacemaking in Africa, 205; perceived
legitimacy, factors affecting, 115; and
preventive engagement, 206–9,
285–86n13; and preventive military
action, 207–8; as source of legitimacy for
U.S. initiatives, 202; successes in conflict
mitigation, 88–89; support of, as U.S.
interest, 114–15; and Syrian civil war,
177; and territorial disputes, 79; Trump
administration funding cuts, 224; U.S.
as largest donor to, 114; U.S. influence
on, 114; and Yemeni civil war, 169.
See also Security Council, UN

United Nations Assistance Mission for
Iraq, 207
United Nations Charter: as code of conduct
for nations, 108, 114; and state
sovereignty norms, 70
United Nations Conventions on the Law of
the Sea (UNCLOS): and China's claims
on China Sea Islands, 135, 136–37; U.S.
need to ratify, 118
United Nations Department of Political
Affairs (DPA), 209, 281–82n13
United Nations Permanent Court of
Arbitration: China's rejection of ruling by,
79, 137, 153; successful arbitration by, 79
United Nations Regional Center for
Preventive Diplomacy for Central
Asia, 207
United Nations World Food Program, as
crisis prevention strategy, 86
United States: balancing behavior toward
China, 99; balancing behavior toward
Russia, 99; cyberwarfare attacks against,
projected continuance of, 99; increased
danger of strategic environment, in
baseline future scenario, 98–100; sources
of concern for, 12; successes in conflict
mitigation, 88; twentieth century
ascendance of, xi–xii; upgrading of
military forces, 5
United States, as guarantor of world order:
and benefits of stable order, xv, xvi; and
dilemma of overextension vs. appearance
of indifference, 1–2; as necessary role, 2;
and twentieth-century faith in liberal
international order, xii. *See also*
commitments of U.S., reduction of; liberal
international order; preventive engagement
United States, projected future of: baseline
scenario, 94, 95–100; in case of
progressive globalization, 103–4; in case
of regressive globalization, 100–103; cone
of plausibility analysis in developing, 94;
and cost, variation by scenario, 105